By His Example

The Wit and Wisdom of
A. C. Bhaktivedanta Swami Prabhupada

By His Example
The Wit and Wisdom of
A. C. Bhaktivedanta Swami Prabhupada

Gurudas
a.k.a. Roger Siegel

TORCHLIGHT PUBLISHING

Copyright © 2004 Roger Siegel

All rights reserved. No part of this book may be reproduced, stored in a retrieval system or transmitted in any form, by any means, including mechanical, electronic, photocopying, recording, or otherwise, without the prior written consent of the publisher.

First Printing 2004

Cover design by Yamaraja Dasa
Printed in the United States of America

Published simultaneously in the United States of America and Canada by Torchlight Publishing.

Library of Congress Cataloging-in-Publication Data

Siegel, Roger.
  By His example : the wit and wisdom of A.C. Bhaktivedanta Swami Prabhupada / Roger Siegel (a.k.a. Gurudas).
    p. cm.
  ISBN 1-887089-36-5
  1. A. C. Bhaktivedanta Swami Prabhupada, 1896-1977. 2. International
Society for Krishna Consciousness. I. Title.
BL1285.892.A28S35 2004
294.5'512'092—dc22

2003019374

For information contact the publisher:

TORCHLIGHT PUBLISHING, INC.
P. O. Box 52, Badger CA 93603
Phone: (559) 337-2200
Fax: (559) 337-2354
Email: torchlight@spiralcomm.net
www.torchlight.com

My Eternal Guide,
Seeing you in person at the San Francisco Airport
on January 17, 1967—
that day was the beginning of my new life,
the most auspicious of events,
when I encountered
SWAMIJI—
A.C. Bhaktivedanta Swami—
the most important person in my life,
my greatest influence,
ardent supporter,
and careful critic.
PRABHUPADA
graces my view
with pure, smiling benediction
from his expansive heart.

Portrait for the first edition of Bhagavad-gita As It Is, *1967.*

Contents

Preface ix

Introduction xiii

1 / Honoring Srila Prabhupada   1

2 / San Francisco   5

3 / Montreal   51

4 / England   57

5 / India   123

6 / Sannyasa   227

7 / Drops of Nectar Along the Path   233

Appendix   251

About the Author   271

PREFACE

All Glories to the Assembled Devotees!

RADHA AND KRISHNA have guided this book, a glorification of His Divine Grace A. C. Bhaktivedanta Swami Prabhupada, the kindest, wisest, most determined, noncompromising, open-minded personality I have ever come in contact with. This book is also for and in glorification of all the devotees who have embarked on the path of Krishna consciousness. My heart goes out to all devotees, you who have become tender-hearted by hearing ancient, transcendental sounds and by accepting Sri Sri Radha Krishna's benediction and effulgence.

We can be compassionate towards one another because we are on the same journey, we have the same goal—to become Krishna conscious. Prabhupada has been our example, guide, inspiration, beacon, and forgiving father. He has left us instructions in his books. If Prabhupada can forgive us, we can also forgive each other's mistakes and meanderings. Lord Chaitanya welcomes everyone and sees past any bodily designations. I respect any devotee who has tried in even the smallest way to serve Prabhupada, Krishna, or another devotee. He or she is special—like the sparrow who drank drops of the ocean to rescue her lost eggs from the sea or like the chipmunk who was tossing pebbles into the sea to help Lord Ramachandra build his bridge to Lanka—the effort itself is success.

I offer my well-wishes to anyone who gets up shivering before sunrise and, still shivering, takes a cold shower. I offer my well-wishes to those who chant at least 25,000 names of the Lord each day, who consider all others "prabhu," who are humble in their practices, who live simply and think of higher goals, and who overcome the tendency for judgmental thinking. I offer my well-wishes to those who renounce material comforts and are more inspired by the sound of karatals, by the sight of pink lotus feet—to those who are struggling to overcome the unending, albeit temporary, attractions of material nature. I offer my well-wishes to those who are eager to hear the nectar of divine pastimes and to serve humanity as brothers and sisters, for again, we are all on the same journey. Let us walk together.

Srila Prabhupada has attracted a fine, diverse international group of people, and the network between us still continues. There are so many personal connections, all due to Prabhupada. If he hadn't come here, we may never have met. He changed each and every life he touched. It is his wish for us to be friendly, to cooperate, and help each other in Krishna consciousness. Devotees are rare, and we must encourage one another rather than criticize and turn others away from the delicate devotional path. Prabhupada said someone who finds fault is like "a fly on sores," while someone who sees good, who sees the soul within, is like "a honeybee (madhukara) going from flower to flower, transforming everything it touches into pure sweetness." Allowing someone to grow, as Prabhupada did for me, is better than faultfinding, which creates resentment and rebellion. Since we are a small family, divisive behavior is counterproductive. There are so few Vaishnavas. We must unite, because we have the same goal: love of Krishna.

* * *

In 1968, I wanted to start a book glorifying the Swami. I intended to call the book *Swamiji*. We discussed it briefly. And then, on June 7, 1968, Prabhupada wrote: *"Your book SWAMIJI may be interesting to admirers and disciples."*

Because of my duties overseeing the opening of the London and Vrindavan temples, and other devotional service, the book was postponed but not forgotten. Later, Prabhupada again brought up the subject of the *Swamiji* book and said that it should be produced nicely and include photographs.

In another letter Prabhupada sanctioned the book:

From Allston, Mass
27 April, 1969
To London

My Dear Gurudas,

Please accept my blessings. I beg to acknowledge receipt of your letter of April 20, 1969, sent along with some pictures. All the pictures you sent are very important. You are doing very laudable service by collecting some old reminiscences, and I shall do the needful in due course; there is no immediate emergency. Your idea of writing a book named Swamiji was formerly informed to me. Unfortunately, because I am traveling in so many places from Los Angeles to Hawaii, then to San Francisco, then again Los Angeles, then New York, then Buffalo, and now I am in Boston. From here I shall go to Columbus, then to North Carolina, then to New Vrindavan, and then I may go to

London if required. At that time I shall give you solid information for both the Krishna book and the Swamiji book."

This book is the result of these earlier efforts. It is not meant to be a biography but rather a transcendental medium that allows both those who knew him and those who never had a chance to meet Prabhupada to experience his humor and compassion, to come into closer contact with his vani and vapu. Prabhupada once said, "Krishna consciousness means happiness." I hope that you may derive some happiness, inspiration, encouragement, and transcendental ecstasy from this rendering.

As I began to put this book together, I became very puzzled by how much of my own voice to include. My first idea was to just glorify Prabhupada without including myself at all. Then I realized that this idea was tantamount to impersonalism, thus stifling the flow of the Vaishnava history I wanted to narrate. Therefore, I include myself, with humility, as these accounts of Prabhupada's glories are perceived through my eyes and convey my impressions of his activities and glories.

I have attempted to share with you the same feelings that I experienced in the presence of His Divine Grace A.C. Bhaktivedanta Swami Prabhupada.

This small but natural offering is in eternal thanks to you, Srila Prabhupada.

INTRODUCTION

London, June, 1999

WALKING THESE STREETS again after so many years, I see you here all over the place, Gurudas: browbeating Michael-X and his goons to move their stuff from the flat so we can move our stuff in; Mr. Charm himself, chatting up Mr. French till he actually convinces himself that the heavy thumping through his walls at 4 A.M. just COULDN'T be our kirtan; double-talking the guard at the Ambassador's gate while we whisk inside to crash his party. . . . You were our Stalwart, the guy who always did the stuff the rest of us didn't have the guts for, with that raw, New York courage, right in their faces. But with a heart of gold, you were our fellow prankster, ridiculous in that unpressed, yellow-gray bed sheet, master of histrionics—sometimes the buffoon—dispenser of comic relief for the pangs of our struggles.

What a team we were in those days, Gurudas! Yourself; and rock-hard (ready to weep at the drop of a sloka), fixed-up Yamuna-devi dasi, my childhood friend; and Mukunda (now Maharaja), musician extraordinaire, our laid-back Paragon, whose Perry Como-like balance kept us afloat through many a stormy session; and his wife, Janaki, who brought passion and tension to the mix; and dear, outspoken Malati, busy as a bee; and baby Saraswati for cute and awe, our reminder of original purity: the London Yatra—together, we pulled off a monster for our Spiritual Master!

"How did you guys do it?" youngsters ask me now. And you know, as I and all the others know who were so blessed by Srila Prabhupada, the secret was and always will be: We simply followed His Example—He who touched us, talked and wrote and phoned to us, SHOWED us by his actions life's highest form of happiness—Serving Krishna at The Edge.

In "Swamiji" we witnessed, and interacted with, an extraordinary person: not afraid of anything, willing to risk it all—someone who never made a mistake, someone who in every circumstance was happy and self-contained, unaffected and at ease. And Hey! We were not so easy to convince—in those days of chaos in the streets, the nights of instant-everything—that a Perfect Man could walk this earth, a Hero for the Age! No. But that he spent so much of his precious time for us, that's the wonder: to lead us little by little, holding our hands at first, then turning forward and boldly striding ahead, stopping, glancing back from time to time, till we were right behind, tucked into his slipstream, into his rhythm, rocketing along in his footfalls....

Now, he said, you fly off alone. I am there, don't fear—just do as I told you, do as I do, dare all to dance at The Edge for Krishna: "In this manner you will see Krishna; He must personally come to help you when He sees His devotee take so much trouble on His behalf. He must personally come."

And didn't we see that! How hindrance after obstacle was swept off by some swift, bluish movement, right before our eyes, how problems insurmountable dissolved (Was that a flute I heard above the traffic's roar?). At The Edge we saw Krishna's love for Srila Prabhupada *force* Him repeatedly to come to our aid, to kick into place an event or a thing or a person: to favor the stage for Prabhupada's work.

His Example was charming—and angry as hell; simplicity itself—and as complex as the universe; effortless to follow—and like walking through knee-deep, wet concrete. Prabhupada was everything, an endless, unpredictable variety of everything, but what remained as constant through his pastimes with us was his unfailing sense of humor and his unchallenged, absolute knowledge: His Wit and His Wisdom. You hit it right on the head, Gurudas.

You were Srila Prabhupada's friend, and a good one at that, the foil and perfect vehicle to reciprocate with him your own grasp of deep meaning in the parable and homily—your own developed sense of the absurd in his slapstick and his jokes.

You of all of Prabhupada's servants remember him in a very special manner. The little vignettes (the universe on the head of a pin, the hilarity in a misplaced word), so quickly perishable in a mind like mine, stuck to your brain cells like glue—and now you've given them to the Vaishnava Devotees forever. Thank you, Gurudas, for bringing Srila Prabhupada back to us in this Book.

—*Shyamasundar dasa*

HONORING SRILA PRABHUPADA

1

"Do something new."
—A. C. Bhaktivedanta Swami

THE MORE I WAS AROUND Bhaktivedanta Swami, the more I loved him. He affected others that way, too. He never demanded respect, yet we all were very respectful of him. We whispered in his presence and let his words set the pace. He demonstrated determination, discipline, knowledge, and humility, woven together with threads of kindness, humor, and enthusiasm. In his presence it was easy to become interested and enthusiastic. He used jokes or stories to illustrate very important spiritual points. He did this with such ease that we absorbed his message and changed without knowing it. For example, he told me a story once about teaching math to students who claimed they couldn't learn the subject. As he told the story, he assumed the voices and faces of both the teacher and the students:

"How many feet are at the rear of the cow?" Swamiji said, taking on the authoritative teacher's voice.

"Two," the students replied innocently.

"And how many are in the front?" the teacher continued.

"Two," the students answered.

Teacher: "So how many feet are on the cow?"

Students: "Four."

Teacher: "Now you know math."

But the students didn't realize that they had learned and exclaimed, "No, we don't!"

At this, Prabhupada laughed and laughed and laughed, and then I laughed and laughed.

In such a manner, Prabhupada taught us everything about Krishna consciousness, without our being aware of it. He taught us how to become God conscious naturally in our everyday lifestyle, as we changed seamlessly from materialists to Vaishnava devotees.

He rarely asked for anything. We asked him if we could become his disciples. If any one of us had an idea and the idea was not wasteful, insane, or unreasonably dangerous, he would encourage the idea and suggest more ideas, giving hints how to bring that idea to fruition.

In this way, my life was changed and a movement was created, a spiritual movement of souls desiring to purify themselves by serving Krishna and thus serving others.

In the beginning there wasn't much money, but somehow donations were given and the things we needed appeared. More than once there was no money for rent, but then someone would walk through the door and the rent would be paid. I saw many mini miracles happen. A miracle is a deviation from the norm, and as I became more disciplined and regulated—"normal"—I felt my life become also miraculous as I developed my relationship with His Divine Grace A.C. Bhaktivedanta Swami.

One of Krishna's most magnificent pastimes was lifting Govardhan Hill. For seven days His cowherd friends gazed at His beauty constantly, while being protected from lightning bolts and the weight of the large hill overhead. Although Lord Krishna, the Supreme Personality of Godhead, had the hill perfectly secured, He acted as if He needed help. In this way, He engaged the cowherd boys and girls in devotional service. Similarly, when I was with Prabhupada, or serving in separation from him, I felt that he was, metaphorically speaking, holding up Govardhan Hill, which was the whole world. And although small, I was helping him.

When the Swami suddenly became ill in San Francisco and we were in the temple praying for his recovery with our plaintive cries—chanting and bargaining with Krishna to make our father well again—we felt the symbolic crush of Govardhan Hill in the form of our beloved Guru's impending death. However, our consciousness was engaged completely in Swamiji and Krishna. As such, we didn't waver, speculate, or get distracted by any of Maya's baubles. We were focused and determined, just like the friends of Lord Krishna at Govardhan Hill. Prabhupada recovered and subsequently led us from one success to another throughout the following years.

Many times Prabhupada told me, "Being jolly is a sign of spiritual advancement." Though Srila Prabhupada displayed discipline and gravity when the time and circumstances called for them, his joy, humor, and quick wit transformed many situations. Whenever there was a chance to add levity, transcendentally tease, or make a joke, Prabhupada would oversee the fun. Sometimes he directed the fun toward me or my godbrothers and -sisters, and at other times even toward himself. Sometimes he made fun of silly acts (e.g., a man sawing a tree limb while sitting outside the cut), and sometimes he made fun of scientists who have "seen" proof by using instruments geared to imperfect senses. Prabhupada often jokingly referred to the wrangling scientists with their "perhaps's" and "maybe's." He was an excellent mimic, punctuating his stories with imitations of character types or animal sounds. He joked: "The scientist claims that such and such poison is odorless and tasteless. How do they know that the poison is tasteless?" Laughing, he imitated the scientist whose final words are "It's tasteless!"

False yogis were another source of jokes. Once there was a yogi who threw gifts he received into the Howrah River to demonstrate his detachment from material goods. But at night he pulled the gifts out of the water in a fishing net. Prabhupada, like Shakespeare, made fun of material life and the many absurdities of this material world. The more time I spent with Srila Prabhupada, relishing his humor, the more love, faith, devotion, and spiritual practice began to outweigh my material ambitions.

As we naturally cultivate our relationship, rasa, with Lord Krishna, so too does each and every disciple have a special rasa with his or her spiritual master. Many devotees can easily understand the mood of awe and reverence, but my special rasa with Prabhupada is friendship. I learned compassion by experiencing Prabhupada's humor and wit. Many times we related through humor, since neither of us could let a good joke pass us by. Prabhupada was accepting and open-minded to all, yet he could make each person feel special and wanted. Even if I had just seen him an hour before, he welcomed me as if we hadn't seen each other for a year. Sometimes he would even ask me for advice. Then, after coming to a solution together, our Jagat Guru of the Universe would humbly ask me, "Is that all right?" Sometimes Prabhupada would confide in me in a soft voice, and I would reveal my inner thoughts, while he allowed our elbows to touch. I drank in the fragrance of saffron, sandalwood, mustard oil, and champa flowers that signified his presence. He cared for me when I was sick, as I cared for him when he was ill. His divine lotus hands even bandaged my wounded foot one night in Vrindavan.

To Prabhupada, the best instruction was by example.

Sometimes he taught by being aloof, and sometimes with understanding and compassion. On more than one occasion my mentor taught me a hard lesson (in ISKCON jargon, by "giving me the sauce"), which I took as great mercy, a rough caress. On learning, Prabhupada taught: "If learned the hard way, it will be remembered well; if learned too easily, it is easily forgotten."

He mercifully granted me so much personal time with him, and sometimes, if I stayed away too long, he would call for me. If I didn't write, he would write saying he had not heard from me. When I had typhoid fever in Vrindavan, he demanded a report on my progress from wherever he was traveling.

We walked side by side, slept in the same train compartment, held hands, stepped carefully into a dark basement and shuffled along groping the wall together till we found the door.

We laughed and cried together. We sang and danced together. I ate maha-maha prasadam, touched by His Divine Grace's lips, which he had slid onto my plate with golden lotus fingers.

We held up a collapsing altar together, rode rickshaws, cars, trains, boats, planes, and walked seven and more steps together side by side.

Srila Prabhupada was the center, core, and zenith of all his students' lives. We wanted to please him and make his path easy and comfortable. We brought him dictaphones, pens, and watches; we cooked special dishes like shukta; we made garlands and knitted sweaters—all to please our Guru Maharaja. When he came to visit us, we gravitated toward him like flowers toward the sun.

This phenomenon is analogous to Krishna and the gopis, a living illustration of how the gopis responded to Lord Krishna. They ran to Him when they heard His flute, just as we ran to Prabhupada when we heard his voice or his singing. The gopis, like Lalita or Vishaka, would leave milk boiling on the stove, or be so attracted to Krishna's Shyama form that they would even leave a baby behind. When they saw Lord Krishna's beautiful, three-fold dancing form, they became so entranced that they swooned in exhilaration. We too became elated and disoriented when Prabhupada merely looked in our direction or sent us out on some spiritual mission. Whoever came in contact with Srila Prabhupada was changed forever. I watched and listened to Prabhupada more than I read our Vaishnava books. I am not a great scholar, but I remember so many moments, so many instructive words, so many looks which seemed to caress me, and so many humorous moments with my dear, wonderful Swamiji!

SAN FRANCISCO

"I am like a cow; I give my milk freely."
—A. C. Bhaktivedanta Swami

Early Days in San Francisco

TIMES WERE CHANGING. It was the sixties—a president was assassinated; racial injustice was challenged; children were running away from home, questioning authority and the materialistic ways of their parents. Young people like myself were searching for answers to the meaning of life, and new ideas were becoming acceptable to those with open minds. So much new information was available everywhere during those times, especially information about esoteric, occult, and ancient traditions of thought, and I began to absorb a wide variety of these principles in my spiritual quest for God, harmony, and world peace. I let my studies guide me down many different paths. I was ready to give my life in civil rights causes. My work both in the North and South during the early sixties with Dr. Martin Luther King, Stokely Carmichael, and Julian Bond was only a prelude for what I would personally experience under the wing of my spiritual father. My experiments, guided by Aldous Huxley, Timothy Leary, D.T. Suzuki, and Chief Black Elk, were only small drops in the pond of enlightenment. Although I felt I was gaining some spiritual insight from all these teachers, and though there was much in enjoyment in my life, I had no direction. I felt like a fish swimming in a lazy river, floating from pleasure to pain, continuing to exist but going nowhere. I found out later that this is called samsara, the wheel of life, spinning in a cycle of birth, disease, old age, death, and again rebirth—a cycle repeating life after life without cessation. Samsara brings to mind the analogy of a hamster in a cage, running and running on its little wheel yet constantly remaining in the same place. After I would meet the Swami, though, my search would take an abrupt turn: He opened the door of my cage, and I got off the spinning wheel of samsara. I would henceforward truly cleanse myself, turn myself inside out and stand on my head, in total readiness to give my life again for my beloved teacher, A. C. Bhaktivedanta Swami.

All the knowledge I'd acquired—from the *Torah* and kabbala, Zen Buddhism and the Bushido code, Taoism and the *I Ching*, and Native American wisdom—was synthesized in Swamiji's teachings and instructions. His wisdom was tried and true; his guidance was punctuated with humor and concern. Sometimes he displayed a childlike glee when we learned, yet he remained transcendent and affectionately detached. He lived simply, and we followed his example. He often looked deeply into my soul and smiled kindly. And my soul smiled back.

"THE SWAMI" DESCENDS

"The Swami's coming, the Swami's coming!" shouted the brightly clad youths. We raced to our vehicles. It was January 17, 1967.

Caravans of painted cars, hippie vans, and motorcycles rode out to the airport to greet the Swami. He was finally arriving from New York! At last I would meet the Swami I had heard so much about. I'd been told how he was wise and kind. I knew he had opened a storefront temple at 26 Second Avenue, in my old stomping grounds on the Lower East Side. I had heard how the Swami welcomed anyone and everyone who showed up at the door and how he had endured the cold New York winters. I had heard how, living in the Bowery and then in Mukunda's loft, he had simply stepped over the sleeping winos outside, or greeted them if they were awake. He was able to see their very souls within their miserable outer shells and accept them, even though they were broke and often drunk. Now he was coming to San Francisco!

About fifty people arrived at the airport with me. Haridas had driven an old Cadillac across the United States, which we had immediately painted with the Hare Krishna mantra. The Krishnallac, as we called it, stood ready to take the Swami to our new temple on Frederick Street. I remember the colorful garb: Max Ochs, folk singer Phil Ochs' cousin, in a Patrice Lamumba T-shirt, I was in my samurai-like robes, and Shyamasundar was in a brocade Moroccan jellaba. We didn't have dhotis and saris then, so we were clad in these multicultural flowing clothes and beads. The air smelled of incense, and the airport resonated with the sound of cymbals, drums, and chanting. A friend later said, "The feeling at the airport was one of loveliness." He recalls that about a hundred people were there, while I remember about forty or fifty. (Maybe he saw the demigods smiling down on us and raining flowers and rose water on the ad hoc congregation!) Some of the New York devotees who'd come ahead to pave the way for the Swami were there. The new, uninitiated San Francisco devotees were there, as were many characters who came regularly to the temple, such as Mr. Matthews, the "man in the suit." He was older than the rest of us, very quiet, very nice and the only one who wore a suit. He respectfully followed the Swami everywhere.

We went to the large observation windows and saw the plane making its descent. Someone ran to inform the others who were waiting by the arrival entrance. We watched as the passengers exited the airplane and walked down the stairs.

No Swami. The line of passengers finished.

Suddenly, we saw a small figure in saffron glide out of the airplane, a halo of light surrounding him. A youth, Ranchor, followed him. Swamiji walked down the stairs slowly and deliberately, and then he crossed the tarmac. It seemed to us as if his feet weren't touching the stairs or ground. His head was raised, and as he walked towards us we were overcome with excitement and ran en masse to the spot where we thought he would enter the terminal. After waiting what seemed like a really long time, the Swami wafted through the door in a regal and confident manner. He was relaxed and happy. And when he saw everyone chanting, he gave us a huge smile, and that smile felt like an ocean washing over and protecting me. When Swamiji smiled, that smile became my beacon and shelter.

He walked to a seat and settled into it as a great bird might settle upon a cloud. Sitting cross-legged, his eyes closed in blessing, and he started chanting. We sat down around him and followed. As we started chanting with him, he wrapped the kartalas perfectly around his hands. I watched him intently as he began playing the now-familiar one-two-sizzle/one-two-sizzle beat with his kartalas. Someone had a bongo drum. Some had finger cymbals. We played with him. He opened his eyes and beamed at us kindly. We continued to clap, bang the drum, ring cymbals, and chant the Hare Krishna mantra, and soon people arriving in the terminal from around the world came over to surround us, watching with curiosity. The Swami stopped after some time and said some prayers to his spiritual masters in a golden, husky voice. We remained silent except for repeating, "Jai!" whenever he said "Ki jai!". The prayers echoed throughout the airport, and when they were over, he thanked us all for coming, showing us a respect that was often lacking in our peers and parents alike. I remember thinking that I had never encountered such a mix of greatness and humility in one person. The throng around us grew bigger, and eventually some airport officials came over to ask us to stop chanting. But as Swamiji had just ended the chanting, the officials simply stood around with nothing to do.

We informed the Swami that the Krishnallac was ready for him. He rose and, in a majestic yet simple way, walked out of the terminal, while we ran after him. Mukunda arrived from the car and embraced Swamiji, who hugged him back. The Swami's demeanor was humble, his mind totally absorbed in Krishna. We didn't know about bowing down to him then. We followed him out to the Krishnallac and watched it drive away, then ran to our respective vans, motorcycles, and cars to follow his vehicle in grand procession. Some cars went ahead to provide an escort to the new, makeshift Radha Krishna Temple on Frederick Street. Swamiji viewed our new temple for the first time and smiled upon us. He singled me out with his glance, looking through my grossness into the very core of my soul-self.

Then and there I knew I had found my Guru.
I knew I would follow him in my spiritual quest.
I knew I would follow him to the ends of the earth.
My search had ended.

Mantra Rock Dance

Within a short time the Hare Krishnas became a familiar part of the Haight-Ashbury scene. If you lived on the street in the Haight, one of the underground secrets of survival was that you could go to the Krishna temple and get a nice warm breakfast in a friendly atmosphere. Chanting became known as a nice way to come down from an acid trip, and the meal of hot cereal, marinated garbanzo beans, and fruit drink or hot milk was always welcome.

When we knew that the Swami was coming to San Francisco from New York, we decided to introduce him to thousands of our fellow members of the counterculture by sponsoring a charity rock concert and dance at one of the venues that were so popular at the time. I was acquainted with Sam Andrews of the band Big Brother and the Holding Company; Shyamasundar knew Chet Helms, proprietor of the Avalon Ballroom, who agreed to donate his hall for one night. Shyamasundar also knew Rock Scully, manager of the Grateful Dead, whom Yamuna and I knew because they lived across from us on Ashbury Street. Chet arranged interviews and, in addition to the Dead and Big Brother, we were able to persuade Jefferson Airplane, Quicksilver Messenger Service, and Moby Grape to perform free as a benefit to support the Radha Krishna Temple. Allen Ginsberg had agreed to fly out from New York to perform onstage and introduce the Swami to the people of San Francisco.

The evening of the Mantra Rock Dance, January 29, I walked into the empty ballroom and yelled, "Hare Krishna!" The transcendental sound echoed off the walls. The rest of the devotees came over to the hall early to take tickets, cut oranges, and decorate the stage with flowers, cloth hangings, and paintings and posters of Lord Krishna. I saw the empty concert hall gradually fill up with life—soon it was bustling with sounds, smells, lights, and joy. Of course Lord Chaitanya was there too, as were all the demigods, who relish attending functions such as this. It felt as if they were throwing rose-petal benedictions upon the place. We had brought all our instruments: kartalas, flutes, trumpets, and a huge timpani drum. We checked the sound and greeted early arrivals. The Swami was to arrive later.

First Moby Grape played, as strobes and colored lights danced. Then the house lights were turned on and various celebrities began to fill the stage. Allen Ginsberg, wearing a long, white robe, climbed up the madras-covered steps and settled onto the stage. Peter Orlovsky sat down too. Tim Leary came in, smiled, and sat cross-legged. Swami Kriyananda, a disciple of Paramahamsa Yogananda, came in with a vina. He seemed comfortable and happy to be there. Then a short man in a silk top hat and sash which read SAN FRANCISCO, who claimed to be the Mayor, came onto the stage. Some Hell's Angels stood in the back of the stage near a large painting of Radha and Krishna. They were our security guards, and no one was going to mess with them.

Yamuna and I were cutting up oranges for prasadam distribution. My friend Easy drifted by, greeted us, and danced away. Allen Ginsberg took the microphone and introduced chanting of the maha-mantra to the congregation. "This mantra can deliver us all," he said. "Just sink into the sound vibration and think of peace." Accompanied by a small harmonium, he then began chanting: "Hare Krishna, Hare Krishna, Krishna Krishna, Hare Hare, Hare Rama, Hare Rama, Rama Rama, Hare Hare."

I jumped up and started chanting and dancing, and gradually, as everyone joined in, the whole hall felt like it was traveling on an intergalactic journey. In our transcendental spaceship, the Avalon Ballroom, we were separate but safe in the universe. The sound swayed around us, sheltering us in its transcendence.

Then Swami Bhaktivedanta entered. He looked like a Vedic sage, exalted and otherworldly. As he advanced towards the stage, the crowd parted and made way for him, like the surfer riding a wave. He glided onto the stage, sat down, and began playing the kartalas. Again the sound vibration entered my heart, and I felt warmed. Others listened, then started softly singing in unison and weaving in dance. The hall filled with the Holy Names. Swamiji beamed down on the crowd. Everyone was cheering, bowing, clapping, swooning, jumping, chanting, and in a general state of bliss. Finally the chanting ended in a wild crescendo. The Swami then rose slowly, and with hands and palms folded in pranams, he walked down from the stage. Again the throng parted and—respectfully, ecstatically—let him through, some bowing and some even taking dust from his feet.

Jefferson Airplane came on stage next, and Grace Slick sang "Do You Want Somebody to Love?" The large faceted glass ball sprayed blips of light to every part of this separate world. It seemed like stars were cascading around in our miniature planetarium. Big Brother and the Holding Company took the stage. Janis Joplin, with her mouth on the microphone, belted out "Ball and Chain." It looked like she was eating the microphone. Sam Andrews played his classic riff to begin "Summertime." Janis whooped and yelled, and the bands all yelled out Hare Krishna at one time or another. Between sets by the famous bands, people were holding onto each other and chanting in a large circle. Everyone was in harmony. We danced into the night, and this amalgamation of mantra and rock worked extraordinarily well.

That night all those people who heard the Holy Names were on the path towards liberation from the material world, making their way towards the loving arms of Sri Sri Radha Krishna and Lord Chaitanya. Surely the demigods showered benediction upon this most wonderful event, which heralded Swamiji's entry into the hearts and souls of multitudes. (Moreover, the $2,000 in proceeds from the Mantra Rock Dance supported our activities at the Radha Krishna Temple in San Francisco for quite some time!)

> *"If we can help one person become Krishna conscious, then our movement has been successful."*
> —A. C. Bhaktivedanta Swami

ALLEN GINSBERG

Allen Ginsberg had always shown friendly and helpful interest in the Society and had agreed to headline the giant Mantra Rock Festival that the temple members held in the Avalon Ballroom to introduce Bhaktivedanta Swami to the hip community. On the day of the concert, the good poet had come to early-morning kirtan (7 A.M.) at the Temple and later joined the Swami upstairs in the apartment his pupils had rented for him. We were sitting in the glow of this holy man, munching on Indian sweetballs cooked by the Swami, when Allen came through the door, a warm smile on his face. The Swami offered him a sweetball, "Take!" he said, and I recorded the following conversation:

[They sat in silence for a few moments, radiating mutual love.]
SWAMIJI: Allen, you are up early.
GINSBERG: Yes. The phone hasn't stopped ringing since I arrived in San Francisco.
SWAMIJI: That is what happens when one becomes famous. That was the tragedy of Mahatma Gandhi also. Wherever he went, thousands of people would crowd around him, chanting "Mahatma Gandhi ki jai! Mahatma Gandhi ki jai!" The gentleman could not sleep.
GINSBERG (smiling): Well, at least it got me up for kirtan this morning!
SWAMIJI: Yes, that is good.

*Allen Ginsberg visits Srila Prabhupada in San Francisco, 1967.
"Krishna consciousness resolves everything. Nothing else is needed."*

[A few days before, the *San Francisco Chronicle* had published an article called "Swami in Hippie Land," in which the reporter asked, "Do you accept 'hippies' in your temple?" The Swami had replied, "Hippies or anyone—I make no distinctions. Everyone is welcome."]

SWAMIJI: Allen, what is this "hippie"?

GINSBERG: The word "hip" started in China, where people smoked opium lying on their hips. [Allen demonstrated.] Opium and its derivatives then spread to the West and were looked down upon by the people in power, who were afraid of the effects. As a result, the hip people created their own culture, language, signs, symbols. San Francisco is a spiritual "shivdas" [meeting ground]. The word "hip" has changed into "hippie" today. But basically, Swamiji, the young people today are seekers. They're interested in all forms of spirituality.

SWAMIJI: Very nice.

GINSBERG: The hippies will all fall by here at one time or another.

[There was some discussion regarding New York's Lower East Side and the Haight-Ashbury district in San Francisco—both of which are locations of Krishna consciousness temples and are well-known to Allen Ginsberg. Then:]

SWAMIJI: You have not had LSD, Allen?

GINSBERG: I have had it.
SWAMIJI: It is dependence, Allen.
GINSBERG: It's like a car—a mental car—to resolve certain inner things.
SWAMIJI: Krishna consciousness resolves everything. Nothing else is needed.
 [They then discussed the upcoming dance at the Avalon. Allen felt that certain mantras would be more palatable to American ears than others, and that he would like to try his tune at the dance. Swamiji agreed: "Very nice." Poet Ginsberg said he was not yet ready to become a devotee, but that he was chanting the maha-mantra every day, and that he would do so until he leaves this Earth. The Swami thanked him for the work he'd already done in spreading kirtan (chanting of the Holy names).
SWAMIJI: And if you are chanting Hare Krishna mantra daily, then everything in your life will be perfect!

Allen then prostrated himself and, touching the Swami's feet, symbolically wiped the dust from them onto his forehead. Then, with a few sweetballs in a paper bag under his arm, he took his leave.

Update: Though I had sometimes gone to his apartment on East Tenth Street on the Lower East Side of New York, the last meeting between Allen Ginsberg and myself occurred some years later on an airplane going from Milwaukee to San Francisco. I wound up on this particular plane only because I let the airline bump me, and much to my jubilation, there was Allen, with Peter Orlovsky! I reintroduced myself, and Allen had Peter and me trade seats. He questioned me about Swamiji and the Hare Krishna Movement. After speaking with me, he said, "You have a few books in you." I told him I had begun researching my memoirs and asked him to write an introduction to the book, as he had for the Swami's *Bhagavad-gita*. Allen agreed.

At this time, Allen has left the planet. I pray that he is situated in a Vaikuntha realm, where his peace may continue without the confusion of the material world.

Tomorrow

I was sitting in a grove in Golden Gate Park, reading the *Bhagavad-gita*, when Yamuna approached me and spoke of marriage. "The Swami says if man and woman are living together, they should get married." After considering the idea for some time, I said, "Yes, I'll marry you." We chose a Franciscan monk, a Buddhist Rimpoche, and Swamiji to perform the ceremonies.

We went to the Swami's apartment, sat before him, and said, "We want to get married. Will you also perform the ceremony?" The Swami smiled at us and answered, "Yes. You will be double the potency. You're both very good devotees, so this will be double the potency." Then he added, "But before you get married, you must get initiated."

I still wasn't sure I wanted to get initiated—or married—and was secretly thinking of declining. But Yamuna and I asked, "When do you want us to get initiated?"

Swamiji replied, "Tomorrow."

His answer didn't give us much time to think it over! I wasn't sure I wanted to surrender. Yamuna was to spend the night at the temple with Harsarani and Janaki while I went over to Coleridge Street to figure things out with an old friend of mine, Leo. There was a Christian fundamentalist there, a friend of a friend who, without even knowing what Krishna consciousness was, was speaking vehemently against it, calling it idol worship and this and that. Maybe this was Krishna's test for me, because I found myself filled with doubts about the whole thing. At first, his ravings against Krishna consciousness made me more uncertain, but eventually it made me stronger, because I knew I didn't want to hang around with ranting fanatics like this guy. When I woke up the next morning, I decided I wanted to get initiated—and married.

"Don't fight with God; He has more arms than you."
—A. C. Bhaktivedanta Swami

INITIATION

The initiation ceremony consisted of Bhaktivedanta Swami singing prayers of purification and glorification to his guru and to the past spiritual masters. A fire was built, and rice and barley soaked in ghee were thrown into it, as well as colored dyes of red, green, yellow, white, and blue. At the end of the ceremony, bananas were put into the fire. All were offerings to Krishna who, with the fire, burns up all past imperfections. I handed the Swami a bulky strand of 108 large, red, wooden beads, and he chanted on them. Somehow the fad of the large, wooden beads became status quo. Some mixed the colors: reds, blues, and yellows. Swamiji just accepted this, without saying anything about tulasi beads. Later when I was instructed by Swamiji in this matter, I replaced the red beads with the traditional tulasi beads, and he chanted on them, too.

As the yajna progressed, my mind was reeling and racing. The Swami handed beads back to another new initiate and said, "Your name is Shyamadevi dasi." He handed me my beads and gave me my spiritual name. Up to that point the spiritual names had all corresponded with the first letter of the name we were given at birth; for example, Robert became Rupanuga, Bruce became Brahmananda, and so on. At first Swamiji said, "Your spiritual name is R___."

So many things were going through my mind at once, I didn't hear the name. The fire was crackling; the crowd was talking and singing; my head was filled with sounds, smells, and a thousand pictures and thoughts. I wasn't sure if I'd made the right decision. Was I giving up my freedom and fun? Why was I suddenly getting initiated when I was a freewheeling, music-playing, go-anyplace-meet-anyone-do-anything adventurer? "Oh well, this is an adventure too," I thought. The chanting started to soothe me, and the sweet smell of the flower garlands and incense calmed me down. Random thoughts surged through me, but as I viewed the Swami's strong, calm face and his expert hands organizing the fire sacrifice, I accepted everything. I didn't know my new name, but it didn't matter.

After a very short pause, Swamiji said, "No, your name is Gurudas." The guests and witnesses *ooh*'ed and *ahh*'ed. Gurudas, the servant of the guru. I liked it. It fit like the top to a pot. As the Swamiji and I became closer and closer, I became Gurudas. That night, after the initiation ceremony, Yamuna and I went in to see the Swami, and he greeted us with his vast, oceanic smile.

"You are both great devotees of Krishna."

We were silent, but comfortable. After some moments, Yamuna asked, "When do you want us to get married?"

"Tomorrow," the Swami replied.

He did it again! He was making me surrender my restless nature. I felt like I was playing hide and seek with Swamiji and Krishna.

> *"A pure devotee never asks the Lord for anything; however, even demigods still possess some material desires."*
> —A. C. Bhaktivedanta Swami

Marriage Ceremony

The marriage ceremony was yet another fire sacrifice. Many guests and visitors filled the temple room, including Yamuna's Aunt Edna from Klamath Falls, Oregon. Janaki, Yamuna's sister, had been running around making preparations and had gotten margarine instead of butter to make the ghee used in the ceremony. To make things even more precarious, wood from fruit cartons was used instead of forest twigs and branches, so that during the ceremony the fire continuously sputtered, even in Swamiji's expert hands. His golden fingers picked just the right pieces of wood and made a tent to start the fire. He dipped each piece into the ghee (clarified butter) first. The fire began to rise and then die down, rise and die down, but Swamiji kept it going, rising and falling, until finally it burst into flame, and a roaring, sputtering fire lit up the whole temple.

Smoke was rising to the ceiling, as more guests came in. Then barley, rice, colored dyes, and bananas went into the holy fire. The Swami was singing ancient Sanskrit and Bengali songs. He said, "This marriage will be like the fire, beginning slowly and then bursting into flames. You are both good devotees; together you will be at least twice as strong."

There was a very spaced-out girl present whose baby, Kaviraj, was lying haphazardly across her lap. His head kept hitting the floor. It seemed she'd forgotten she even had the child. Everyone in the room seemed to notice this except the mother. Even the zonked-out hippies were catching it. The Swami remained aloof, but the baby's head kept hitting the ground and hitting the ground. Eventually, even the Swami could not remain detached.

"It will be a strong baby," he remarked.

Then Swamiji beckoned for the mother to hold the baby so his head would remain in her lap. Incidentally, this was one of the girls who wanted to marry Swamiji. After a lecture, during the question-and-answer period, she would burst out, "I want to marry you!" She had simply fallen in love with the Swami, who remained detached and transcendental. He would simply say, "I am sannyasi." Of course, the girl's actions were totally understandable to us, as we had all fallen in love with the Swamiji.

After the wedding ceremony we all sat down to a huge feast of samosas, puris, rice, vegetable preparations, sweet rice, and dahl. The Swami ate and laughed with us. "Make sure everyone gets enough to eat," he said.

We were happy in the presence of our divine father.

Family

The Swami had been received nicely in San Francisco and New York, so he wanted to get an immigration-status visa. One way to obtain an immigration-status visa was to be adopted. Swamiji joked to Nandarani and Dayananda, "You can adopt me as your child. But then they will say, 'What you are doing with such an old child?'"

Sri Sri Radha Krishna Temple

Now, instead of waking up in community crash pads next to new bodies every day, I rose in the mornings with Yamuna, with the Holy Names upon my lips, feeling spiritually clean and purified. The morning shower was refreshing, and so was the walk up Ashbury Street as we headed towards the new Radha Krishna Temple on Frederick Street. All-night parties spilled out of the Grateful Dead house across the street as we walked by, and Jivanada and Harsarani would join us as we turned right on Frederick Street and ambled

I felt excited by the newness of it all, but I also felt content, part of a family.

down the hill past brightly painted Victorian houses with little gardens in the front. We would cross the large, four-way intersection at Stanyan Street, past the doughnut shop, and half a block later we were in another world, another time, another consciousness. As we entered, the sounds of hushed talking greeted us. It was almost time for the morning kirtan. The smiling countenances of Uddhava, Ramanuja, Subal, Govinda dasi, Haridas, Rayarama, Krishna devi, and Halidhar turned and welcomed us. I'd sit in the middle against the left wall. The karatals and finger cymbals started clanging as the Swami strode through the double Dutch doors.

I felt excited by the newness of it all, but I also felt content, part of a family. Since we first cleaned, painted, and decorated the storefront on Frederick Street, it had evolved magically into a temple. Every day something was acquired—a poster from India, a painting by Gaurasundar and Govinda dasi, a picture of Christ from Brother David, plants from neighbors, a totem pole, and more musical instruments (many homemade) for kirtans. The totem pole, newly carved by Haridas, stood to the right of the altar, its totemic animals grinning at us. Swamiji would eat oranges and then—splat!—throw the peels on the totem pole. It always amused me when he did that. Eventually, the totem pole was removed to Haridas' apartment.

At first there was no special vyasasana for the Swami to sit on, so he sat right on the altar. He was the father of our budding family, spoon-feeding us doses of spirituality such as the concepts of karma, transmigration of the soul, and "you are not this body." He explained things by means of stories and, in this way, enlightened us with eternal truths. There were not many books at the time—only the three volumes of *Srimad-Bhagavatam* that the Swami had printed in India; a small, plain-covered pamphlet entitled *Easy Journey* to *Other Planets;* and an occasional *Back to Godhead* magazine that had been mimeographed and put together on the temple floor. Most of what we learned was transmitted orally, as it had been handed down from guru to guru for generations, like a ripe mango handed down branch to branch from the top of a tree.

The Swami also had a knack for finding out our talents, dreams, and wishes and then engaging them in Lord Krishna's service. "Everything we do," he told us, "we can do for Krishna; we can offer our food in thanks and, Gurudas, you can photograph beautifully, and Yamuna can write in her nice handwriting (calligraphy)."

He would lead kirtan and speak in the temple on Monday, Wednesday, and Friday mornings at 7:00 A.M., and evenings at 7:00 P.M. The atmosphere felt otherworldly and ethereal. We would sing together, and then the Swami would talk for a while, then answer questions.

One night I was filming in the temple, and Saradia and Ali Krishna were wearing new saris. They were dancing together in unison from side to side. Swamiji saw them and pointed to the camera and then to them, indicating that he wanted me to film them. His seat became the director's chair. Our problems and old dreams of the past fell away, like the impurities in ghee that rise to the surface and disappear. Our dreams, as well as our day-to-day activities, became transcendental. As we grew in this way, I felt spiritually happy; I felt I was doing something worthwhile for myself and for others.

Yamuna and I moved into a nice apartment on Willard Street, with hardwood floors and a piano, just half a block from the temple. Lilavati, Murari, Jivananda, Harsharani, and my dog Que Tal moved in with us. Each married couple had a small room, and we shared a common living room and kitchen. I used the photo center run by the S. F. Parks and Recreation Department on Scott Street to develop film and print photographs. Some of us, including Jayananda, Shyamasundar, Krishna dasa, and myself, worked at jobs and gave some money for maintaining the Frederick Street temple. Others cleaned and cooked or did other service in the temple. I had a clerical job during the day and started teaching vocational English classes for the Department of Vocational Rehabilitation. The classrooms were in a business school on Market Street. About twelve students from various parts of the world attended each class. Although I was the teacher, I was the youngest person in the room. The average age of each student was about 48 years. One woman from Chile was 68. I would take any opportunity to bring up the subject of God-consciousness to them, and preaching became a normal part of my everyday life.

Finally, my life had structure, goals, and lots of love. My innocence was still intact; I felt purer every day, and I smiled a lot.

18   By His Example

THE FIRST HARINAMA SANKIRTAN

Gradually, I became accustomed to the new simplicity and regulation in my life. I hadn't dodged any bullets lately, or been zapped with electric cattle prods, or evicted from a domicile, or thrown off the planet. I was spending more time with the Swami, and I liked the wholesomeness of my companions on our mutual spiritual path. Most of them were good people, upbeat and somewhat innocent.

In my dreams—and during chanting—big blocks of past garbage floated up and away forever, as if my subconscious self was doing a spring cleaning. A general feeling of purification replaced my nescience. I asked Swamiji about this feeling. He said, "This is the purification process working. As you serve Lord Krishna, all unwanted things will go away." Although my inner self was being thus purified, I never liked too much cleaning. "You don't want to throw out the baby with the bath water," I told myself. "Go slow, go easy."

The new devotees were getting ready for our first all-day festival in the temple. It was to celebrate the appearance day of Lord Chaitanya Mahaprabhu, the Golden Avatar Who is Lord Krishna Himself, and Who came to Earth 487 years ago. The sight of Lord Chaitanya, His eyes turned towards heaven, His arms upraised in trance, the Holy Names of Krishna and Rama on His lotus lips, graced us from many Indian paintings. At the Swami's request we gathered produce, grains, and other foodstuffs to be prepared and offered for our biggest feast yet. This feast was to be served after the day-long festivities, which included congregational chanting, japa, and reading from *Srimad-Bhagavatam*. We gathered together early in the day and softly chanted our sixteen rounds of morning japa to ourselves. Later we shared the stories we had heard about Lord Chaitanya's life, pastimes, and miracles from Professor Sanyal's book. After about an hour of reading—about all our short attention spans could digest at one sitting—we started chanting loudly with instruments. Then we started the cycle again.

Early in the afternoon we were again performing kirtan loudly, and as the sun was streaming through the front window and open door, I started to get restless. I looked over at Jayananda, Jivananda, and Uddhava. Jivananda silently indicated, "Let's take this outdoors in the streets like Lord Chaitanya." While the temple kirtan was going on, the four of us headed for the door with cymbals and drum, inviting others to follow. Everyone else stayed put, and I wasn't sure at all if we were doing the right thing. We turned left and then right on Stanyan Street, up the hill, past Subal, Krishna devi, and Ramanuja's apartment. Then we turned right on Parnassus, chanting and marching to the sound of drum and kartalas.

We ended up under the window of the flat on Willard Street where

Yamuna and I had formerly lived, now occupied by the Swami. Our singing got louder and we hoped it would attract his attention. Soon Swamiji appeared at the window and looked down on us. He motioned with his hand in a downward thrust. Once, then twice, and then again; we thought he was motioning us back to the temple. Dejected, we started slowly down the hill but still managed to continue our chanting, although it sounded more like a dirge. We realized that we were supposed to stay in the temple all day and, having ventured outside, we thought that we had made Swamiji angry.

Chastised, we made our way down the hill. Upendra then came speeding out of the building, made a rounded turn to catch up with us and said, "The Swami wants to see you." We were confused, and then Upendra added, "When Swamiji waves his hand downward that means come here. That's how they do it in India." Relieved, yet still apprehensive, we went up the stairs. The Swami was in the front room. He beamed at us and said huskily, "Come on." Again he waved his hand downward. We sat in a crescent near his feet. He smiled even more. "Lord Chaitanya has given you the intelligence to chant outside in the streets so more people can hear the Holy Names. Lord Chaitanya always chanted in the streets, so now you can do this every day." Then with his golden graceful fingers he handed us gulabjamuns (sweetballs), all the while gracing

Our first kirtan was held at the cable car turn-around near Aquatic Park.

us with his munificent smile. Upendra then signaled that we should leave, so we bowed down and silently left.

When we returned to the temple, we told the others what had happened, and from that day on we went out with banners, signs, poster photos, instruments, and the mimeographed copies of *Back to Godhead*. Our first kirtan was held at the cable-car turn-around near Aquatic Park. I photographed the event. On other days we went to Union Square or Market Street near the cable-car turn-around. The enchanting sounds of the Holy Names wafted through the streets of San Francisco, bringing joy and healing via their transcendental vibrations. "Stay High Forever" said the article in *Back to Godhead*. The outdoor chanting became a gentle part of San Francisco life, and in a newspaper poll 67% of the citizens were not only favorable towards Hare Krishna but said also that they agreed with the Krishna conscious spiritual path.

No one felt coerced or pushed into anything. The example of Swamiji's enthusiasm, and our new faith in Krishna, were our beacons. A fresh wind of peace from the East came to us in the form of A. C. Bhaktivedanta Swami.

"You know Krishna through guru, and you know guru through Krishna."
—A. C. Bhaktivedanta Swami

I Just Want You to Be Happy

When conservative Vaishnava tradition mixed with the new hippie rebellion, sometimes there were small conflicts, minor rebellions, or outcries against racism or restrictive lifestyles. The initiated devotees also had some questions, like why animals couldn't come into the temple room or why couldn't we let our beads touch the ground since Krishna made the Earth too? We were a tight group, learning, struggling, chanting, and laughing together. New souls were joining every day, and we all liked being with the Swami, and with each other.

One of the most rebellious was Ravindra Svarup (Robert L.). He was an ascetic, bearded artist from New York. He was married to Halidhar and was outspoken when something didn't seem right to him. Ravindra Svarup's bewilderment was due to a theological difference, as he wanted to find Krishna directly and didn't think he needed to go through a spiritual master. One night, our spiritual family was together at evening kirtan, and Swamiji was sitting on the new vyasasana. Suddenly, in the middle of the service, we heard sobbing. I looked around and saw that it was Ravindra Svarup. He was so distraught, he just cried out loud. The Swami saw this, motioned to Ravindra Svarup, and said, "Come here, my boy."

Sobbing, Ravindra Svarup crawled slowly on all fours up to Swamiji, who motioned for him to come right up on the vyasasana. He crawled up next to the Swami and put his head on his lap, blurting out through heavy painful sobs, "I have to leave."

Swamiji caressed his head softly and said, "There, there, my boy. I just want you to be happy."

Within moments of receiving the Swami's comforting touch, Ravindra Svarup got up, slowly went to the door, turned towards the Swami, and said, "I love you, but I have to reach God directly. I cannot do it through anybody else." He ran out of the temple room, leaving the front door open.

No one could speak, and many of us were also crying. I was touched by Swamiji's compassion but sad at the loss of one of our family. We started chanting. It was our third "bloop"—our third instance of a devotee leaving. Another "devotee" who left our early budding movement was Brother David, whose eclectic altar burnt up in the basement of the Frederick Street temple. A large handlike burn mark remained on the wall jutting down towards the debris of his altar. He left in the middle of the night and started the Children of God group. The second bloop was my dog, Que Tal, who, according to Jivananda, used to walk right in the temple, stand on his hind legs, and dance and howl during the kirtans. Devotional life and vegetarianism turned out to be too tough for him, and one day he walked out of my life forever. Swamiji told me many times that "Krishna consciousness means happiness." If one is truly Krishna conscious, then he will be happy. Swamiji wanted his children to be happy.

When, Oh When

The Swami always looked regal, his face turned towards the sky. Outside the temple, I often stood on tiptoe to make myself look taller and bigger so that he would see me. However, everyone else was attempting this very same thing, so I just blended in again. Maybe the right idea was to become "smaller." But Swamiji wasn't ignoring me at all—he just seemed to be inside of himself. It was as if he could look and not see, or look and see everything. He could see right inside you, or notice and focus attention on things that others missed—little things, like opening a window so a butterfly could go back outdoors.

He went inside the temple and bowed down. The rest of us stood around, waiting. Then some of us followed the Swami's example and bowed down too. The double Dutch doors were wide open to the street, and the temple room quickly became crowded with visitors who wanted to see the Swami from India. I stood by my favorite photo of Lord Krishna on the left wall of the temple room. The Swami sat and looked on all of us in the room. When he saw me he smiled even wider, and I was encouraged.

Maybe he knew my mind and how I yearned to become his close disciple. Everything else about devotional service was indeed very nice: the prasadam was good, the godbrothers and -sisters were all right, being with Yamuna was great, chanting was effectively purifying, and the stories were instructive and exotic. But I really felt that for me the best means of spiritual advancement was with, and through, Swami Bhaktivedanta. Sitting on the low altar next to a painting of Lord Chaitanya, Whose eyes were raised in the trance of chanting, Swamiji set the rhythm and began singing the Holy Names: Hare Krishna, Hare Krishna, Krishna Krishna, Hare Hare, Hare Rama, Hare Rama, Rama Rama, Hare Hare. Deep in concentration, he closed his eyes in rapture. Every once in a while his eyes opened a bit wider, just a slit, and he would glance around. Sometimes his eyes opened wider, and sometimes closed again smoothly and slowly like a turtle doing tai chi. When he noticed me through his transcendental eyes, I chanted louder, trying to feel and look more spiritual. After the chanting, Swamiji's voice respectfully intoned the names of past acharyas. Most of the initiated devotees bowed down, and many of the congregation followed. This was the Haight-Ashbury, its flower children fully engaged in our spiritually charged atmosphere.

Then the Swami began addressing the congregation: "When you do things to please the Lord, you become pure, and what you do becomes spiritualized. If Krishna gives you a certain talent, and you American boys and girls are very intelligent, and you utilize your talent for Krishna, then you will be blissful, sat cit ananda. We are constitutionally sat (eternal), cit (all knowledgeable), and ananda (blissful.) Our real nature is covered up when we serve maya (illusion), or that which is not. We serve our own temporary pleasures and then we desire more pleasure. This samsara wheel (the cycle of birth, old age, disease, and death) never stops turning round and round." (I visualized a hamster on a wheel turning endlessly and thought to myself, "I am moving, but going nowhere.") "When you chant Krishna's Name," Swamiji continued, "He is with you, in your heart. He and His Name are connected, for it is a transcendental sound vibration. When we chant 'water, water,' that is a material sound, and our thirst is not quenched, but when we chant the Hare Krishna mantra, the sound "Krishna" and Krishna are the same. This process is so easy, even a child can do it. So please chant and be happy."

The Swami swept out of the temple room, and it was as if a great vacuum had replaced the wonderful ambiance created by his divine presence. The lights were brightened, and people started to tidy and clean, but I was hesitant to break my mood. An experiment began to form in my mind.

Outside, in front of the temple, Haladhar dasi, blond and pretty, came over. She asked, "Did you understand what the Swami was saying?"

"Some of it," I said, and I walked away from her and everyone, so I could think to myself. We were living in an unreal world, I knew that; but some things—like love, learning, music—seemed more real than other things. I had already experienced alternative worlds, so I knew what Swamiji was saying. I had already felt drops of spiritual ecstasies and peered into mysterious realms. I needed heavy, incontrovertible truth.

Que Tal and I walked home to the Willard Street apartment. No one else was home, so I began the following experiment:

I decided to walk through the wall.

I figured that if, like a yogi, I concentrated on the illusion of the wall, I could walk through it. I emptied my mind and walked towards the wall.

BOOM!

I connected with the wall, but not in the way I'd envisioned.

Yes, I became one with the wall, but as the sound of one forehead clapping. Shaking the stars out, concentrating even more,

I chanted Hare Krishna loudly.

BAM!

This wall may be temporary, but its rigidity is real.

Later I learned that temporary can mean a span of many years, or a lifetime, like a past civilization that eventually crumbles, decays, and returns to the dust from which it came.

I tried once more, but not as fervently.

BONK!

The wall met me again. I have to ask Swamiji about this, I thought, if I ever get to talk to him in person. This illusion and reality stuff is an enigma.

"We are not this body, we are spirit soul," he says. Oh yeah, I thought; then what was this that just slammed into the wall? Que Tal was looking at me quizzically. "You are not this body" kept running through my mind.

"Eternity is not subject to time and fashions," the Swami later enlightened me. At this time, however, my dilemma was unresolved.

> *"Something learned with difficulty is not easily forgotten;
> something learned easily is soon forgotten."*
> —A. C. Bhaktivedanta Swami

FACE TO FACE WITH SWAMIJI

The next day at the temple Mukunda informed me that the Swami wanted to see me! I had started going on a few morning walks with him, though most of the time the Swami was silent as he walked. Now, I would have a private darshan with him.

I cleaned myself and went up to his quarters. He was alert and smiling. "You know about photography and cameras. Is Asahi Pentax a good one?" This wasn't what I had expected. Maybe some wisdom from the East, but certainly not a discussion of camera brands. "A friend in India has asked me to bring him one," the Swami said and put an airmail letter with small, colorful stamps in my hand.

"Yes, Pentax is a good camera," I said.

"What kind do you use?"

"Nikon, Swamiji." I showed him the Nikon. He felt the heft, looked it over, and pointed to the light meter. "What is that?"

"This measures light, so we know how to set the camera."

I showed him the f-stops, aperture, and shutter settings. He was absorbed and looked like a young boy. Then I picked up the light meter and covered the photo light cells with my finger. The dial arrow went down. With a slight flourish, I took my hand away, and the dial seemingly sprang to life. Swamiji's eyes lit up. I gave him the light meter, and he tried the same thing. The arrow sprang up. Delighted, he played with the meter over and over again, for close to ten minutes.

I sat there enjoying the Swamiji's mood with curiosity, enjoyment, and contentment. He was taking me into his world, wherever it may lead. Feeling comfortable in the shelter of his association, I mustered enough courage to ask him, "If this world is illusion, why can't I walk through the wall?"

He laughed and said: "The material world is illusion because it is temporary. Love for Krishna is real because it is eternal. I am simply saying you can be continually happy by chanting Hare Krishna." Now I understood the real meaning of temporary. After some time, Swamiji asked me to bring him catalogs with the models and prices of both Pentax and Nikon. I told him I would do so and departed in ecstasy, because now I had a connection with him through a particular service. From then on, I photographed for Krishna more and more.

I also started to arrange radio and television appearances for Swami Bhaktivedanta, since Mukunda had informed me that Swamiji was interested in sharing Krishna consciousness with everyone through these forums.

I had soon figured out that if I took a step towards Swamiji, he would likewise take a step towards me. The way he looked into me was as important as what he said. Actually, Swamiji took many steps towards me. According to him, Krishna will take ten steps for each one of ours. Swamiji guided my faltering steps and pulled me up straight and strong. I was now ready to jump into the transcendental waters with both feet.

Portrait for the Books

I acquired price lists of various 35mm cameras, including the Pentax prices that interested Swamiji. I submitted these to him, and he accepted gracefully. I watched him scrutinize the lists. Then he put them aside on his desk, looked encouragingly at me, and said, "Brahmananda has asked that we make one portrait photo for our books." He held up a letter and tossed it into the air for me to catch. By Krishna's grace I caught it deftly. The letter from New York requested an official formal portrait that could be used as a frontispiece in all published items. As I handed the letter back to Swamiji, our hands touched, and I felt the warmth of his comfortable and protective touch.

"Do you want me to take the photograph?" I asked.

"Yes."

"When?"

"Tomorrow."

"Where?"

"Here is fine. Is that all right?" he asked.

Since I had lived at the Swami's Willard Street apartment before him, I knew when and where the sunlight best illuminated the back room. I also knew that Swamiji's morning schedule was taken up with writing, a massage around 11:30, followed by a bath and lunch. After this, he would take a short twenty- to thirty-minute nap (even with this nap, he slept only three-and-a-half to four hours in every twenty-four!)

Upendra told me that the best time for Swamiji would be at four in the afternoon, and this was fine with me because the light was good at that time in the late afternoon, softening everything into a pastel, velvety glow. The back room facing the ocean was well lit, and I could use available natural light, which was softer and less shadowy than artificial light. I arrived at 3:45 P.M. to find everything already prepared—Bhaktivedanta Swami was to sit on a mattress covered with a tasteful madras.

He came in smiling and, like a nesting bird, gracefully sat down on the cushions. The flowered early American wallpaper behind him was distracting, so I suggested that we needed something to cover the wallpaper, as it was too busy and would take away from the portrait. At first no one moved. Then Govinda dasi went out to search for something in another room. Swamiji took off his charcoal-gray chaddar (shawl) and asked, "Will this do?" Even though I thought that a white background would be best, this was what Krishna had supplied, so I agreed to try it and secured it to the wall with pins.

I was anxious to complete the session as quickly as possible so as not to inconvenience the Swami, whose time was so valuable. He sat with his right hand in his japa bag and started to chant quietly. Then he motioned for the

26   By His Example

A smoky golden aura, a special light, emanates around Swamiji in these portraits, instead of the charcoal gray of the chaddar hanging behind him.

three *Srimad-Bhagavatam* volumes to be placed to his right. In one camera I had a few color exposures left, and in another I had loaded black-and-white film. Swamiji watched as I took the light meter readings and, by the look on his face, it seemed as if he wanted to come over and play with the light-meter again. He remained seated on the mattress, however, as I staggered the f-stops (used different lighting sequences) so I could be certain that at least some of the photos taken would produce good negatives. I included some close-ups taken from the ground so that his compassionate face looked down upon me, blessing me. I was so taken with his mercy that I had difficulty functioning. When I developed the black-and-white shots and printed them, they all were sharp. A smoky golden aura, a special light, emanates around Swamiji in these portraits, instead of the charcoal-gray of the chaddar hanging behind him.

Beauty

Someone said to Swamiji, "You look so beautiful today."
He replied, "Why just today?"

Don't Let Gurudas in

I found any excuse to go to his apartment and see the Swami. I wanted to be near him, no matter how petty the reason. Seeing me with Swamiji so often, his servants Satchitananda and Upendra talked it over and advised him, "Don't let Gurudas in so much." Yet I still found ways to be near the Swami, because to me this association was the sum and substance of my Krishna consciousness. When they were out of the room for even a brief moment, I would slip in.

He would greet me warmly, expressing real happiness to see me. I had never experienced such acceptance from anyone else, ever. He would sit comfortably, cross-legged, with a huge smile and a welcoming gesture. I would sit on a cushion on the opposite side of the simple, low coffee table which served as a desk. On this desk were a goblet of water with a lid and the three original volumes of *Srimad-Bhagavatam*. There were papers neatly arranged, as well as a pen-and-pencil set, some note paper, his glasses, and, at certain times, some fruit or sweets on a large, stainless-steel thali plate. If it wasn't on his hand, his japa bag was nearby. Between conversations he would chant constantly, almost silently. Upendra and Satchitananda would come back from somewhere and find Swamiji and me sitting there talking and laughing.

Glossolalia*

One time a crazy fellow somehow got into Swamiji's apartment and was ranting and raving. Mukunda, who lived next door, rushed over and asked the person to leave. The guy finally left but yelled, "*Ooga booga, ooga booga!*" all the way down the hall.

Swamiji turned to Mukunda and asked, "What is this Maha Buddha?"
Mukunda replied, "He was saying ooga booga, not Maha Buddha."
"Oh," said the Swami and went back inside his apartment.

Hell's Angels, Diggers, and Jagannath

A steady congregation of characters was now flowing into our storefront Radha Krishna Temple for the nightly sessions of rocking, chanting, dancing, feasting, and transcendental information. Jerry Garcia of the Grateful Dead had just donated a huge, new stove, so we now had breakfast, lunch, and dinner programs on a regular basis. There were so many folks coming that the temple would be filled from the front altar all the way to the back of the room and out the double Dutch doors to the sidewalk.

One night the temple door opened and a shaggy-haired, gap-toothed

---

*In some religious practices they have this word, which means "speaking in tongues."

youth in a homemade dress came in. He called himself Rabbit and didn't bother closing the front door. Behind him came Israel, a gaunt, scholarly-looking man in his late twenties. Israel wore wire-rimmed glasses and a topknot trailing down to his waist. Trumpet in hand, he was ready to wail and chant.

Then three soiled, blanketed cherubs walked in silently and went to a far wall. They stood together, not talking, not looking around, just waiting. They had begun showing up every day, especially for feasts. They rarely spoke, but they muttered and motioned that they would like to help out around the temple. In the front window were some potted plants and flowers donated by the Patels, a local East Indian family. I asked the three to water the plants with a can, and I filled it for them. All three stepped up onto the store-window platform and proceeded to spill water all over themselves and everywhere else except on the plants. One of them even stepped right on the plants! I saw this and nicely asked them to please just sit down and chant.

They turned out to be airy-headed "space cadets." They muddled any simple job they were asked to do, or left it in midstream. If it was licking envelopes, they would end up sticking the envelopes all over themselves; if it was cutting vegetables, we had to protect them from cutting themselves. So we assigned them to just hang around the temple and chant. If they were stationary and content, so were we. We eventually nicknamed them the Three Wise Men because they looked like a scruffy version of the three visitors to baby Christ in the manger. Since we didn't know their names and they never told us, we called them Frank, Incense, and Murray.

Surendra, a youth from Bengal, was one of the regular guests at the temple, and he was always gaping at the scantily-clad and beaded flower girls who danced in the temple room with abandon. Emaciated, sullen, self-absorbed, poetic-looking folks crept in, as did sleek girls that came to dance, first gyrating and then, after some words of instruction from the Swami, swaying like bamboo in the breeze, their eyes closed in the Hare Krishna trance dance. Many street people came only to fill their bellies, yet they eventually took to the chanting.

Each night the newly initiated devotees would file into the temple. Mukunda appeared with a conga drum, and Yamuna came in looking confident, like the mother of the temple, her beautiful, long, black hair flowing straight down her back. She smiled at her friends, as her sister Janaki, animated and giggling, followed right behind her. Govinda dasi and Gaurasundar, one of the first married couples, brought one of their new paintings of the Swami and hung it on the wall for everyone to admire.

Uddhava, with his curly beard and open face, arrived ready to sing out. A contingent of devotees from New York arrived: large, blustery Hayagriva in front, with a horn he had fashioned from a length of dried kelp; Ranchor and Rayarama, quiet and shy. Malati walked down the four steps from the back kitchen room with a huge kettledrum in her arms. Brother David (who later founded the Children of God cult), soft-spoken and slow-moving, walked up from the basement where the brahmachari students lived.

At 7:00 P.M., Swami Bhaktivedanta walked in, head raised slightly, simultaneously noble and unassuming. Upendra stumbled in behind him like one of Snow White's dwarves. The Swami was not looking directly at anyone but embracing us all. He then smiled, went to the altar, and sat down right under our new painting of the Panca-tattva. The five avatars, with Their arms raised, eyes to Krishna in Goloka Vrindavan, dancing serenely: Lord Chaitanya, Nityananda, Sri Advaita, Gadadhar, and Shrivas catalyzed our mood. As Swamiji sang the "Vande Ham" prayers to his line of spiritual masters, it soothed and calmed us. The prayers ended as the sunset and the last rays streamed through the front door and window, bathing the temple room in orange-yellow light. I was nestled cross-legged on a pillow with my back straight. All eyes were on Swamiji. He took out some bell-metal kartalas, looked around without looking at anything in particular, and began a three beat: *chah-chah-cheee, chah-chah-cheee*—the third beat sizzling. In husky, sonorous tones he sang out: "Hare Krishna, Hare Krishna, Krishna Krishna, Hare Hare, Hare Rama, Hare Rama, Rama Rama, Hare Hare." We couldn't stay seated and jumped up almost in unison. Hayagriva blew the kelp horn, as the booming kettledrum created a throbbing foundation rhythm.

The mantra was starting to grow on me, and singing with Swamiji leading the congregation was really fun. Kirtan usually lasted more than an hour, the sound rising, subsiding into sweet, low tenderness, and then ending in a joyous crescendo that left me with an afterglow—a clean, elated feeling.

The Swami's eyes were closed, and his head was swaying from side to side. My hands went up towards the ceiling, and, in a trance dance, I swayed like wheat in the wind. As the sounds grew louder and slightly faster, Israel jumped up and down. He danced in a circle and bleated his trumpet like Cat Anderson of the Duke Ellington band. A blond girl, naked beneath a homemade dress, rose and started dancing, her dress falling provocatively off her shoulders. I became distracted and saw I wasn't alone. Eyes darted in her direction, and I saw bramacharis peeking through supposedly closed eyes. This innocent, chanting wood-nymph was unaware of the agitation around her. Sensing what was going on, the Swami opened his eyes. The girl was right in front of him now, shaking all over as if she were at the Avalon Ballroom. Swamiji didn't change his expression and continued chanting.

When it was the congregation's turn to chant he called me over. "That girl must be covered," he told me.

I didn't know what to do, as only a few weeks before I would have been dancing with her at the Avalon Ballroom myself. I got an old sari worn for cooking and draped it around her. "Now to deal with her dance style," I thought to myself. I didn't have to say anything though; her consciousness was made more gentle simply by the shelter of the sari.

The kirtan built up again. Yamuna yelled, "Hari hari bol!" her voice piercing the temple room with its pure, spiritual strength. Janaki echoed her sister. Mukunda played the drum expertly, catalyzing everyone with driving rhythms. I felt like I was leaving my body. We got into a steady, flowing ecstasy. After some time, the Swami speeded up the karatal beat, and we responded faster. The whole room was bursting; the whole city was rocking; the whole world was vibrating; the whole universe was in balance—and I was experiencing transcendental bliss!

The bongos, kettledrum, cymbals, kelp horn, trumpet, and African instruments all stopped in one unified beat. Swamiji called out, "Gaura premananda hari hari bol!" In a voice that was simultaneously sweet and grave, he recited paeans glorifying the past preceptors in our spiritual lineage. We collapsed on the floor, bowing down. Swamiji settled into his raised seat. "Thank you very much—all of you such nice young boys and girls—for coming and . . ."

We heard pounding on the wall. A loud thump from next door suddenly resonated on the wall. Framed pictures shook. Again there was a thump.

". . . chanting this Hare Krishna mantra with us."

The Swami didn't miss a beat. He stopped talking, called me over, beckoned me closer. My ear was right near his mouth. I felt privileged.

"What is that sound?" he asked.

"I don't know," I answered.

"It is coming from next door."

Next door was the God's Eye Ice Cream Parlor, which was the hangout and hideout of the Hell's Angels as well as headquarters for the Diggers, an anarchistic organization run by Emmitt Grogan and Peter Coyote, which believed that all goods and services should be free. The police raided the place frequently, and when this happened the Angels would whip out movie cameras without any film in them and pretend to film the raid. The police, fearing they would be on the evening news, always left quickly and quietly.

The banging continued.

"Go see what is making that noise," Swamiji requested. "Ask them to stop."

"Why me?" I thought. I'm wearing a robe, I'm high from the kirtan, and now I have to face the Hell's Angels. Cloth versus leather, finger cymbals versus knives. The Swami again addressed the congregation.

"I see you, so many bright-faced people chanting and feeling blissful by chanting these Holy Names..."

Excusing myself, I went out into the cool, night air and started to breathe more easily. I heard loud laughter from inside the God's Eye. Yes, I thought, inside God's eyes certainly Krishna would protect me. But my throat was dry as I knocked on the door. Sonny, scar-faced yet handsome, opened the door. He wore swastikas and lots of black leather. He stared at me. I held his eyes and stared back. Six more Angels encircled me. Then a tattooed 13 AND BORN TO LOSE arm waved me inside.

Resolutely but quietly I said, "The Swami is about to speak. He was wondering if you could party less hearty." They didn't say anything. I persevered. "The thumping on the wall interrupted him. Many folks would like to hear him speak, and you can come too if you like."

Sonny stared at me a while longer. Then he smiled and said, "It was your singing that made us dance, but the wall got in the way! Hey, if the Swami wants to speak, that's okay with us. Your guru is heavy, man!" His gapped-tooth smile embraced me. I thanked them all.

As neighbors, we would eventually come to know each other and get along well. They came over for free feasts, a stick of incense, or for a cup of sugar. After my meeting with them they always quieted down when they heard the kirtan stop, because they knew the Swami was speaking. I could sense their presence behind the wall. "The Swami is going to speak now; shut up." The Angels became our security guards at the Mantra Rock Dance and at many of our other large gatherings, like the Jagannatha Car Festival.

> *"In any effort we must take time, place, and circumstance into account."*
> —A. C. Bhaktivedanta Swami

A Tribute to Jayananda Prabhu

Swamiji told me that when you see a Vaishnava you automatically think of Krishna. Jayananda was steady in his devotion. Jayananda was one of the most unselfish people I have ever met. Jayananda Prabhu was most known for his tireless work every year to make the Jagannath Festival a success, but his passion for all types of service was evident from the first day I met him in San Francisco. He motivated many of us by his stalwart example, doing as much as he could by himself before asking anyone else to help.

Jayananda once gave Swamiji five thousand dollars to keep our budding San Francisco temple blossoming. He drove a taxicab and became a celestial

32 *By His Example*

Jayananda Prabhu was most known for his tireless work every year to make the Jagannath Festival a success.

chauffeur by driving Swamiji to radio and television programs and to various places in Golden Gate Park for his morning walks. I witnessed the respect Jayananda felt for Swamiji. I saw the love brimming from his eyes when he viewed his spiritual master. Although Jayananda presented a simple demeanor, his tremendous mind retained many details at once.

In a playful mood, Jayananda once asked me to name any street in San Francisco and he would tell me the adjacent streets, what stores or residences were on the street, and even what colors the buildings were. I picked obscure streets, but he could accurately identify what stood on any given street, road, lane or boulevard. He remembered whether a house was a Victorian, and he knew the cross streets. I relished my association with Jayananda during his presidency of the first San Francisco temple. After I was elected vice-president, we would ride together to the Farmers' Market or the flower outlets and plan events for the temple.

Jayananda gave Yamuna and me his apartment on Ashbury Street across from the Grateful Dead house, while he moved into the stark basement of the Frederick Street temple where the bramacharis lived and slept on the floor with them. Our small family was close, serving Krishna, learning and building together. Later, I went on to London. Jayananda was needed elsewhere, so we drifted apart.

Around 1974, Jayananda and I wwould be reunited when I was given charge of a Radha Damodara bus that traveled throughout the Pacific Northwest. We put on three to four programs a day. During lunch we would set up a stage, prasadam counter, and book table. Jayananda would man the prasadam booth, and Paravrajakacharya and I would speak about the chanting and philosophy in student unions from Reed College to the University of Nevada.

From Tuesday through Saturday, Jayananda would lead the satellite sankirtan party chanting through the streets. He took care of the two vans that we used, and I always trusted that the party was secure under his guidance. Even though I was officially in charge of the traveling party, I considered Jayananda the spiritual leader. The servant is the master. Jayananda Prabhu called me Maharaja, but with so much friendship and so little formality that he endeared himself to me. He cut through pretense in order to get to the heart of our mutual goal: devotional service. While others were parading or posturing, Jayananda was working. He taught by his example.

Free Passage

Swamiji wanted to speak on radio and television, so I arranged it. I called the radio station KRON and reserved a time slot. The program format consisted of an interview with call-in questions and answers. Swamiji arrived with Subal, Shyamasundar, Jayananda, Mukunda, and myself.

After we had settled in, the interviewer asked some general questions about Krishna consciousness and then asked about our tilak markings. We had arranged that some of the devotees would call in some questions to the show, so when he opened up the phones Uddhava called, asking, "Swamiji, what is the meaning of life?"

"Ah, the meaning of life is to cultivate your love of God, Krishna. . . ."

Swamiji answered the question for fifteen minutes. Then Gargamuni called, asking, "What are we here on Earth for?" Again, the Swami launched into a long explanation.

The interviewer soon figured out what was happening and said, "We want callers other than from your organization to call in."

Then another question from radio land: "What does Hare Krishna mean?" Swamiji answered this question also.

Then a lady with a raspy, sarcastic voice called in and asked, "Why is your so-called temple in the Haight Ashbury district?"

Swamiji replied, "So-called temple? We have Deities, worship, chanting—ours is a real temple."

She said, "Then why is your temple in the Haight Ashbury?"

"Inexpensive rents. That is why my disciples choose that place."

Then she asked, "How did you come to the United States?"

Swamiji replied, "I received free passage."

She asked, "Who paid for it?"

He countered, "Free passage means there was no payment involved."

She then asked, "Are you a freeloader?"

Swamiji had never heard the expression before and thought she meant "free passage."

He said, "Yes."

We could hear her surprise and silence. There was no retort.

Understanding what had transpired, even the interviewer got angry and cut her off abruptly. However, the rest of the show went smoothly.

Buzz Word

Once, preparing for a television show in San Francisco, Swamiji was sitting peacefully while technicians readied the lights, cameras, and sound. There was a mysterious hissing in the sound lines. The soundmen frantically tried to find and erase the buzzing sound. For an hour they followed lines, searching for the source of the murmur. Finally they followed all the wires to Swamiji. The technicians pointed to the beatific soul in orange cloth and said, "It's him. The sound is coming from him."

The murmuring sound was Swamiji quietly chanting the maha-mantra while he waited to go on TV.

Restricted Love

A girl remarked, "If I eat meat, it becomes a part of me."

Swamiji replied, "Then why don't you eat your father?"

The girl was momentarily stunned. She countered, "Because I love him."

Swamiji said, "Your love is restricted. You eat animals but not your father, your brother, or your friend. In Krishna consciousness we love and respect all living entities."

She replied, "If you eat vegetables, you also kill."

"Yes, that is the law of nature. One entity kills another for survival. But we eat vegetables because we love Krishna and we eat what he likes, and Krishna says in the *Bhagavad-gita*, 'Offer a leaf, a flower, a fruit to Me.' That is why we eat vegetables."

She said, "That is a very nice answer. Thank you."

KARTAMASI ON HAIGHT

For many months we had longed to have a Deity of Krishna for our altar at Frederick Street. We didn't have a clue where to find such an item. One day, I was walking down Haight Street near the temple—and Krishna was standing right there, in the window of a shop called Phoenix! This shop sold everything from drug paraphernalia to beads, Indian posters, incense, etc. But their most attractive item was the beautiful, two-foot high painted plaster statue of Krishna.

I went in often and asked them to donate Him to our new temple. The shop owners were friendly but, being businessmen,

"It's him. The sound is coming from him."

refused again and again. I persisted. Then one day Krishna was no longer in the window. Alarmed, I went inside and asked where Krishna was. They said they had moved Him upstairs to the workshop. Again, I beseeched them to give Him to the temple, where He would be cared for nicely. To my surprise and happiness, they agreed that I could have Him for $35.00. But I didn't have $35.00.

Since Krishna is my father, my son, and my friend, I immediately went out onto the street and begged passers-by, "I need money to get my father out of jail," or ". . . my friend out of jail," or ". . . my son. . . . " Very quickly I had the money and gave it to the shopkeepers. I wrapped Krishna in a blanket and carried Him home. Yamuna, Harsarani, and I cleaned Him up and gave Him a bath, and then presented Him to Swamiji, who was very pleased.

"We shall name Him Kartamasi—feed Him some nice prasadam."

I had photographed Kartamasi immediately after I got Him out of the shop. At the shop I had noticed a small burn in His base. After showing Him to Swamiji, and after offering prasadam and a rest at our apartment, I photographed Kartamasi again. And through the lens I saw a remarkable difference: He was happier looking, and his bluish color shined. Swamiji remarked on these changes, and others saw the differences too. Later I showed the slides to Swamiji and he said he was very happy that Kartamasi had changed in the home of His devotees.

Morning Walks

Walking in the early morning with Bhaktivedanta Swami was a special treat. Swamiji would say, "Regulation is the preventative for disease," and he practiced this principle by going to sleep at 10:30 P.M., waking at 1:30 A.M., bathing, chanting, translating, and then taking a walk at 6:00 A.M.—each and every morning.

Walking by his side I felt secure. He walked and chanted with a bead bag on his right hand and a walking cane in the left; and when he stopped to point to something in nature, his words filled my heart and soul. He would glance at me, and it felt as if we were all alone. The other four or five devotees, all that could fit into a car, became a peripheral part of my consciousness.

We especially liked to go to Stowe Lake in nearby Golden Gate Park. One morning two carloads went, and as the Swami and ten others walked in the early morning fog, some ducks were sleeping on the pathway. A wellmeaning devotee started yelling at the ducks, "Make way for the Swami—get out of the way!" Quacking, the ducks grumpily got to their feet and half staggered to the side of the wide, cement path towards the lake, where other ducks were still in peaceful slumber. The loud, bold devotee came back to Swamiji and reported, "We have moved the ducks so they won't disturb you."

With a laugh in his eye, Swamiji replied, "As you are thinking they are disturbing us, they are thinking we are disturbing them." I burst out laughing. I couldn't help it, because I was thinking that very same thought. I liked the way Swamiji could be so compassionate and open-minded and see all sides of a situation.

At Stowe Lake Swamiji would walk up and down, turning around as he got to one end of the wide, cement road. Instead of going around the scenic lake he would be satisfied to just walk back and forth on one shore. Usually whenever Swamiji turned, all ten of us would continue as if we were going around the lake. Then suddenly realizing that he had about-faced, we would run back to catch up with him, angling closer to see who would walk right next to him. It was like the roller derby in slow motion, people subtly elbowing out their fellow prabhus.

Jayananda and I decided that at the next opportunity we would take Swamiji all around the lake, as it was very pretty, with an ornate bridge, a little stream, and earthen paths. The next morning I got to go on the walk again; this time I motioned to Swamiji to walk around the lake, which he did. I watched his face as we came upon some particularly beautiful spot, expecting it to change—but his face remained constant in the same

"We would run back to catch up with him, angling closer to see who would walk right next to him."

transcendental mood. The next morning he resumed his walking up and down one side of the lake, and I realized that his contentment was not dependent on a beauty of nature or on any situation or environment—his peaceful constitution was dependent only upon Lord Krishna. Regarding Stowe Lake he said, "This place reminds me of Bombay." The more I walked with him in the mornings, the more friendly he was to me; and when he looked toward me, he looked right into me—it was nonjudgmental, just looking and making me feel good. Sometimes we took the Swami to different places in the park. Once, in a wooded section of Golden Gate Park, deep inside the forest, a policeman came driving slowly through the woods on a cement path. The cop leaned out of his car and said, "Hi-ya, Swamiji," waved, smiled, and drove on.

Swamiji turned to us and said, "He has seen me on television."

> *"Morning sun gives strength, afternoon sun takes away strength."*
> —A. C. Bhaktivedanta Swami

Do-Nots

Walking down Stanyan Street one day, Swamiji saw a sign advertising "Do-Nuts" (doughnuts) and asked, "What are these do-nots?"

Perhaps he thought these were posted rules for what not to do in America.

A Question to Swamiji

"Can Krishna do anything?" someone asked.

"Yes," Swamiji answered.

"Can He make a mountain so large that even He can't lift it?"

"Yes. And then He will lift it."

"If You Are Photographed..."

In San Francisco I was photographing all the new activities: the street sankirtan, love feasts inside the temple, my wedding with Yamuna, the Mantra Rock Dance. But I enjoyed photographing Swamiji most of all, more than anyone or anything. I photographed him at the beach, chanting with us, and during morning walks in Golden Gate Park. Each expression, each moment, was so full and so graceful. He was becoming so dear to me. Not wanting to miss even the slightest change in his transcendental mood, I would snap the shutter rapidly to keep up with him. Each one of his movements was a singular joy. He rarely posed, yet the photos appeared perfect.

One day, walking at Stowe Lake, he looked down at me through the camera lens and said, "In India, there is a superstition that if you are photographed it will shorten your life span." I stopped abruptly, and the camera fell from my hands like Arjuna's Gandiva bow. I felt so ignorant.

"What do you think of that?" he asked.

I thought for a moment and replied, "It is more important what one does with his life than how long one lives."

"Yes," he laughed. "That is just an Indian superstition."

He then motioned that it was all right to continue taking pictures.

Appetite

With a twinkle in his eyes, Swamiji entered the kitchen where Harsarani and Yamuna were making samosas. He began eating some, and then more.

"How many of these can you eat?" Harsarani asked.

"More then you can prepare."

Swamiji laughed, eating another. Then Swamiji said he liked cooking for himself.

"Why?"

He replied, "There is no one else to find fault."

Yes, No, Very Good

Swamiji told a joke about a man from India coming to the West. The man said to his friend in Hindi that he was afraid to go to America because he didn't know English. His friend told him, "All you need to know in English is yes, no, and very good." When the man who knew only "yes, no, and very good" arrived in the West, he managed for awhile and was even employed.

One day the boss' watch was missing.

The employer asked the new arrival, "Did you take my watch?"

The man replied, "Yes."

"Give it back then."

"No."

"Then you will go to jail."

"Very good."

7-Up

Swamiji was given a 7-Up soda. Later, wanting to try the soda again, he asked, "Is there any 7 o'clock?"

Brainy Boy

Swamiji was addressing a class for nine-to-thirteen-year-old children at the YMCA in San Francisco. He looked out into the audience and asked, "Who is the most intelligent child?"

A boy, proud of his brain, stood up. Swamiji pointed to the boy's head and asked, "What is that?"

The boy answered, "My head."

Swamiji continued, "Yes," and pointed to the boy's arm. "What is that?"

The boy said, "My arm", smiling now, thinking the Swami to be simple. Swamiji then pointed to the boy's leg and asked again, "What is that?"

The boy, now thinking this was beneath his intelligence smirked, "My leg."

Then Swamiji said, "That is your head, your arm, your leg—but where are you?"

The boy was surprised, and stumped. Swamiji went on, "You are spirit soul; you are not your body. Your body will change, but you are the same inside. We don't say 'I body,' we say 'my body,' because you, soul, are the owner of your head, arm, and leg."

Cowboys and Indians

Govinda dasi was essential to the San Francisco temple in many ways. One of her services was painting nice renditions of Prahlad-lila and portraits of Swamiji. Her parents were visiting from Texas and thought Krishna consciousness just another weird, hippie thing, even though by now the temple was well-established and frequently mentioned in newspapers and on the radio. Members of the Indian community (even the cultural attaché) regularly came to our evening services. One evening, right after the last kirtan, Govinda dasi's father walked right up to the Swami sitting on his new vyasasana and said in a loud, Texas drawl, "Why does my daughter have to have an 'Injun' (Indian) name?"

People were standing and milling about, and they crept closer to hear and see the commotion. The whole Patel clan stood right behind Govinda dasi's father. One elder Patel had a shiny silver tooth that was reflecting light. The Swami looked at the outraged father and quietly said with a laugh in his eyes, "You do not like Indians?"

The father saw he was surrounded. He must have felt like General Custer. He said, "Well, yeah, I like Injuns all right."

Swamiji pressed his advantage and said, "If your daughter is happy, why do you object?" Then Govinda dasi's mother shook Swamiji's hand and said something to him that I couldn't hear. The father was rendered speechless and quietly led away by his wife.

False Devotion

An Indian entertainer, a member of the Baul caste from Bengal, was in San Francisco. He attended our temple and sang songs to Krishna and Lord Chaitanya. He was a friendly man, so one time we invited him to perform first on a double-bill kirtan with us at the Straight Theater on Haight Street. He started chanting, then at one point he swooned and fell on the floor in a fit of so-called spiritual ecstasy. However, he revived just in time to give a talk into the microphone. It all seemed so phony to me.

When later I recounted the incident to Swamiji, I told him that he had risen just in time to speak. Then I asked Swamiji what to do in similar situations when we suspected someone of faking it, and he said: "Kick him." He made a kicking motion with his foot and continued, "If he is faking, then he will get up; and if he is genuine, he won't feel the kick."

Lord Jagannath in San Francisco

Krishna works in mysterious ways. Even several months after its opening, the Frederick Street storefront temple was almost bare, with only a painting of Govinda on the wall, a statue of Kartamasi Krishna, and a piece of Madras cloth. Yet Lord Jagannath would soon miraculously appear in the midst of our new San Francisco temple by way of chaitya-guru, or the spiritual instruction from within. One day Malati prabhu was shopping at Cost-Plus Imports, a huge, warehouse-type store on Fisherman's Wharf, full of knick-knacks from all over the world. A large bin full of two-inch wooden carvings, richly painted and obviously from India, caught her eye. She acquired one of the small statues (some say she got a five-finger discount!), thinking she would go up to the Swami's room and ask him what it was.

When she placed the figurine on Swamiji's desk, we watched in awe as the great Swami bowed down humbly before the little statue, mumbling something. After paying his respects, then sitting back lightly on his cushion, he said, "That is Lord Jagannath." Pausing, he then said, "That is Krishna. He is worshipped in the temple of Jagannath Puri, Orissa, in India. There, He resides with His sister, Subhadra, and His brother, Balaram." He told us that every year the Lord leaves the temple for a trip to the ocean, and how in Jagannath Puri there is a great procession where thousands and thousands of people come from all over India to see the Lord traveling to the beach in His car. When Lord Chaitanya first walked into the temple and saw Lord Jagannath, he said, "Here is Krishna." Then He fell into a trance of ecstasy and did not leave the temple for days.

Swamiji continued, "Lord Jagannath has come of His own accord. We did not have to search Him out. This is most auspicious. It is Krishna's will that we have Lord Jagannath in San Francisco. Now we can also take Lord Jagannath once a year out of the temple for a visit to the ocean." He proceeded to tell us the story of the carver Vishvakarma, how he was commissioned by the king to carve Lord Krishna, Subhadra and Balaram, but only on the condition that he not be disturbed in his work. When the king, no longer able to contain his curiosity, interrupted Vishvakarma before he was finished, the sculptor stopped his work. Thus, Lord Jagannath, in the form we know Him, is the result.

Shyamasundar perked up as Swamjii beckoned him closer, "Can you carve this, big size?" "Yes, I will try," Shyamasundar replied eagerly. Swamiji then asked if there were two other such dolls available, and Malati returned the next day with the little figures of Balaram and Subhadra. Swamiji requested Shyamasundar to carve Krishna's brother and sister in large size as well. Shortly afterward, Hayagriva found and purchased somewhere a sixteen-inch Lord Jagannath, Lady Subhadra, and magnificent Balaram. I walked in and They were sitting right on Swamiji's desk. Many of the fledgling devotees started wearing Lord Jagannath or the holy triumvirate around their necks, which required twisting a small screw-hook into Their Lordships' crowns. When Swamiji saw this he pointed out that, "One should not put any screws or nails into Lord Jagannath." Then others showed up with little ropes like "hangman nooses" around their necks. Nara-Narayan prabhu was wearing a huge, dangling eight-inch Lord Jagannath.

We were new and innocently ignorant of many things which the Swami taught us. Swamiji taught us a new prayer to Lord Jagannath: "Jagannatha swami nayana patha gami bhavatume." Translated into English this means, "Lord of the universe, kindly be visible unto me." One day I walked over to Shyamasundar's apartment on the corner of Haight and Lyon Streets. His neighbor across the hall, a member of a rock band called The Misunderstood—and later to be initiated and named Rishikeshananda—was there also. I had dropped by to visit and to check out the carving progress. Shyamasundar chiseled away on the Supreme Lord to the sounds of Bob Dylan or the "Happening" Hare Krishna record.

On the way back to the temple, I saw Uddhava prabhu selling *Oracle* newspapers on Haight Street and stopped to chat about how nicely the carving of Lord Jagannath was progressing. On Frederick Street, a feeling of bliss filled and enveloped me as I entered our welcoming temple, which was growing like a new plant emanating small, fresh buds. The temple fed many and had also become a cleansing house for sojourners coming off LSD trips. Jayananda and Brother David were serving the prasadam that Yamuna, Harsharani, Janaki, and Malati prepared on the new gas stove with a griddle for chapatis, donated by Jerry Garcia of the Grateful Dead.

Shyamasundar soon completed the Jagannath Deity at his Haight Street apartment and invited Swamiji over to see Him. All the devotees squeezed into the small apartment and eagerly waited Swamiji's arrival. We cooked a feast, all new preparations taught to us by Swamiji. When he arrived, Swamiji proceeded directly to the reclining Deity and bowed down. When he got up, he looked very pleased. He settled into a rocking chair and led a kirtan with shining eyes. He also praised the cooks for the fine prasadam and requested Shyamasundar to make an altar in the temple for their Lordships. A few days later, a nice altar of redwood had been fashioned, with flashing psychedelic spotlights, and Haridas had painted the temple walls in bright colors.

On the day of the installation, we raised Lord Jagannath onto a broad shelf above the altar. Then we watched as Swamiji performed a ceremony we had not seen before: he offered incense, fire, water, cloth, and flowers.

"This is called arati," he explained. "Now the temple is for worshiping." Then Swamiji sat below Jagannath and, playing bongo drums, led us in chanting the maha-mantra for at least an hour. Hayagriva blew the kelp horn; Israel the trumpet, Mukunda played kartalas, and Haridas banged on a rented tympani drum. Yamuna's piercing "Hari Hari Bol!" resounded through the room.

The day after the installation, some devotees took Lord Jagannath into Golden Gate Park and started a kirtan. Soon, enthusiastic people gathered and encircled the Lord, all the while chanting and dancing. When the Swami heard from someone about this occurrence, he walked over to the park at a very fast pace to the place known as Hippie Hill—and when he saw Jagannath, he offered his obeisances. Then he sat

Srila Prabhupada leads the chanting on Hippie Hill in Golden Gate Park.

beside the Lord and led the chanting. More and more people arrived. Mukunda and Shyamasundar ran back to the temple for the tympani drum and portable microphone.

Later, Swamiji firmly but kindly told us that "Lord Jagannath always stays in the temple. People come to the temple to visit the Lord, but Lord Jagannath does not go out to see the people." We were sitting in a circle around the Swami when he told us again of the yearly car festival in Puri where each Deity is taken out, riding on their own ratha, or car. This was his way of forgiving us. While speaking with us, Swamiji was looking out of his apartment window, and he saw a flatbed truck. He drew us a simple diagram of how that could be made into a cart for Lord Jagannath.

Maya's Attack

Shortly after the Jagannath installation in San Francisco, in early April, 1967, Swamiji returned to New York. On the last day of May, 1967, the news came over the phone from New York: Swamiji had suffered a stroke and was going into Beth Israel Hospital!

The awareness of Swamiji's ailing health spread quickly through our small community. We were devastated, lost, a dysfunctional family without our father to guide us. We were like the walking dead. I was relishing my new and exciting Krishna conscious life when everything just stopped. When the Swami became ill and suffered this stroke, our little community changed drastically. We prayed continuously to Lord Krishna for Swamiji's recovery.

We quickly decided with the devotees in New York that when the Swami got out of the hospital, he would recuperate better in a quiet place on the West Coast. Mukunda was able to rent a small cottage on Stinson Beach, about twenty miles north of San Francisco, for Swamiji's convalescence. When the Swami arrived by air on June 25, he was very quiet and visited the temple briefly before leaving for the cottage. No one knew whether he would live or die. But from his retreat at Stinson Beach, Swamiji encouraged us to continue our Krishna conscious activities, especially the proposed first annual Rathayatra Festival for Lord Jagannath. He directed us to prepare "such-and-such a car" and proceed in a nice procession, chanting on our march to the ocean. If we had not had this festival to arrange, we would have moped in an ocean of despair. The Swami seemed unconcerned about his own health and more intent on glorifying Lord Jagannath.

July 9, 1967, the date of the first Ratha Yatra festival arrived. We had rented a U-Haul flatbed truck for the occasion. Jayananda Prabhu astounded us with his energy as he, Haridas, and Shyamasundar worked around the clock to build a pavilion and altar on the bed of the rental truck. The Diggers, our next-door neighbors, loaned us their flatbed truck (with OM emblazoned on the hood and DIGGER YOU painted on the front bumper!) to haul the devotees behind the Deities' truck. Yamuna, Janaki, Harsharani, and Malati decorated the trucks. I went with Jayananda to the Farmer's Market for oranges and apples. Ramanuja and Uddhava came with armloads of flowers.

The parade started on Haight and Central Streets. The police wanted Shyamasundar, who was driving, to speed up. They reckoned that ours was like all the other hippie parades and demonstrations, and they wanted to put an end to the celebration as soon as possible. Swamiji, however, had told us to go slowly, which is just what we did. Shyamasundar told the police that he didn't want to run over anyone in the crowd, which was now dancing and singing around the cart. The police calmed down and later admitted that our parade was one of the most peaceful events they had ever experienced.

I photographed the cart as it moved down Haight Street, attracting more and more dancing and singing souls. Murari and Subal, both with their heads newly shaven, danced in front of the chariot as we proceeded through the streets. At one point, as Lord Jagannath rode up a steep hill, the truck stalled and almost rolled back down, out of control—but suddenly the clutch caught,

Haight Street, San Francisco—the first Rathayatra parade in the West.

the motor roared, and the cart glided to the top and turned down Irving Street towards the sea. After this first Rathayatra festival, the devotees drove the truck out to Stinson Beach so that Swamiji could see Lord Jagannath. We sat around him while the Swami described the festival in India. "Lord Jagannath has His own mind and stops many times during the festival in Puri. Once, when Lord Jagannath would not move, Lord Chaitanya pushed the cart with His head!"

In this way, Lord Jagannath bestowed His benedictions upon all of us.

A Test of Maya

Shortly afterwards, Swamiji sent word that his illness was worsening and that we should pray all day in the temple for him.

When we gathered the next day, we realized that we had never before prayed for anything with so much intensity and purity. Perhaps for the first time in our lives we were completely selfless, and we stayed in the temple praying all that day and night. It was cold and leaky in the Stinson Beach cottage, so the next day Swamiji returned to his apartment in the city. He requested us to gather in the temple room. Swamiji didn't restrict the meeting to initiated devotees, and the room was packed.

He came in helped by Upendra and Mukunda. He walked slower than before, but his face was confident and composed. With assistance from the devotees, he very slowly climbed the steps of the vyasasana. First he led a kirtan, and we all joined in with tears brimming, hopeful and respectful. After, the room became super silent as we waited for Swamiji to speak. He coughed and said softly, "Thank you so much, my beloved disciples, for praying so nicely for my recovery. I am feeling a little stronger now." A feeling of great relief flowed through the temple. "Maya has tested me again. Whenever there is spiritual progress, Maya attacks. All you boys and girls have been making nice progress. So Maya has attacked me."

We Are a Movement

Swamiji continued: "I may die at any moment."
We gasped out loud.
Sporadic sobs were coming from all parts of the room.
"I want you to continue my work for Lord Krishna. Now we are a movement. I want to open 108 temples. If we continue to serve Krishna so nicely, I will get better. Now go and start new temples all over the world. He stopped there and said, "Let us chant."

He turned and looked with pleasure and sadness towards our storefront refuge.

Sad Departure

In late July, 1967, my magnificent mentor left for New York and then Vrindavan, India to regain his health. As he started to leave for the airport, he turned and looked with pleasure and sadness towards our storefront refuge. I saw his many expressions rolled up into one and was saddened myself, since I didn't know if I would ever see him again. My heart was burdened at the thought of Swamiji's illness. I had already experienced great loss when my mother died when I was seven. The two senseless assassinations of President Kennedy and of Martin Luther King Jr. were still fresh in my consciousness.

Swamiji Returns!

Soon after, we received optimistic reports from Kirtanananda in India about Swamiji's health. After some setbacks, he was eating again and began to improve so rapidly that his doctors were amazed. After a few months, on December 14, 1967, Swamiji arrived again at the San Francisco airport. He had returned to us.

As Swamiji's health and vigor returned, soon he was back to his usual schedule. He resumed writing while we slept, and he often led us in an at Golden Gate Park as two concentric circles of ecstatic, young flower children danced around us, all the while propelling us into the glorious future of the

48   *By His Example*

new movement. The Krishna consciousness movement was now like a plant flowering with many bright, young faces.

Krishna Murari works in many merciful ways.

Janaki Takes Swamiji's Ticket

Once again, in April of 1968, we found ourselves gathered at the San Francisco airport. This time Swamiji was leaving us for a tour of his new temples in New York, Boston, and Montreal. He gave Janaki his ticket to hold, but since Janaki didn't want him to leave, she held it back. "I am not going to give

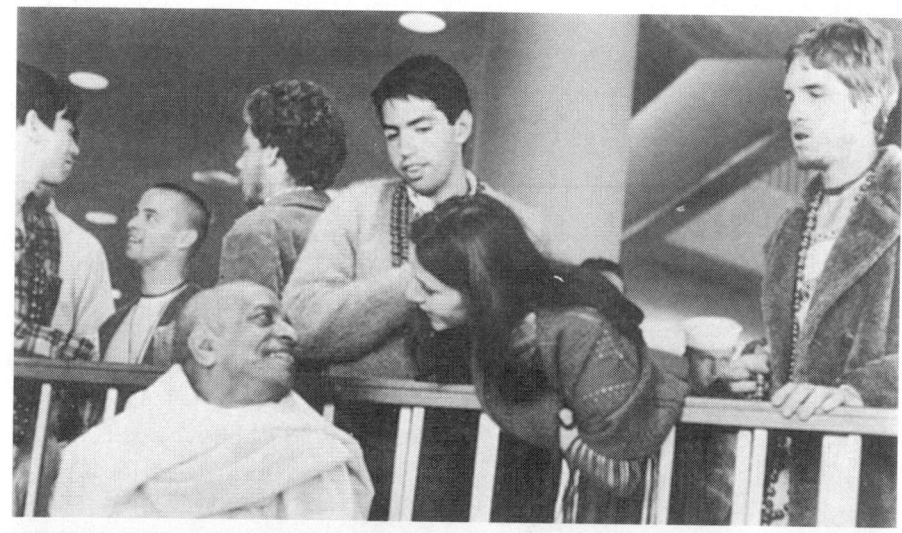

"I am not going to give you your ticket," she said, holding it in the air.

you your ticket," she said, holding it in the air.

Swamiji calmly said, "They have a record of my name on the airship, and I have my passport. I can go." Janaki gave the ticket back but was frustrated, and her face showed it. I photographed the sequence. The last photo of four is one of Swamiji smiling broadly, having had the last laugh. It is this expansive expression on his face that appears in the photo on the back of the *Govinda* album.

MONTREAL

"What great men do, others will follow."
—Bhagavad-gita

Psychic?

In August 1968, on our way to London, six of the San Francisco devotees—Mukunda, Janaki, Shyamasundar, Malati, Yamuna, and myself—stopped off to meet the Swami in Montreal, to celebrate Janmastami and Vyasa Puja. Swamiji always made Krishna consciousness a great adventure. He had invited us to Montreal to be with him and to receive advice, encouragement, money (a loan of $1,000 from his own lotus hands for our London trip) and, more importantly, Brahmin threads. It was a lovely time. New devotees (we were all new, actually) were coming from all over, and Hansadutta and Himavati, who were in charge of things in Montreal, were very hospitable. The temple was a converted bowling alley, and "rooms" were created by hanging blankets on ropes slung like clotheslines. We could hear everything Hansadutta, Himavati or anyone else in their cubicles talked about, and they could hear us also. We communicated through the thin, cloth walls. This exemplified to me how sound vibration was the most important of the senses because, as we heard and spoke to each other, I realized that seeing was not as important for our functioning. The sense of sound is higher than the sense of sight. Transcendental sound vibration is the most effective way of reaching out, I thought.

The morning after our arrival I went for a japa walk. Though I had never been on the streets of Montreal before, I felt that something was pulling me. Guided by instinct, I turned this way and that, not knowing why. Then, for some unknown reason, I found myself standing in a driveway. I felt strongly that this was where the Swami was staying. I had no address or directions but, when I looked in the window cautiously and saw a picture of Krishna, I knew I was in the right place. Many months had transpired since I'd seen Swamiji in San Francisco. I announced myself, and as always, the Swami was glad to see me.

"What news?" he inquired.

"Mukunda, Janaki, Shyamasundar, Malati, Saraswati, Yamuna, and I arrived last night. We are ready to go to London—and it is wonderful to see you again!"

He was silent.

I was still amazed that I was able to find the house where he was staying. I said, "I found you and this house with no directions or address. Is it due to some psychic energy?"

He answered immediately, "It is due to Krishna's grace."

This reminded me of an exchange I observed once in San Francisco:
Vishnujan: "I see a pink glow around the food, what is that?"
Swamiji: "Just eat. It is prasadam, it is Krishna's mercy."

"A child takes protection of mother even after she slaps him; similarly we take shelter of Krishna, even if slapped by Maya."
—A. C. Bhaktivedanta Swami

Strength

Malati had given birth to a baby girl in San Francisco in June 1968, and Swamiji had named her Saraswati over the phone from Montreal, pronouncing her the first child born to ISKCON parents. Now Malati had brought her to meet her spiritual master.

Swamiji held baby Saraswati up in the air with one lotus hand; he was so strong.

Gaurasundar then came in with a camera and began to photograph. Prabhupada put his garland around her and held Saraswati up again and said, "They will say, what kind of sannyasi am I?" He beamed on all of us like a proud father.

First Janmastami in Montreal

Janmastami is the annual celebration of the birth of Lord Krishna. Kamsa, an oppressive tyrant who ruled the region where Krishna was born, was desperate to kill the newborn child because of a prophecy that one day Krishna would kill him. So, on Janmastami, all day and night the devotees await baby Krishna's perilous crossing of the Yamuna River in his father's arms to escape death at the hands of Kamsa. Around the world, devotees wait for midnight with more anticipation than those waiting for the New Year's ball to drop in Times Square.

Vyasa Puja, the celebration of our Spiritual Master's birthday, always occurs the day following Janmastami. Though we had observed makeshift versions of Janmastami and Vyasa Puja in San Francisco the year before, while Swamiji was recuperating in India, this was to be our first real Janmastami with the Swami personally present to guide us. Swamiji made suggestions on how to prepare everything. He even supervised all the food preparations for the Vyasa Puja feast to be served the next day. On Janmastami day we were instructed to remain in the temple room, chanting, telling stories of Lord Krishna, and fasting until midnight. At midnight we would all celebrate Lord Krishna's safe passage of the Yamuna River and welcome Him to Vrindavan, followed by a small break-fast. "What better way to celebrate Janmastami and Vyasa Puja than with Prabhupada here," I thought to myself.

On the morning of Janmastami, I hung up photos of Lord Krishna (that I had brought with me for our London yatra) on the walls of the temple room. Gopal Krishna dasa, a young motivational researcher for the Coca-Cola company in Montreal—and Swamiji's first initiated Indian disciple in the West—bowed down at every photo of Lord Krishna. The Swami silently walked into the temple room. We all felt the anticipation and elation and a sense of shelter. As he began to speak, one groupie girl in the congregation yelled out that she wanted to marry him, and she was very loud and insistent. I looked at Prabhupada to see his reaction. He was transcendental and totally ignored her. He told us the story of Lord Krishna, Kamsa, Mother Devaki and Father Vasudeva, and of Krishna's crossing the Yamuna River to Vrindavan. He also spoke of how chanting can take away maya, illusion.

The groupie girl had quieted down while the Swami lectured, but during the question-and-answer period she again stood up and proposed to him. Swamiji nicely and quietly said, "I am sannyasi—I have renounced family life." She was finally satisfied. After this, a brash gentleman proposed that it was not proper to bow down. Swamiji looked at him and said, "As you are thinking they should not bow down, they are thinking you should. This is a democracy, so majority wins." We all cheered, the man was reconciled, and the room became quiet again. I went to sleep that night with visions of Krishna in my head and Swamiji in my soul.

First Vyasa Puja in Montreal

The next day was Vyasa Puja, celebrating the appearance of Bhaktivedanta Swami. (My theory is that Swamiji stayed inside his mother's womb until the day after Janmastami so that his birth would not take any attention away from Krishna's birth!) Feeling refreshed, even after only a few hours of sleep, I went into the temple room and started taking down the photos of Lord Krishna and replacing them with photos of Swamiji that I had also brought for our London excursion. There were shots of A. C. Bhaktivedanta Swami walking by

Stowe Lake with the ducks, as well as color photos from his walks around South Lake. I placed both color and black-and-white portrait photos on the altar. We were surrounded by loving reminders of our Spiritual Master as I hung the photos of Swamiji chanting with us in Golden Gate Park, Ocean Beach, and other spots.

After preparing most of the feast himself, Swamiji came into the temple.

Swamiji then handed each of the six devotees from San Francisco a five-inch by six-inch piece of paper with the Gayatri Mantra prayers typed on it and told us to memorize them. We didn't know what they meant. He then personally, with his divine golden lotus hands, placed sacred threads on Shyamasundar, Mukunda, and myself. Then he handed them to Janaki, Yamuna, and Malati. Wow! He told us to recite these prayers three times a day. Then he explained that Vyasa Puja was the day for disciples to speak about and glorify their spiritual master. Suddenly he looked at me and said, "Gurudasji, please speak something." I was taken completely by surprise, slowly regained my composure, and managed to speak about him in glorification. He smiled upon me at that moment, and I have been glorifying my Spiritual Master ever since. After several others also spoke, we had a wonderful feast presided over by Srila Prabhupada from his Vyasasana, making sure that everyone received some of each of his preparations. With great animation we were feasting with our spiritual father, just as Krishna feasted with His friends.

The room was now quiet, as everyone was eating and relishing the prasadam feast. Swamiji was sitting on his elevated seat, occasionally looking up from his food and smiling down on us. One of the many holy preparations was dahi bharats, fried balls of dahl in a yogurt sauce. I bit into this divine cuisine and could not stop myself from exclaiming out loud, "This tastes great!"

Swamiji looked up again, puffed up his chest, and pronounced, "I made them—they are called bharats!"

CHARLIE CHAPLIN TEACHES BY EXAMPLE

Before we left for London, the Swami often invited the three married couples from San Francisco into his rooms, where his encouraging words and instructions inspired and motivated us for our upcoming mission. One time, a new *Back to Godhead* magazine was lying on Swamiji's desk. The cover showed a painting of Lord Nrsimhadeva killing the demon Hiranyakasipu by tearing him apart. For some unknown reason, I asked, "Can we wear Lord Nrsimhadeva masks on harinama sankirtan [chanting in the streets]?"

The Swami smiled and replied, "Oh, yes—what great men do, others will follow. Soon everyone will be wearing Lord Nrsimhadeva masks!"

Instead of following up with a verse from *Bhagavad-gita*, Swamiji used a

Charlie Chaplin film to illustrate his point: "Fifty years before, I saw a cinema of Charles Chaplin. He was at a ball dance, prancing in his tailing coats. Someone stepped on his tailing coat and it split a little in the back. Charles Chaplin went into the private room [lavatory] and looked in the mirror at his ripped tailing coats. Then he tore the split tails all the way up to his neck." The Swami imitated Chaplin's bemused, comic expression as he told the story.

"Then Charles Chaplin came out of the private room and started dancing very vigorously." From a sitting position, Prabhupada imitated Charlie Chaplin's energetic dancing.

"Other people saw his dancing and they thought it was a new style, and they went into the private room and tore their tailing coats up to their necks also and returned to the ball dance and simulated Charles Chaplin's dancing style. So, yes, you can wear Lord Nrsimhadeva masks on harinama sankirtan."

We were surprised and inspired. It was another example of Swamiji's open mind and humor.

A devotee told me that once he was on an airplane with Swamiji, and a Charlie Chaplin film was showing. All the disciples accompanying Prabhupada went to sleep or chanted to themselves, trying not to look at the screen. The devotee peeked up to see what our spiritual preceptor was doing and found him watching the movie and laughing, tears streaming down his face!

Another time, while I was sitting in the presence of His Divine Grace, he turned to me and said, "I like the Charles Chaplin cinema where he is intoxicated and he can do everything better."

"*Easy Street*," I offered.

Swamiji laughed and said, "He was able to walk better, but he couldn't get his key into the lock."

As was often the case, he suddenly went onto another topic, and the conversation was over.

In 1977, I visited Charlie Chaplin at his home on Lake Geneva in Switzerland, right before his passing. I gave the aging comic a *Bhagavad-gita As It Is* via his wife, Oona O'Neil, and told her the three above stories. She laughed, thanked me profusely, and rushed to Chaplin's sick bed to retell them. The great comedian died a few days later.

Srila Prabhupada

About this time, late summer of 1968, we started calling the Swami "Srila Prabhupada," or "Prabhupada."

My guru's spiritual master, Bhaktisiddhanta Saraswati, was also named Srila Prabhupada, which means "At whose feet all masters sit." Now the mantle was passed on to my guru, A. C. Bhaktivedanta Swami Prabhupada.

ENGLAND

*"I have come here to teach you
what you have forgotten: love of God."*
—A.C. Bhaktivedanta Swami

London Arrival

SIX NEW DEVOTEES AND A BABY were on their way to England to start a new ISKCON center for Srila Prabhupada. We had less than $1,000 among us, after paying our one-way airfares, and two addresses in England: one for an East Indian named Dr. Kholi, and one for Tom Driberg, a Member of Parliament. Allen Ginsberg had given us an introductory letter to Mr. Driberg, who was a fellow poet. The British government, quite well known for being stroppy, required married travelers to carry a certain amount of money per couple—just about all the money we had among us!—if they didn't have return tickets. Tourists without sufficient funds just weren't considered eligible to enter the country, since they had no money to invest in the British economy.

We decided to go to the Netherlands first, as their entrance restrictions were less stringent. We arrived in Amsterdam; Holland had a quaint and friendly feeling. Shyamasundar and Malati set out for London first, with all our money. They were let into England without any difficulty. Shyamasundar opened a bank account, then wired the money back to us through the bank. Then Yamuna and I took all the money and rode the Hoek van Holland ferry to Dulwich, England. By Krishna's grace, we were also allowed to enter. We met up with Shyamasundar and Malati at Piccadilly Circus at noon. The four of us then sent the money back to Mukunda and Janaki in Amsterdam, and they arrived the next day.

We were all together again!

We first decided to visit Dr. Kholi, to see if we could stay with him for a while until we became acclimatized to Great Britain.

Dr. Kholi lived in Herne Hill, a suburb of London. We boarded the train in Waterloo station and rode through Brixton (a ghetto), past Clapham and other manicured suburbs, going out towards the Crystal Palace. As the conductor announced Herne Hill, we saw old-fashioned, winding lanes surrounding the Victorian train station.

We found the street where Dr. Kholi lived, in a nice, large detached house. (In Britain, a charming, cottage-type, detached house denoted wealth, for many houses clung to one another, especially in industrial cities.) He and his family greeted us and let us stay for a few days. He took us to a nearby empty house he owned, and we negotiated a rent that was a little high, but we trusted in Krishna to provide. We rented the separate house on a temporary basis, allowing his family to get back to their routine minus the ashram we had created in their living room.

About this time, Prabhupada sent a letter to me in London from San Francisco:

14 September, 1968

My Dear Gurudas,

Please accept my blessings. I was in due receipt of your letter dated Sept. 3, 1968, and now I have received a letter from Mukunda, and I am pleased to learn that you are now together, all six. So please try to start the temple as soon as possible and call me for your service. Offer my blessings to Yamuna as well as to Malati and her husband and the little child. I have sent one newspaper cutting to Shyamasundar; that is a very nice article, if you get it photostatted, you can use it for propaganda work. Hope this finds you in good health.

Your ever well-wisher,
A. C. Bhaktivedanta Swami

Shaved Heads

We were committed now, and devotional service filled our days. Shyamasundar, Mukunda, and I decided that it was time for us to take another step in overcoming our attachment to vanity and appearance. It was time to shave our heads! By throwing our hair on the ground, we cast out attachments to personal appearance, personal wealth, or wishes for respect. Plus, we figured that the British public would certainly notice these bald-headed blokes, and this kind of recognition would be vital to our preaching efforts.

We sat each other in chairs, and shaved all the hair off. All that remained was the hairpiece, hanging down the back of the head. This tuft of hair is called the sikha. When asked about the sikha, Swamiji replied, "This sikha is there so that Krishna can pull you up to Him easier." He demonstrated pulling his own sikha up. Now that my head was shaved, it felt clean and fresh.

Visitors

An Indian gentleman named Prem Sayal, who sang devotional songs with exaggerated movements, came to our meetings at Herne Hill, along with a Mr. Govind. They both introduced us to some leaders of the East Indian community and took us to the Hindu Centre, where meetings and shows were held. Devotees at the Hindu Centre always requested Prem Sayal to play harmonium and sing bhajans. He resembled Charlie Chaplin, and sometimes he would stop his songs in mid-refrain, roll his eyes back, and speak devotionally. His intense, exaggerated movements and gestures, and the way he would throw his hair back, made us laugh, and Shyamasundar, Mukunda, and I would poke fun at him by imitating his movements.

Soon, Andy, a young English lad from Watford, joined us. I don't remember how he heard of us, but one day he just showed up and became a part of our group. He was friendly and humble, one of thousands of youths searching the globe for enlightenment at that time. He stayed with us for a while, followed our rules and regulations, took part in the morning and evening services, and helped with the cooking. Andy liked being a vegetarian, asked meaningful questions, and was making progress, but eventually he left because he missed his life of desire, gratification, and struggle.

We held small intimate programs at Dr. Kholi's and in the suburban homes of other Indian families around London, but, soon decided we should look for a place of our own, more centrally located. We searched central London in Shyamasundar's red Ford pickup, and eventually we met some people in the center of the city who published an underground newspaper. We had seen their paper, *International Times*, on the newsstand, and attracted by its eclectic articles, we visited their headquarters at 22 Betterton Street.

We found the small street in the heart of Covent Garden, central London's bustling wholesale fruit-and-vegetable district; we located the four-story office building and rang the doorbell. An American with curly hair answered. He, like the rest of the staff at the newspaper, was young, hip, and very friendly. As they welcomed us, I had a communal feeling like being back in San Francisco. I felt we had finally arrived.

22 Betterton Street

"All you need is love."
—The Beatles

At *International Times* we met one gentleman named Graham Keene, who was very kind and especially interested in our Movement. We asked him if he might know of a place where we could live. Graham (who is still my good friend today) informed us in his quiet, mannerly, and imaginative way that, as they were moving their offices to Endell Street, around the corner, the Betterton Street building would be used only for storing back issues of *IT*. He thought that one or two floors would become vacant. He then supplied us with the name of the landlord, Nigel Samuels, and his phone number in Portsmouth Square. Graham ventured that Nigel might let us live at 22 Betterton Street if we asked him nicely, so he rang Nigel up and introduced us on the phone. We arranged to meet him that night.

Portsmouth Square is in one of the ritziest parts of London. The Square itself is a private park, fenced and locked, surrounded by townhouses and large apartment buildings for the affluent. We located the address. The building's doorman inquired who we were visiting and rang up for Nigel's confirmation. We rode an elaborate, art-deco elevator all the way up to the penthouse and stepped out of the elevator into a huge living room with a 360-degree view of London. Nigel got up and bounded over to greet us. He was very slim, almost emaciated, very white-skinned, and had a heavy, upper-class English accent. I appreciated his friendliness and overlooked his limp handshake, as he made a special effort to be cordial. I was impressed by Nigel's civility, though he was a little shy and awkward. Samuels had a locating service for rare books, named Bibliophile, so after some small talk, like "How do you find England?", we talked about books. "Have you read *Bhagavad-gita?*" I remember asking.

We talked about the seeming phenomenon of "unity" that we were experiencing in the underground community. We noted how alike London was to San Francisco in terms of social change and the growing openness to other forms of philosophy and spirituality. I spoke a little about our mission in London. It was prearranged that I would do most of the talking, but I wanted the other devotees to talk also, to rescue me from having to carry the conversation. Sensing my feelings, the others also participated in the conversation. Finally, Nigel asked, "What can I do for you?"

I replied, "We need a place to live in central London, and we were hoping we could stay in your building at 22 Betterton Street?"

He thought a moment and said, "Yes, that is possible, why not? You can use the second and third floors. Sometimes I come to my office on the top floor, and sometimes another tenant shares the top floor with me, but we won't bother you."

"I won't charge you any rent," he added. We shook his hands profusely and thanked him.

Our new residence, 22 Betterton Street, was situated in the center of the

Covent Garden district, where wholesale fruit, flowers, and vegetables were sold. The surrounding neighborhood was gradually being converted into chic cafes, restaurants, boutiques, art studios and lofts. The walls of 22 Betterton Street were exposed bricks, which reminded me of many Greenwich Village pads. The building was a warehouse, not zoned for living. It had no heat, and the taps supplied only freezing water, but at last we had a large space for a temple room, and as a shelter it was marvelous for us. We had to move around bundles and boxes of past issues of *International Times*, and sometimes we used these boxes as tables or furniture.

I was delegated to ask a group of Black Muslims, who were camped out all over the warehouse, to move. By Krishna's grace, they moved out without protest.

We had the use of two floors: one of the floors was the temple room, with the kitchen behind it; the floor above was our living quarters. Shyamasundar built our *sh-sh*-shower in the garage on the ground floor, and Malati and Saraswati lived down there in a huge cardboard box.

Young people from a place called the Arts Lab around the corner on Drury Lane, along with hippie squatters from nearby buildings, began to visit regularly. Three enthusiastic youths began to help out and then moved in with us. They were named Colin, David, and Tim. Eventually they were initiated and became Kulashekar, Digvajaya, and Tirthapada. Our 22 Betterton Street temple location was great, right in the heart of London, near the British Museum, the Swedenborg Society, the Theosophical Society, the rare and metaphysical book dealers, the theater district, Piccadilly Circus, the embassies, and the BBC. We were at the hub of the world, the center of the universe.

KRISHNA CHANT STARTLES LONDON

Now that we had a building and a temple room, we could invite all the new friends we were meeting every day to chant and hear holy subjects and to share prasadam with us. London seemed to vibrate with the same exciting energy that originated in San Francisco.

London's atmosphere was like a small town. The hip leaders in their fields all knew each other and tended to congregate together, so we were able to meet many of these prominent people in a very short time. The two newspapers *International Times* and *Oz* (a Berkeley-type weekly) disseminated information about the scene—music, underground events, philosophy, cartoons—including articles about the arrival of Krishna consciousness in England.

Hoppy, famous for producing what are now archival videos and films of the London scene in the Sixties, recorded the moment. Hoppy shot videos of the Rolling Stones, as well as the squatters who occupied unused buildings. He experimented with video when it was a new medium by recording our chanting in parks, along thoroughfares, and at events around and about London. Miles, a hip young writer and proprietor of the trendy Indica Bookstore, was interested in Eastern knowledge and carried our books in his shop. Avant-garde leaders like Jim Haynes and Bill Moore of the Arts Lab welcomed us, and we began chanting at the Arts Lab regularly.

Skirting the theater district in London's Drury Lane, the Arts Lab was a multistoried loft building, which was really more of a scene than a building. Artists, poets, squatters, buskers (street musicians), inventors, thinkers, as well as Christine Keeler (famous for her role in the Profumo scandal) all hung out there. Although we were practicing monks, we were accepted along with everyone else and felt comfortable visiting the Arts Lab. We chanted and spoke three nights a week and were very well received.

We met John Peel, a popular disc jockey, who talked about us on the radio and urged us to record our music. David Frost, the well-known and intelligent talk-show host, invited us to appear on his television show.

At one point we decided to print some handbills. We cut Swamiji's eyes out of one of my close-up photos and put a border around them. The caption read, "Krishna Consciousness Is Coming." We printed two thousand of these and dropped many of them from a rooftop down onto Oxford Street, London's main thoroughfare. A month or so later, we printed another handbill showing the San Francisco devotees chanting, with arms and faces raised. I used a reverse negative print. The caption read, "Krishna Consciousness Is Here."

Then a reporter from *The London Times* interviewed us. The article was extremely favorable and open to our ideas. We told him that we were considering chanting in front of the London Stock Exchange, as well as other sites. The reporter wrote: "The devotees of Krishna are considering chanting in front of the London Stock Exchange. What effect that will have, Krishna only knows."

The international wire services picked up on this article, and one day someone saw the headline "Krishna Chant Startles London" in the *San Francisco Chronicle* and showed the article to Swamiji, who telephoned us, overseas, to tell us he was very pleased. By some little effort on our part, and by Prabhupada's and Krishna's immense grace, Krishna consciousness did indeed startle London in a very short time.

Krishna Consciousness Is Here

I was becoming accustomed to the new and interesting sights, smells, and sounds of England: double-decker buses, red telephone kiosks, subways that were the "underground" or the "tube." The men's room signs read "gents," and the lavatory was the "loo"; people were "in hospital" instead of "in the hospital." Thanks became "ta" and I was called "luv" and "gov." The British populace was very well-mannered in general. There were small parks, or "commons," every few streets, dotting the city. Viewed from above, London seemed like a gigantic, green maze. The London community was made up of circles of friends that knew one another. These tribe-like connections were communal rather than geographical and provided us a good chance to meet people with similar interests again and again, even though we were in a large metropolis.

The city of London was becoming familiar to me, like a comfortable greatcoat, and I felt like I had been there in a past life. Although I liked London, I could have been anywhere, as our temple lifestyle was monkish, insular and completely engrossing. Our spiritual mission, my five friends, and baby Saraswati—these were my world, not the tourist sights or theaters.

As the Holy Names began to take root in the British Isles, I reflected on how my life had changed since meeting Prabhupada and learning about Krishna. Not only did I look different, with a shaved head, dhoti and sikha, but my right hand was often inside my bead bag and the Holy Names were on my lips. I chanted between conversations, while waiting for a bus, or in the

Meeting with Sri Pant, High Commissioner of India.

temple room. Krishna had also blessed me with a chance to meet people from all segments of an exotically different society. I was experiencing new adventures. I was realizing transcendental insights. I was in ecstasy and shared this joy with others. I was changing people's views, their lives. I was helping attract many new students to move into our temple, simply by speaking about Prabhupada and Lord Chaitanya and Sri Sri Radha Krishna.

I felt guided, and rather detached; Prabhupada's dream was coming into being, effortlessly.

We became acquainted with diplomats like Sri Pant and S. S. Dhawan, the High Commissioner for India, and with other important members of the Indian community. It seemed as if the Indian people were happy at last to be worshipping as they did in India, but right in the heart of London.

Tom Driberg, a Member of Parliament, was advising us, especially in the matter of registering ISKCON as a charity in the U.K., and he wrote several letters of commendation on our behalf. One time Mr. Driberg invited us to an historic English church where he was giving a guest sermon, and from this ancient podium he several times quoted from *Bhagavad-gita*.

We were being accepted by people from all walks of British life as an important part of the London Renaissance. Krishna consciousness, I thought, is indeed here.

A letter from Prabhupada:

Seattle
16 October, 1968

My Dear Gurudas,

Please accept my blessings. I am in due receipt of your nice letter dated Oct. 11, 1968, and by reading the contents it was so much encouraging, for me. Previous to this I received one letter from Mukunda and that was also very encouraging, so I am sure combined together you will have a great success in starting the ISKCON temple in London. I have also received one letter from Ginsberg. Mr. Tom Driberg is an intimate friend of Ginsberg and he has already written to him promising all help to us. So by Grace of Krishna there you are meeting nice gentlemen, interested gentlemen, and I hope it will become a very grand success.... So by the Grace of Krishna this mission is going on nicely, and I shall be glad to hear from you further good news. Please offer my blessings to your good wife, Yamuna, as well as all other devotees, Mukunda, Shyamasundar, Malati, Janaki, and Sarasvati devi. I hope this will find you in good health. Thanking you once more for writing me.

Your ever well-wisher,
A. C. Bhaktivedanta Swami

Ravi Shankar

Ravi Shankar, the famous sitar master, had scheduled a well-publicized concert in London. *The London Times* announced that a post-concert party would be held in his honor at the home of the Indian High Commissioner, S. S. Dhawan. After hearing of this, the six of us had a brief discussion and decided to "crash" the party. We hoped Ravi would remember us from previous encounters in San Francisco and at the Monterey Pop Festival, and that he would be glad to see us. And we wanted to meet High Commissioner Dhawan as well. Prabhupada had taught us that meeting dignitaries was helpful in spreading Lord Chaitanya's mission, as the *Bhagavad-gita* states that what great men do, others will follow.

We crowded into Shyamasundar's little, red pickup truck and drove to the High Commissioner's Kensington Street mansion. The iron gates protecting the ambassadorial enclave were open, so we drove in and parked the truck. Autumn leaves crunched under our feet as we found the address. We heard names being bleated out as we approached the decorated doors, not Holy Names but names of Britain's elite peerage.

A butler in livery was announcing the entrance of each celebrity in a clipped high-class British accent: "Lord and Lady such and such." Seven beautific devotees entered. We scribbled INTERNATIONAL SOCIETY FOR KRISHNA CONSCIOUSNESS on a card, and the steward loudly announced, "International Society for Krishna Consciousness!" as we walked into the room. All heads turned. Startled, Ravi Shankar put something down and came forward to greet us warmly, followed closely by the High Commissioner. Ravi recognized us from San Francisco and asked how we were. We chatted for a while, and then the High Commissioner interrupted our pleasantries and, ignoring the other guests, invited us upstairs.

Mr. Dhawan led us into a simple room, sat on the floor cross-legged, and motioned for us to sit beside him. We sat and talked, and he was very friendly. We also showed him some slides of our worldwide ISKCON activities. The High Commissioner then enthusiastically invited us to a late dinner. We stressed that the dinner must be pure vegetarian without garlic or onions.

Mr. Dhawan was intelligent and thoughtful; he enjoyed conversing with us and took notes during our discussions on a little pad he kept in his pocket. He was an avowed communist, so we didn't discuss politics. In his role as High Commissioner, I subsequently called upon him to help us many times in our mission. I also met him again years later in Calcutta when he was Governor of Bengal. (In Calcutta he hosted a wild kirtan where one devotee disappeared and a Cabinet Minister had a heart attack—but that's another story, one which I will relate in the India section of this book.)

California Contingent

By late 1968, London and San Francisco had become twin epicenters for the worldwide hippie movement, and we tried to stay in touch with friends and events in the Bay Area. One day Shyamasundar got a surprise phone call from Rock Scully, manager of the Grateful Dead. He had just arrived at Heathrow airport "with about ten friends" and wondered if we could put them up for a few nights until they got situated! They had come to London to meet the Beatles and generally to check out the London scene and establish liaisons between San Francisco and London hippie leaders and motorcycle gangs.

Shyamasundar went to the airport to meet them in his tiny red Ford pickup. We cleaned the temple and prepared a feast. I was in the kitchen cutting vegetables when they arrived. They sounded like a stampede of bulls at Pamplona coming up the stairs.

The first one to arrive was Rock, skinny and alert. Mukunda stood at the top of the stairs with me, "So we meet again. What's happening in San Francisco?"

Rock informed us, "It's gone down, man. Since you all left there's been rioting on Haight Street. But we can survive."

"There's always good people still around," I said.

"Yeah, but many are leaving," Rock said.

A petite, pretty girl named Frankie came in. She wore her hair cropped and was wearing tight leather pants and a red jacket. She looked tough and could have been hanging out on a stoop in the Bronx, but when she smiled you could see her heart showing. After Frankie, Sonny Barger stomped in—President of the Oakland chapter of the Hell's Angels motorcycle club. He had a bored, detached look on his weather- and fist-beaten face. A swastika hung around his tan neck. His muscular arm sported a tattoo of a hand holding a knife. His leather jacket's colors said HELLS ANGELS OAKLAND.

I asked that everyone please leave their shoes by the door.

Sonny hesitated, then reluctantly took off his thick, black engineer boots. Behind Sonny came Frenchie, also in Angel colors, accompanied by his "old lady," Angie. When Angie leaned down to put her boots alongside the rest, her purse opened and the handle of a gun popped out. She pushed it back in and closed the purse.

Next came Ken Kesey. I greeted him, "Hey man, haven't seen you since the Be-In." Kesey smiled his gap-toothed smile. He strode in with confidence, followed by an American-born Buddhist, who tried to be friendly but acted mostly aloof. I think he felt out of his element in our midst—he was no longer the authority and missed it. I still tried to make him feel welcome.

Exchanging news and happenings, I learned that the Haight scene was essentially turning nasty and that many shops had boarded their windows and closed down. The Grateful Dead were becoming even more popular, and a roving community called The Dead Heads was beginning to follow their concerts from town to town. Sonny Barger said that the Angels were being continuously hassled. The Vietnam War was bombarding everyone's senses on the evening news.

They asked us what we thought their chances were for starting a branch of the Hell's Angels in London. We had to be tactful. Shyamasundar said he thought that, yes, they would find some willing bikers here. "Perhaps some skinheads?" (I had to laugh to myself—I thought it ironic that sometimes inebriated British drivers would yell out of their car windows, "Skin 'ed!" (skinhead) when they saw us monks with shaved heads walking on the street.)

I said, "Here in London it's like it was in Frisco before the summer of love in '67: the streets are full of rebellious, searching, kindred souls. They are re-enacting here what we did in San Francisco a year ago."

"The Hell's Angels are famous; I think you will find some people who are interested," Mukunda added quietly. (If you persevere long enough in your belief, people will become interested, I thought. It's simply a matter of getting your message out. Even fan clubs for serial killers, absurd as they are, exist. And here we are exchanging knowledge with them as if they were opening one of our temple branches.)

Joking, I asked, "Did you bring your hogs?"

They pointed outside.

Surprised, I went and looked out the window and sure enough there were two Harley-Davidson motorcycles tied up in the back of Shyamasundar's truck.

"We paid five-hundred pounds air-cargo for each one," said Sonny proudly.

They sat, and we served prasadam. They were hungry after a long airplane trip, and they ate with both hands. All the girls—Janaki, Malati, and Yamuna—were advancing quickly in the art of KC cuisine, and the food was delicious. Then, like a well-run basketball play, we broke off into little groups: Yamuna and Janaki with Frankie, Malati with Angie, Shyamasundar and Mukunda with Rock, Sonny and Frenchie. I sat down near a window with Ken Kesey. The Buddhist guy sat by himself. Conversations filled the room.

Ken asked me, "Why do we need a guru? Why can't we find the way ourselves?"

I answered him this way: "We can find the path ourselves, but if we find someone who has experience, who has already reached enlightenment, we can learn very quickly how to become liberated. It's faster following a teacher. One way is taking the stairs, the other the elevator."

"Why not learn from nature, or books?"

I continued, "Nature is very nice to learn from, and books help, but which ones do you pick? Your method is one of trial and error and may take many lifetimes. A guru teaches by his example and gives you the correct holy books. If you were becoming a doctor, wouldn't it be better to learn the methods and books at a medical school rather than by the trial and error method? As a patient, I would certainly rather go to a doctor who was trained by another doctor." Then, imitating a doctor, I said, "Mr. Kesey, you must have appendicitis, I think. It has to be removed. Do you remember what side it's on?"

We laughed, and he said, "Hmmmm, I will think about what you said." He then asked, "How do we know which guru to pick?"

"Pick the guru that resonates in your heart, and someone who you feel can teach you. Choose someone that you are ready to accept as someone who can answer all of your questions and, most importantly, choose someone who practices what they preach. My own guru says, 'You must test the guru; there are many false gurus.' A guru is someone you can feel a loving connection with forever."

Then Kesey gave Prabhupada a great compliment: "Your guru is the heaviest." Translated, that means: "The deepest, most natural, determined, noncompromising, real, not-afraid-to-say-what-he-thinks, brightest star in the honorific galaxy of living saints in the universe."

Quietly I said, "One of the Sanskrit meanings of guru *is* 'heavy.'" Ken was delighted by that tidbit, and we smiled knowingly into each other's minds.

Malati interrupted. "We're showing a movie. Would you like to come and watch it?" We got up and went to another part of the room where a white bed sheet was hung on the wall. An 8 mm film had arrived in the mail the day before from the Boston temple, and it chronicled some of Srila Prabhupada's visit there. Jimmy Doody, a young English boy and aspiring devotee, had brought a projector from the Arts Lab, and we started watching the film. We saw Prabhupada walking the snowy streets of Boston, along with two devotees. This clumsy homemade film gave us great joy, but it probably seemed totally boring to anyone who didn't know Prabhupada. Occasionally His Divine Grace would look towards the camera or point his cane at something, and we would *ooh!* and *ahh!* I looked through the darkness and saw that the Hell's Angels and their friends were asleep, looking like angels. Rock Scully was nodding off too. Jetlag had finally caught up with them. As we continued watching, we were excited by even the slightest twitch of Prabhupada's eyebrow—

and so was Ken Kesey, who continued to watch with keen interest.

Upon waking, the San Francisco bunch was restless, and they asked where the action was. I didn't know what action they were thinking of exactly, but I suggested they start off at the Arts Lab, a local hippie hangout. They thanked us, and as they left, the roar of the Harleys echoed and resounded like bowling pins off the walls of quiet Betterton Street. Along the fog-shrouded, late-night street I saw lights flash on in many flats, and heads peered out to see what caused the noise. The entourage turned left at the corner of Drury Lane and disappeared into the night. Later we heard from Jack Moore and Jim Haynes, founders of the Arts Lab, that the Hell's Angels did pick up some converts that night, and then, because it was their nature to do so, they also trashed the place a little.

Prabhupada sent me an encouraging letter:

Los Angeles
15 November, 1968

My Dear Gurudas,

Please accept my blessings. I am in due receipt of your letter dated Nov. 7, 1968, and I very much appreciate your sincere endeavor for preaching our Krishna consciousness Movement. I have received one letter from Dr. Athvale whom you met in Amsterdam, and he was so much pleased with your behavior and talk that he has been induced to see me at Los Angeles. A qualified disciple increases the importance of the Spiritual Master. So I find in you some good qualities. You think yourself as very humble but you appreciate the services of your Godbrothers and I am very much pleased on your such behavior. I have received the news cutting. This is also very nice attempt, and by your sincere endeavor you have now got a nice house to stay free of charges till it is sold. So all this encourages me that you are doing your best, and Krishna will bless you for your noble attempt.

I hope his meets you in good health, along with Janaki, and Malati and Shyamasundar, and Miss Sarasvati. Please continue to keep me informed.

Your ever well-wisher,
A. C. Bhaktivedanta Swami

Meeting the Beatles (Flower Arrows for George)

We had talked about trying to meet the Beatles, especially George Harrison, even before leaving San Francisco for London. As to how we eventually met the Fab Four, nearly one year later, it happened like this.

Underground movements, from the avant-garde '20s through the Beatnik '50s, tend to remain hidden, and spread out geographically. But the '60s underground movement expanded in London, much as it had in San Francisco, in an explosive, public manner—basement doors were flung open, people came out of their garrets and went into the streets and parks. Surrealists met rebels; bohemians became friends with the new pop-intelligentsia.

All sectors of the underground community were linked: a writer for *International Times* knew an editor at *Oz* magazine, who in turn knew a filmmaker (Hoppy), who knew a Member of Parliament (Tom Driberg), who knew a poet (Allen Ginsberg), who knew a writer (Miles), who knew a disc-jockey (John Peel), who knew a TV personality (David Frost), who knew Prince Charles—and all of them wanted to know the Beatles. We did too.

About the same time that we moved into the old *International Times* offices at 22 Betterton Street, the Beatles were going through their own changes. There was some disappointment with the Maharishi (they all had the same secret mantra), and the Beatles were weary of holy people bringing gifts. They were rethinking things.

Then the Beatles decided to organize themselves as Apple Corporation. They made their headquarters in posh Saville Row, adjacent to the custom tailors and high-fashion men's clothing shops.

They decided to get back to some of their original ideas and spontaneity, both musically and in their lives. They opened a boutique on Baker Street and made themselves accessible to new ideas, projects, and people.

Soon the Beatles were inundated with self-proclaimed Messiahs, inventors, and garage music tapes. This is when we came on the scene.

We had been going to the Arts Lab and practicing a version of the *Brahma Samhita* prayers, sung to a tune Mukunda had written and arranged. We went through the arrangement a dozen times, and finally we made a demo tape on a small tape recorder. We were not in a studio, nor did we have proper engineering or professional musicians. What emerged sounded like a group of innocents with lots of heart and devotion. A copy of this tape was sent to Apple Records.

Apple Corp's open invitation for new talent and ideas was a chance for us to also send some *pushpana* messages (arrows made of flowers) to the Beatles. We mounted a campaign to send them something—a flower arrow—every day for a week. That should get their attention, we thought.

Our unspoken hope—though it seemed impossible at the time—was to someday record the Hare Krishna mantra with the Beatles.

These are the flower-arrow messages we sent:

The Beatles had recently published an advertisement picturing all four of them in concert, with the caption: "Send Us Your Ideas." So the first envelope we sent included a photo I had taken of the devotees in New York, with smiling faces and arms raised in their chanting pose; we captioned the photo: "Come Sing With Us."

The second day we sent the Beatles part one of a two-part illustrated article about Prahlad Maharaja that we had recently published in the *International Times*. I had written the text about Prahlad, the great child devotee who overcame the attempts of his demonic father to dissuade him from worshiping Krishna. We illustrated the narrative with Gaurasundar and Govinda dasi's paintings of the Prahlad story, painted on wooden rectangles.

On the third day we sent the second part of the Prahlad story.

On the fourth day we sent a walking, wind-up apple toy we had found at a kirtan program held at All Saints Church in Nottinghill Gate. We wrote HARE KRISHNA, HARE KRISHNA, KRISHNA KRISHNA, HARE HARE in gold paint on the back of the red apple and sent it, along with one of our "Krishna Consciousness Is Coming" handbills, to the Apple offices.

Yamuna had designed and written in calligraphy a cover for *International Times* which featured the Hare Krishna mantra in Sanskrit devanagari script. So on the fifth day, we sent Yamuna's Sanskrit cover, plus our handbill showing Prabhupada's eyes: "Krishna Consciousness Is Here!"

We had been sending the flower-arrow packets and envelopes to Peter Asher, the artist-and-repertoire person for Apple. Peter is the brother of Jane Asher, the actress. We never knew what he did with our presentations, as we never heard from him or from anyone at Apple Records. So, on the sixth day, we decided to make our daily presentation in person: We baked an apple pie and then cut letters depicting the maha-mantra in the top crust. We brought the maha pie, still fresh and steaming, to the Apple Corp offices. We inquired about our demo tape and tried to find Peter Asher, but we couldn't find out about either. No one knew anything. We then brought the apple pie to Chris O'Dell, an assistant to George Harrison. She was from Los Angeles, about our age, and happy to meet some fellow Americans. We talked for a very long time and were tempted to break into the apple pie, but no, this pie was for the Beatles. Chris promised to get the pie to George and the others and to follow up on our public relations packets. We gave her a copy of the demo tape as well. A few weeks later we would be sitting in George Harrison's home, having kirtan.

Regarding the two Prahlad articles in *International Times*, Prabhupada wrote:

From Los Angeles
1 December, 1968

My Dear Gurudas,
Please accept my blessings to yourself and to your good wife, Yamuna

Devi. With the greatest satisfaction I have read your letter of November 25th and just yesterday I received our published pictures of Prahlad Maharaja. I thank you very much for your sincere endeavors and I am sure that Krishna will bestow upon you all blessings for your notable service attitude. This is the key to progressing in Krishna consciousness that one learns to serve Krishna and the Spiritual Master in humble attitude and this attitude in you shall certainly bring you further and further in perfecting your life. In humble submission the devotee finds such sweet transcendental pleasure that no more he is interested in the nonsense material world and no more he is affected by the influence of the inferior energy, maya.

Your idea of arranging meeting with all of the influential people who are interested in your activities is excellent suggestion and may prove very good results. So certainly Krishna is guiding you in your thoughts and activities. This is very nice, and all very encouraging to me. As you may have heard, our *Bhagavad-gita As It Is* was published and can be ordered from the New York temple by writing to Brahmananda. Please try to popularize this book throughout England as much as possible. Because if these books are read, there is no doubt that many sincere souls shall be attracted and will join you in your work for Krishna. So please try for selling these books, it shall be considered as the greatest service.

You have requested of me to write one letter for opening the "board meeting" so when the meeting is arranged definitely I will send the same. So far as the dictionaries go, the Niruktih is the better of the two. I think that you may send me few more of the published Prahlad Maharaja prints so that other temples may be inspired and also may try to republish them in some American papers.

Once again I thank you for your nice labors and hope that you are all well.

Your ever well-wisher,
A. C. Bhaktivedanta Swami

Contact!

One day the phone rang at Betterton Street. It was Rock Scully calling for Shyamasundar. He talked quietly in the corner for a few minutes, hung up the phone, threw his arms in the air, and started shouting "Hare Krishna!" and dancing around the room.

"Wow!" Shyamasundar exclaimed, "That was Rock calling from their new place in Earl's Court. He and Kesey and the gang have got a meeting set up down at Apple tomorrow with the Beatles—and he said I could tag along!"

The next day Shyamasundar was really nervous as he prepared to leave

On the roof of Apple Studios.

for Apple. The girls had baked a cake topped by a green apple and the words HARE KRISHNA made of frosting. We soothed his nerves with comments about how Krishna would help him, and saw him off down the stairs.

Shyamasundar describes his first meeting with George Harrison.

> I had some trouble getting admitted into the Apple offices—finally Yoko Ono drove up in a white Rolls and told the guard it was okay to let me in. I told the receptionist I was with the group from San Francisco, and she said, "Oh, you mean those, er, fellows with the, uh, motorcycles?" and pointed up some stairs to a large reception room. When I walked in, the place was packed with about fifty people—rock stars, elegant ladies, Carnaby Street hippies, guys in suits—and our San Francisco crew spread out among them. I greeted Rock, then took a seat at the far end of the room, away from two doors at the opposite end, behind which everyone said the Beatles were having a meeting and would be out shortly. Hours passed; no Beatles.
>
> Finally, one by one, Paul, John, and Ringo each stuck their heads out of one of the doors then quickly bolted for the exit, not pausing or speaking to anyone. A few minutes later, George poked his head out, and those famous, intense dark eyes quickly scanned the room and alighted on me. Before anyone could react, George had shot out of the door, crossed the room, and come straight at me, grinning and saying, "Hare Krishna! I've been waiting to meet you!"

He sat down, and we started yakking a mile a minute, as if we were old friends meeting after a long time. The other people in the room were stunned and came over to gawk silently while we shot the breeze. Rather than nervous, I felt marvelously fluent, chosen, and wonderfully happy! George related how he often listened to the *Happening* record of Prabhupada leading Hare Krishna Mantra with the New York devotees. He described an incident that had happened to him a year before, when a light plane he was in suddenly lost altitude and started to crash, and George began shouting "Hare Krishna!" at the top of his lungs, and the plane leveled out just before hitting the ground. I answered some of his questions about philosophy, we had a few laughs, then he invited me out to his home in Esher on the coming Sunday and sketched a map to his place on a napkin. I also invited him to Betterton Street to meet the other devotees when he could find the time.

Krishna Progress

Some mornings I would not want to get up so early and had no desire to leave the shelter of my warm blankets and jump into a cold shower, then stumble into a large arenalike room to have the loud sounds of chanting interrupt the dream I left behind.

However, on most mornings, the names of Lord Rama and Krishna danced upon my lips, and being filled with the encouragement of my beloved guru and Their Lordships, I bounded out of the sleeping bag, freshened up in the invigorating waters, and ran into the temple room to share in the sound of the Holy Names with like-minded souls. After morning kirtan, we would hear the pastimes of Lord Krishna from the *Srimad-Bhagavatam*.

And on some mornings, during the *brahma-muhurta* time (an hour and a half before sunrise), I would go on my morning japa walk with thoughts centered on Srila Prabhupada, even though he was far away. This pastime of separation from my guru was analogous to the separation the gopis felt when away from Krishna.

The air in London was now very cold, and another overcast sky was predictable. Prabhupada was not here to go with me on morning japa walk. But this morning I feel alive and hopeful, and I'm bounding out of bed, because today is the day we're going to meet George Harrison!

George

With great anticipation and excitement, we prepared a sumptuous feast on the appointed day. Later that afternoon a slick blue Porsche sports-car roared into Covent Garden and stopped in front of our Betterton Street warehouse. Watching from the window above, I saw George emerge from his chariot wearing blue jeans and a denim jacket. He checked the address and rang the bell. Shyamasundar greeted him downstairs; when he arrived upstairs, Mukunda, Yamuna, and I were introduced, and we greeted him warmly.

George took off his shoes and put them with all the others. He entered the temple floor and went before Lord Jagannath, bowing his head reverently and gazing at the altar for a few minutes. Standing by his side I felt elated, for he was a great musician, an elevated person, and a voice for our age. But I soon popped my awe-bubble and began to treat him just like anyone else. He was also just another spirit soul on the planet.

We walked out of the temple room into the dining area. I introduced the new English brahmacharis (celibate students): "This is Colin, David, and Tim." They *pranamed* (folded their hands), a little awestruck. I had suggested to everyone at a meeting earlier that day to restrain our urge to worship George, but I knew we all felt like he was a demigod. "George will appreciate us much more if we act ourselves and not fawn all over him," I said. "People must do that to him all the time, causing him to always take the role of the celebrity. This is not fair to him. We will impress him with our natural demeanor and with our Krishna conscious philosophy, nothing else. Prabhupada treats everyone equally."

Malati came zooming out of the kitchen, her hands covered with samosa dough. I introduced her: "This is Malati." Her eyes looked all over as she flashed him a quick smile.

George and I both smiled as she walked away in a gangly fashion. His was a simple smile, almost self-effacing. He was an unassuming, regular person, fun and interesting to share things with, who became my good friend. He seemed genuinely interested in learning new things, and there was an intrinsic spirituality about him.

"Who owns this building?" George asked.

I said, "Krishna." And we all laughed in agreement.

He rephrased the question: "In whose name is the building?"

"Nigel Samuels," Mukunda said.

"Nigel has so kindly donated the two floors for our use," I said.

George asked, "What was the building used for before you came?"

Shyamasundar said, "It was the original *International Times* office."

Malati piped in, "Now it is used to store their old magazines."

I added, "The top floor is being shared by Michael-X and the Black Muslims with a rare-book company run by Nigel called Bibliophile."

George had a bemused look.

Yamuna came out of the kitchen with her beatific smile, holding the plate of mahaprasad, and beckoned us into the temple room, where she placed it on the altar.

We handed out kartals (hand cymbals), and George took a pair. I wrapped the cloth strings from the cymbals around two fingers and watched as George did the same. "Let's chant!"

Mukunda began with his swinging drumbeat. I clanged *da da daaah*, and George picked it up immediately. Yamuna led the kirtan with her strong, sweet, soulful singing. "Hari haribol," yelled Janaki. We chanted in bliss for a long time. George was truly moved by chanting the holy names.

Malati took the offering off the altar and invited everyone to respect (eat) prasadam. We sat in an oval around a long table mat we had laid out. "Are you hungry?" I asked gently, and George said, "A little."

At that point Janaki started bringing out pakoras, Yamuna followed with lassis, and Malati came with fruit.

Just in time for dinner, an intense, young English boy came in and left his sandals at the door, smiling self-consciously. "George, this is Jimmy Doody, an artist and inventor," Mukunda said. "He has just invented a light machine that projects images of colored oil and water mixtures on a wall."

George listened with interest and then asked, "Is Krishna the only name for God?"

"There are many names for God," I answered. "Just like you have different names such as 'George,' or 'son,' or maybe someday 'father', and they are all you. If someone chants with devotion any bona fide name of God, it is the same as chanting Krishna. Krishna and His name are nondifferent. When we say Krishna, He is actually dancing on our tongue. It is a transcendental sound vibration."

George looked thoughtful and said, "That's lovely." Then he inquired, "Why is the Hare Krishna mantra called the maha, or great, mantra?"

"Because Lord Chaitanya has made it easy and available for everyone," Yamuna said, as she brought in a large plate of basmati saffron rice.

Malati frenetically put plates in front of everyone, while Janaki followed with water in stainless steel glasses.

The plates were heaped with dahl, two different vegetable preparations, puris, and salad. George ate with gusto. As soon as he finished one item, one of the ladies would replace it. Finally, George tried to cover his plate, but Malati slid some more puris between his hands, just like the East Indian community had been doing to us for some time. We all had a laugh. I was hoping no one would milk the joke and keep piling prasadam on his plate. We were all still a little restrained and on our best behavior.

George looked like he wanted to get up.

I led him to the sink, and as we washed our hands together, side by side, I perceived him as a friend rather than a musical demigod.

I handed him a clean towel, and he looked me straight in the eyes and said, "I am inspired here."

We walked back out to the main room, and George said to everyone, "I had a really nice time, and the prasadam was great. I especially liked the lassis."

We said something like, "It was wonderful for you to be our guest; please come again."

As he was putting on his tennis shoes, George said, "I must go to a mixing session at the Wardour Street studio now, but could all of you please come down to my house in Surrey soon and be my guests, and we can chant there too?"

"Yes, that would be nice," we chorused.

Kirtan at George's House

On the agreed date, we rode down to George's house in Surrey in the back of Shyamasundar's truck. It was a sprawling, Western-style, ranch house in a stately suburb. Though the rooms were quite spacious, it seemed all in all to be an ordinary house—until we came into the living room: A large altar hugged one wall graced by pictures of Krishna, Srila Prabhupada, Lord Shiva, Sri Yukteshwar, and Sri Yogananda. On another wall hung a picture of assorted dogs playing and cheating at poker. The contrast made me laugh.

Billy Preston sat at the piano-organ, smiling, his hair swept up in a huge Afro. Our friend Frankie from San Francisco sat next to him on the piano bench.

Patty, George's pretty, blond wife, came in and was very gracious. George invited us to sit. We sat in a circle on the floor. "Shall we chant?" George asked.

With special excitement we got out our kartals and medina drum, while George picked up an electric guitar, doodled with it for a minute, then laid down an introductory riff. We played the drum and cymbals, George led the singing, and Billy Preston chanted and filled any musical gaps with a rhythmic, gospellike organ pulse. Our voices rang out, and I felt that the roof might fly off this suburban house *satsang* (spiritual gathering) at any moment! The trees outside seemed to be dancing and raising their armlike branches to heaven. Yamuna's "*hari hari bol!*" pierced the sedate Surrey countryside.

In our first meeting with George Harrison, we did not mention the demo tape that we had submitted to Apple Records. Mukunda, Shyamasundar, and I had discussed it, and we had decided to play it by ear whether to bring the subject up or not. Instinctively, we moved very carefully and slowly when dealing with George, as nobody likes to be preached at; and due to our patience, the relationship between us flourished. Just before we left his house, out of the blue, George said, "I love this chanting. You all sound so great! 'The Radha Krishna Temple!' I want Apple to record you guys chanting the Hare Krishna mantra, if it's all right with you."

A recent reunion at Friar Park Manor, George Harrison's home in Oxfordshire, England. From left: Shyamasundar; George; George's son, Dhani; Mukunda Goswami; Gurudas; and George's business manager, Derek Taylor.

We all said, "Yes, that's all right."

George Harrison displayed great respect for Srila Prabhupada. He bowed before Prabhupada at each of their meetings, even though he was never formally initiated. I witnessed in at least six of their meetings how George demonstrated so much love towards Prabhupada and how he was treated like a son in exchange. George also backed up his convictions by rendering services such as financing *Krishna* book and giving us Bhaktivedanta Manor.

John Lennon

John and the other Beatles became more favorable towards us, and we chatted from time to time and soon became friends. Each Beatle approached us from a different perspective. George was always the friendliest; however, John and I also became friends through the many discussions we shared.

I was fond of talking with John, because he would want to talk philosophy. He challenged organized religion in general, pointing out various tainted incidents in the theological history of Western civilization. He spoke about injustices and made some good points, such as how religion can subjugate people's creativity and the sales of indulgences by early Christians. I submitted that spirituality can also enhance one's creativity. "If we create for God, the result becomes eternal." Regarding the sales of indulgences, I told John that I was not an apologist for Christianity, but that anyone on the spiritual path must try to be pure in his intent. I added that there are also many false yogis and swamis who misuse their power.

John always wanted to hear my answer if he asked a question. If someone challenges just to challenge, nothing is accomplished. But to try to understand another's point of view is the essence of life. The Native Americans have a saying: "Never judge me until you walk a mile in my moccasins."

John and I slowly got to know one another. First, he had to trust me before he opened up. On one hand I really didn't want to hear conversations unrelated to Krishna, but I thought back to one time in Prabhupada's room when we had to listen to a man rattle on and on about some construction work—yet Swamiji remained interested and even asked questions. Prabhupada was inquiring and curious about people and the nature of human interaction. So, following his example, I entered into talks with John and Yoko freely.

I had heard that John and Yoko were interested in macrobiotics. One day, as I turned a corner on the third floor at Apple Records, going towards the copy machine with some bhajans (prayers) to reproduce, I met John again. We smiled at one another, and I said, "I heard that you and Yoko are interested in a macrobiotic diet."

John answered, "Yes, we've been eating macrobiotic food for two years now. It feels good."

"That's nice," I said, "Have you tried the ten-day rice fast?"

"Not yet—there's not ten days in a row I have off," John said.

I replied, "Yes, it requires at least ten days, and then it helps to have a few days before to get ready and then a few days after to readjust to a busy schedule like yours."

John was becoming interested and asked me if I had tried macrobiotics. "Yes," I answered, "first in New York in 1963. Some friends were studying with D.T. Suzuki. I read *You Are Sepaku*, and two macrobiotic restaurants opened on the Lower East Side where I lived, so I decided to try the diet. A few months later, I tried the ten-day rice fast."

"So how did it make you feel?"

"For the first three days or so I had to get used to a half cup of brown rice, six ounces of water, and a little tamari (soy sauce). Sometimes thoughts of other kinds of foods invaded my mind. I wish I had known about chanting then—I would have been able to control my tongue a little easier! But after the third day, the rice became pleasurable, appreciated and, although simple, it appeared and tasted like a small feast."

John was silent and engrossed.

"At first the days wore on slowly; however, after three days, the meditation became almost effortless. Basically, I read, reflected, ate the small bowl of brown rice, and drank my six ounces of water. Then I started to feel more ethereal and light, and I actually became naturally high, like I do now when I chant. The experience was quite nice, actually."

John was very interested now, but he was also in a hurry. He apologized, "We'll talk some more another time."

Next time we talked about music, specifically Chuck Berry and early rock and roll. Sometimes we just joked around. He was bright, peace-loving, cynical, loyal, imaginative, irreverent, thoughtful, and someone you would want in your corner.

I miss him.

The Beatles

Paul was always very busy and a homebody, preferring to spend time with his family. So, although we had so many things in common—I went to high school with his wife, Linda Eastman—we never had a chance to cultivate a friendship.

Ringo would bounce in here and there, make a simple statement, and smile. They liked us. We liked them. We all liked each other.

One day, Ringo wanted to know about reincarnation and whether or not he could come back next life as a cat. We asked, "Why a cat?"

"Because I like cats," he said, and laughed. I thought to myself that we humans have had to endure so many animal births in order to reach a human birth. I kept the thought to myself.

George was truly a spiritual person. He was my true friend. George was a real person, and when he could have been vain and filled with airs like many wealthy and idolized people, he was instead very unassuming. George was caring, sensitive, honest, a great conversationalist, deeply reflective, and spiced with a keen sense of humor. Because he often visited us, ate with us, and sang with us, he became our friend. His wife, Olivia, calls Shyamasundar, Mukunda, George, and me "the old gang."

George not only supported us by his friendship but by his deeds as well, his many selfless services to Srila Prabhupada. He encouraged our "Hare Krishna Mantra" and "Govinda" recording projects from the beginning. Among so many other services, he financed Prabhupada's *Krishna* book, bought valuable slabs of exotic marble for our altars, and gave us Bhaktivedanta Manor.

Alchemical Wedding

Jack Moore was one of the main catalysts of the London renaissance. He was an expatriate from Texas and cofounder of the Arts Lab. One day he came over to our temple on Betterton Street to talk. I had always liked Jack; he was very smart, witty, and a great innovator of events and ideas.

We all sat together, Shyamasundar, Mukunda, Jack, and I. Jack began: "Jim Haines and I want to stage an event to call all the people together, and we would like you guys to be part of it."

"Yeah, like a gathering of the tribes," I said.

"Exactly," Jack continued. "We want all types of people from London to gather in Royal Albert Hall and sit in silence together. Will you join us there?"

We conferred briefly. "Yes, we can all be there but, according to the *Vedas*, we should be able to chant because chanting is also silence."

"Well, okay. But please come anyway and add your charm to the mix! I'm making handbills. I'll drop one by when they're ready, alright?"

On the night of the event we dressed in our finest dhotis and saris and set out for the program. Our party consisted of Shyamasundar, Malati, and baby Saraswati crammed into the cab of the tiny truck, and Mukunda, Janaki, Yamuna, and me, along with all our musical instruments, in the open back. Fortunately it was springtime, and the air was refreshing. We found a parking place in Knightsbridge and walked to the huge, round, beautiful music hall, usually reserved for the London symphony and other headliner concerts.

We found the entrance and went in. The middle of the floor was empty of seats, like a Roman theater in the round. A large, white stripe—Jack's idea—was painted down the middle of the sunken area. Seats surrounded the empty circle, all the way around the hall and into the balcony. We were scheduled to start the program by chanting the maha-mantra, accompanied by our instruments. I had a camera slung over my shoulder and kartals in my hand, and I was ready for something to happen. Our plan was for the six of us to split up and each walk singly down one aisle, chanting. We would start from the top seats and then proceed down into the pit itself at a time which would "reveal itself."

I settled into a seat at the top of an aisle and watched as Royal Albert Hall buzzed and filled with thousands of people, the leading characters of the London underground movement, decked out with feathers and beads, and wearing big hats. The colors of the rainbow adorned the clothes of the swirling and weaving girls and boys.

Six Hell's Angels came in, did a scouting lap like lions in a zoo cage, looked around, and slumped themselves over eleven seats. Ken Kesey and

Rock Scully came in and sat down near the Angels. John Peel, and then Miles, dressed in a long Edwardian coat, came into the huge, circular hall.

A huge, white cloth bubble, probably containing John Lennon and Yoko Ono, "walked" out onto the central open area and stopped (see next story).

As the lights were lowered, a general pall fell on everyone, as if an invisible sound barrier net was thrown over us. In the darkness, shadow people slowly emerged as my eyes adjusted to the dimness. No one said anything; no one knew what to do. A few minutes passed in hypnotic silence.

Suddenly a screech from one of the Hell's Angels pierced the silence and minutes later an isolated voice shouted, "Strawberry fields forever!" Then someone yelled, "*O-O-O-M-M!*" Realizing this must be our signal, I start ringing the kartals: one-two-sizzle, one-two-sizzle—Mukunda boomed the medina and laid down the rhythm. The other devotees joined with kartals, and we slowly, evenly, walked down the aisles. Malati carried Saraswati and played kartals at the same time.

Very soon, people joined in. The holy sounds built, and transcendental Names surged towards the high-domed ceiling. No one was supposed to cross over the painted white line, so we stood tall and humbly defiant, lined up right on the line. A nonverbal electricity of understanding energized the hall. Janaki raised her arms and began gracefully dancing the Swami Two-Step, then we all started dancing with upraised arms and increased the volume of our singing.

The arena suddenly exploded with a mighty kirtan, and the lights flashed on. People jumped up and started dancing with us. We moved away from the white line and ambulated in a circle through the crowd that joined us. I played kartals and swung my camera out and rapidly photographed the joyous commotion around me. Someone handed me a microphone, and I began singing over the sound system. It turned into an improvised twelve-bar, blues-raga kirtan. This spontaneous, transcendental symphony was totally blissful and ecstatic. I continued to sing and photograph simultaneously.

The traditional building rocked like never before. Then, after what seemed like hours, some officials turned off the lights and the sound; but still the chanting went on, slowly becoming softer, dwindling, and eventually stopping. We decided a hasty exit was appropriate, and we went back to the temple feeling contented.

I immediately went to Fleet Street, where a friend at the *Daily Telegraph*, a major newspaper, let me develop my film. When the negatives were ready, I viewed them on the light table. Strangely enough, six other reporters and photographers gathered around the table too. This is a unique story, I thought; I'm glad they are interested. Then they took out a large magnifying glass. One of the men said, "I found it." They all crowded round. "I found her."

Apparently, some girl was so excited by the happenings that she'd taken her clothes off! Disrobing in public happened often enough in San Francisco but was a rare occurrence in London, and these lechers were more interested in that angle than our spiritual viewpoint. They offered me eighty pounds for the photos. "If you'll disassociate our temple from her, you can buy the photos."

The Daily Telegraph ran an article picturing Yamuna and Janaki chanting in ecstasy, plus one or two other photos, and a blow-up of the naked girl wearing only a large, straw hat. The picture was so blurry, it was a very cheap thrill. The headline read "Mad Rave-In at Albert Hall." I cropped out the word "Mad" (so that it read "Rave-In at Albert Hall") and the naked-girl photo, and sent the article to Prabhupada in Los Angeles.

The *International Times* wrote about us as follows: "In their vegetarian loveliness, they turned a corporeal event into heaven." Prabhupada loved the article. From that time on, due to the success of the event, we became an even bigger part of the underground scene in London.

From Los Angeles
24 December, 1968

My Dear Gurudas,
 Please accept my blessings. I beg to acknowledge receipt of your recent letter (undated) along with copies of the syndicate contract inviting for newspaper reproduction of the Royal Albert Hall chanting and they are all very encouraging.

 I am sure that Krishna is helping you all around for your honest and sincere endeavors. Just previous to your letter I received one very encouraging letter from Shyamasundar reporting of his meeting with George Harrison, who I understand has promised to give us a five-story building in one of the busiest quarters of London. You have arranged for the convocation and I have seen the list of invitees. It is very encouraging. Please conduct this convocation carefully and try to recruit some sympathizers for our nice London center. I am dispatching one tape by separate registered airmail, in which you'll find my speech for this occasion. It begins with "Ladies and Gentlemen." I think this speech will be nice and it is recorded on speed 3¾.

 Regarding your analogy of sowing KC seeds, I may inform you that there is a Bengali proverb: Sa Bure Meoya Phale. This means that fruits like chestnuts and pomegranates, or similar other valuable fruits and nuts, take some time to be fructified. So any good thing comes in our possession after hard struggle and endeavor. So Krishna consciousness is the greatest of all good fruits. We must therefore have necessary endurance and enthusiasm to get the result. We shall never be disappointed when things are presented in reversed order. Anyway, your honest labor is now coming to be fructified. Always depend upon Krishna and go on working with enthusiasm, patience, and conviction.

Our policy of Krishna consciousness is very nice. We are offering people good family life with faithful wives in Krishna consciousness. Similarly, able husbands in Krishna consciousness so that the younger generation will be happy to have nice home, nice wife, nice food, nice dress, nice philosophy of life, nice culture, and ultimately, nice Krishna. So this movement is the nicest of all other movements. Simply the ministers should be ready, intelligent, honest, and sincere. Then surely, the Krishna consciousness Movement will be accepted by all considerate men and women. Thank you again for your letter and I hope this finds you in good health.

Your ever well-wisher,
A. C. Bhaktivedanta Swami

John and Yoko's Bubble

John and Yoko had made for themselves a round, white-canvas, bubble-like structure that covered them from head to toe. They could walk inside the bubble but remain completely covered. By attending events in their bubble, they were at some place, yet isolated at the same time. Zen-like, they could be there and not be there, just like the Irish expression "They are in the tall grasses," meaning nearby but unseen.

The couple conceived the idea when a pushy music person scheduled himself to meet with Yoko. "John and I are shy people," she stated to Dick Cavett during one interview. She described how she covered herself with a cloth so that she could meet the music agent yet remain hidden.

John added, "There is no prejudice when you're in the bag. If a black man goes for a job in the bag, no one will know he is black. We both go to many press conferences in the bag; the press looks funny interviewing the bag."

One time John had to go to the dentist, so he asked Yamuna and me if we would replace him and Yoko inside their white balloon in order to trick the press at an art gallery opening. I wanted to do it, but since I was temple president at the time and very busy, I declined; instead, I offered Suridas and Jotilla, two devotees from the Paris temple who were visiting London, the opportunity to pose as John and Yoko in the bag. Jotilla spoke with a strong American accent, and Suridas had a French Algerian inflection. What made the event even more comical was the fact that she was taller than Suridas and had to pose as John with her American accent, and Suridas as Yoko. Suridas recounts that when they arrived at the art gallery in John's white Rolls Royce, many flashbulbs greeted them, and it was very hot inside the bubble. Still, the press believed it was John and Yoko who attended the event!

Abbey Road

George Harrison wanted us to record the Hare Krishna mantra on the Apple record label. We didn't need much rehearsal for this, as we sang it all day anyway: to ourselves on a bus, in our hearts, or together in the temple—the maha-mantra was always dancing on our tongues, the Holy Names our constant companion. But we got some musical instruments—a harmonium, an esraj—and began to practice the standard Happening Records melody. We called ourselves "The Radha Krishna Temple."

The recording session was scheduled one evening at the EMI Studios on Abbey Road, behind the famous zebra crosswalk on the Beatle's album, *Abbey Road*. Inside the studio, we took a leisurely prasadam, chatted, and had a good time in general just lolling around. George was extremely patient, but eventually he reminded us that the studio cost forty-five pounds (£ 45/-) per hour.

The recording went well, with Yamuna and Shyamasundar leading, our backup rhythms supportive but not overpowering. George laid down a beautiful guitar introduction, and the chanting built up nicely in tempo and volume to a wonderful crescendo that ended with Malati clanging a hanging, brass gong. Our collective hearts stopped because the *CLANG!* sounded out of time—we hadn't rehearsed it. We thought we'd have to do the whole recording over!

George was calm. Mal Evans, the roadie, didn't move a muscle. George then led us back into the engineering booth for a listen.

I sat next to George as he put the earphones on.

As we listened the mantra sprang forth, sounding fantastic and inspiring. George began sliding levers up and down, adjusting sounds on the various tracks.

Paul and Linda McCartney came into the booth. We hardly noticed them, intensely waiting for the clang at the end. Once again our chanting came to a crescendo climax—and the gong clang was perfect in its timing and added a nice, conclusive, exotic ending!

George asked us to go back into the studio and sing over our own choruses, which we gladly did three more times. It was fun, and the six of us became 12, then 24, and finally 48 voices. It sounded great to me. George asked us back to the control booth to listen. The mantra rang out purely and joyously. I was completely encouraged and excited by the holy sounds we had rendered.

Linda and Paul, too, were nodding with the beat and smiling. They indicated that they liked the sound, and soon they were singing along.

I turned to Paul and introduced myself: "My name is Gurudas."

Paul introduced himself and said, "And, of course, this is Linda."

I looked directly at Linda McCartney, once Linda Eastman, and said, "Yes, we were in the same homeroom together in high school."

She looked startled with disbelief.

"I attended Scarsdale High School, too, in 1955," I added.

She looked suspicious. (After all, I could have gleaned those facts about her from a music magazine; "Yeah, I sit around the temple reading movie magazines, seeing who got married and divorced last week in Hollywood," I thought sarcastically to myself.)

"We were both in Mr. Steele's homeroom."

Now she believed me, because that was a little-known fact—(as was the fact that she seemed to be a snob in high school, but I didn't mention that, as she seemed so friendly now). I also remembered that we stepped on each other's toes at school dances.

She looked at me now, in robes and shaven locks, and replied, "I didn't think anyone from affluent Scarsdale would become a monk and renounce their wealth!"

I retorted, "Why not? Material wealth is only temporary, and besides, Krishna owns Scarsdale too. He is, after all, God!"

Linda was quite surprised, but seemed to understand what I was saying.

Her reply then surprised me: "Paul is my God," she said.

Then she changed the subject: "I've become vegetarian and want to offer precooked vegetarian meals to the public some day."

I encouraged her: "That's wonderful! The more vegetarian meals available to the public, the better. Being vegetarian is karmically benefiting, and healthy also."

We listened to the final takes of the record until George was satisfied. Paul and Linda left. We packed up our instruments, blankets, prasadam plates, and babies, and departed Abbey Road.

A few weeks later the transcendental sound vibration of "Hare Krishna

Mantra" was released by Apple Records, and the results were overwhelming. On our first attempt, *Radha Krishna Temple* had crashed all geographical and political barriers, and the sound of the "great mantra for deliverance" had ebbed into the hearts of all who heard it, despite any flaws in our singing voices and our outward appearances. People all over the world looked past their differences to accept the unity of chanting the maha-mantra.

Because they struck an eternal chord, the Holy Names flowed even through and across the Iron Curtain. For a few weeks our "Hare Krishna Mantra" single became the fastest-selling of *all* the Apple Corporation's releases, including those of the Beatles.

In Czechoslovakia, the single reached #3 in the sales charts; it reached to #9 in the British music polls. We were in the Top Ten in Japan, Yugoslavia, South Africa, Australia, Germany, and many other countries. This was very rare for a first recording.

But since this mantra has come down to us from time immemorial, via Narada Muni, the eternal spaceman, the record's magnificent success didn't really surprise me at all. This was our first effort as essentially nonprofessional musicians, but because we were sincere devotees who were simply doing what we did best, all-attractive Krishna danced in the collective ears of all who listened to this record.

Govinda

"Govinda", the second single made by The Radha Krishna Temple was recorded at Trident Studios, in an alley off Wardour Street near Piccadilly Circus. For this record, George consulted with George Martin, who was also known as the fifth Beatle because his arrangements so enhanced the Beatles' music. For example, the violin and cello background in "Eleanor Rigby", with a symphony orchestra counterpointing the Beatles' guitars, bass, and drum, was arranged and produced by George Martin. We visited him at his home, and he was a soft-spoken English gentleman, very efficient with his suggestions for embellishing our "Govinda" recording. He thought that strings, choruses, and a harp would go nicely with Mukunda's original arrangement.

During this recording session, our mood was a bit more intense and uncertain. We rarely sang the "Govinda" (*Brahma Samhita*) prayers, we hadn't practiced much, and we now had to coordinate about twenty-five devotees instead of the original six who had recorded the Hare Krishna mantra! Furthermore, the "Govinda" arrangement includes several verses and choruses and complex Sanskrit words and phrasing, totally unlike the Hare Krishna mantra we were used to chanting 25,000 times a day.

Here are the verses to "Govinda", with translations:

Verse 1
*venum kvanantam aravinda-dalayataksham
barhavatamsam asitambudha-sundarangam
kandarpa-koti-kamaniya-vishesha-shobham
govindam adi-purusham tam aham bhajami*

Translation: I worship Govinda, the primeval Lord, who is adept in playing on His flute, with blooming eyes like lotus petals with head decked with peacock feathers, with the figure of beauty tinged with the hue of blue clouds, and His unique loveliness charming millions of Cupids.

Verse 2
*angani yasya sakalendriya–vritti-manti
pashyanti panti kalayanti chiram jaganti
ananda-chinmaya–sad-ujjvala-vigrahasya
govindam adi-purusham tam aham bhajami*

Translation: I worship Govinda, the primeval Lord, whose transcendental form is full of bliss, truth, and substantiality and is thus full of the most dazzling splendor. Each of the limbs of the transcendental figure possesses in Himself the full-fledged functions of all organs, and eternally sees, maintains, and manifests the infinite universes, both spiritual and mundane.

George Harrison directed the whole session, and even though we were under pressure to do our best with this less familiar mantra, he was a master at guiding our large group. George arranged a series of large, sound-diffusing panels around clusters of our singers and instrumentalists. Ishan played the trumpet a bit off-key and too loud, so George sent him out into the hallway. Yamuna sang the lead verses. Mukunda was the lead medina player, and I was the lead kartal player. I played my rhythmic riff on kartals near the end of the song. Shyamasundar played the esraj, and Hari Vilas, who was born in Armenia, played the oud, his Middle-Eastern notes cascading between verse and chorus. George played harmonium and guitar.

George Martin directed the harpist and other members of the London Philharmonic, who created the huge ethereal wall of sound that makes "Govinda" so unique. The recording was well accepted, it sold well, and again

The Radha Krishna Temple made the charts in many countries.

To this day, this recording of "Govinda" is played every morning to greet the Deities in every ISKCON temple on the planet. And still, whenever I hear the chorus building up at the end of "Govinda", tears come to my eyes.

THE RADHA KRISHNA TEMPLE

It took some time, but eventually we set the reporters and news media straight—our group, The Radha Krishna Temple, was perceived as a religious group that happens to sing, rather than a one-hit-wonder rock band. At first, we were considered quite a novelty with our constantly changing personnel (e.g., "Bibhavati has to take care of her baby, so she can't be at the concert tonight."). We had no groupies hanging around the front of the temple, nor did we take drugs or do the things most other music groups did. And yet we were accepted all over England.

Our two hits were another coup for George, for he had sponsored the fastest-selling single record that Apple had ever produced, even among the Beatles' hits. On the spiritual platform, George had helped introduce the great chant of deliverance into the hearts of millions. George Harrison also wrote and recorded many of his own songs with spiritual, Krishna-conscious themes. Literally hundreds of devotees have approached me, asking me to convey to George how his music helped them to become devotees of Krishna and encouraged them in their spiritual journey.

Reporters from the British music magazines started coming around the Bury Place Temple for interviews. They were sent up to me in my office on the top floor. I would be sitting cross-legged on a cushion across from a part-skeptical/part-curious interviewer:

Question: "How long has your group been together?"
Answer: "Some of us have been together for a year, and some joined two days ago."
Q: "So your group changes personnel a lot?"
A: "Yes. I don't allow our celibate students to go to nightclubs with us for live engagements. We are first of all devotees of Lord Krishna; we live simply, like monks. These songs are our prayers. Other people like them too—that is why our Hare Krishna mantra is a success."
Q: "Who is the leader of the group then?"
A: "My guru, A. C. Bhaktivedanta Swami, is the leader of our group."
Q: "Which one is he?" (We are looking at a promotional photo.)
A: "He is our guru, our teacher. See, we are holding up his photo in our photo."
Q: "Does he sing too?"

A: "All the time. He taught us the songs we sing. However, I understand what you are getting at; yes, he is always with us in our hearts and souls, but His Divine Grace was not actually in the recording sessions we did with George."
Q: "Where did the song come from?"
A: "The song came from Narada Muni, passed down to us through the ages stemming from the Satya-yuga, or Golden Age—about 380,000,000 years ago."
Reporter: "Oh."

The Radha Krishna Temple group was featured in all the European and British pop music magazines. Other worldwide magazines began interviewing and writing about us as well. Reporters came from as far away as Egypt and Argentina. An Italian movie company filmed Mukunda and me walking across Trafalgar Square. Another time, a movie producer came to my office to arrange a pilot film-shoot with Vanessa Redgrave. Terms for payment were settled, and on a foggy, steamy night, fourteen devotees and I chanted on the East London docks. Vanessa Redgrave was being chased. She came upon us, found refuge, shook my hand, and ran off. I don't know the title of the film or if it ever got made.

Derek Taylor, the PR man at Apple Records, once rented a large marquee tent in Plimpton near the Crystal Palace to announce the launching of our new hit single, "Govinda". We cooked vegetarian samosas, rice, and subji prasadam. Dozens of reporters milled around looking for alcoholic drinks and found only juice nectar. At first they simply picked at the food, and then they ate heartily.

Another time, Derek rented a marquee for us at an international rock-music festival in rural England. We chanted outside the main venue, and there I ran into my old friend Jon Hendricks, the jazz singer. Jon was glad to take prasadam with us again; I had not seen him since we shared prasadam in San Francisco in 1967.

Top of the Pops

The most popular show on British television in the late '60s was called "Top of the Pops," a sort of variety-musical, half-hour evening show. Young and old, a significant portion of the country's viewers watched "Top of the Pops," as there were only two channels at the time, BBC and ITV (Independent Television).

The first time we went on the show we sang the Hare Krishna Mantra without paraphernalia or incident. The second time we appeared on "Top Of The Pops," we came with more people and more instruments and props.

We brought slides of Radha and Krishna, Bhaktisiddhanta Saraswati, Bhaktivinoda Thakur, Gaura Kishore das Babaji, and Garuda, temples in India, etc. I arranged the slides in order for a projector to flash them on the telescreen.

We laid down a madras cloth and sat cross-legged in a semicircle on the stage. The director of the show asked us to do a sound-check rehearsal. As we began to sing, some "go-go" dancers got into cages suspended above us and started gyrating to our sound. I looked up at them and realized that the *Brahma-samhita* prayers and go-go dancing are simply not compatible! I raised my hand for us to stop all activities. As I was temple president, everyone stopped singing immediately. I said to the director, "We don't require the dancing, especially since we have supplied supplementary visuals with the slides."

He was silent, and we seemed to be at an impasse.

Finally he said, "They are union dancers and must dance every song."

I said, "But that kind of dancing is incompatible with our prayers."

The director, who was pulling out his already scanty hair, said, "Then I don't know what to do!"

I then replied, "What will you do with four minutes of blank TV space?"

I motioned to our entourage to pack everything up and said, "Let's go." We started to leave. The director knew we were serious, and since it was a live show with ten minutes until airtime, he begged me to reconsider.

I had an idea. I said, "Get some long cloths, like saris, and we will dress the dancers and teach them the Trance Dance."

This was a win-win compromise.

They found some long lengths of cloth, and Yamuna, Mondakini, Janaki, Jyotirmayee, and Malati assisted the dancing girls. We gave them a quick course in the side-by-side Trance Dance—or Swami Two-Step—and they loved the novelty and sashaying ease of the dance. The musical intro to "Govinda" came on, we were on the air, and we began to lip-synch with the words, pretending to play our instruments, which was easy for us. We had fun miming it. Slides of Krishna continued to flash on the monitor sporadically.

The nicest aspect of the whole production, however, was how angelic the dancing girls looked, swaying like wheat in the wind to our ancient prayers. Everyone was happy, including the director, and our appearance on the show was a great success.

People stopped me on the street and said, "I saw you on the telly."

Some of the British pop magazines featured articles describing our beliefs and practices. These articles attracted many interested young potential devotees to our doors.

The Radha Krishna Temple on Tour

I also worked with a booking service that Derek Taylor told us about, named Red Door Agency, and they started booking us into all sorts of venues, all around Britain.

Nearly every night of the week we would ride into a town—anywhere from eight to twelve of us—and do a one-night gig, including getting the audience to chant with us. We sang the same tunes that were on the Apple recordings, but, as we were now performing live shows, the personnel were often different for each engagement. I would not allow the bramacharis (celibate students) to go to the nightclubs. When we went to concerts in the Krishna van, I would make sure there were a few empty seats in case anyone wanted to return with us to our London temple. Usually, two or three people would ride back with us.

We had a no-meat clause in our contract, stating that if we were to be offered any food in our dressing rooms, it was to be strictly vegetarian. Although sometimes we were treated quite nicely, there was usually only a tiny dressing room, or no dressing room at all, and no food.

Sometimes we were the sole act, but often we did shows with other holy men or with other artists. Once we shared a stage with Swami Satchidananda. Saraswati cried when he held her.

At Harrow Town Hall we had a joint kirtan with Quintessence, a well-known Anglo-American, psychedelic, mantra-rock group. I became good friends with Shiva, the lead singer, and Stanley, the manager, who I knew from the Lower East Side of New York. Quintessence did a set, we did a set, and then we chanted Hare Krishna together at the end of the show.

We were often booked at the Roundhouse in London and shared bills with unlikely groups like the Fugs, Joe Cocker, Deep Purple, and some guy that smashed his guitar.

After many successful engagements in Great Britain, we started to get bookings in Europe as well—venues like the Konzertgebouw in Amsterdam, a huge rock festival in southern France, and many others.

I particularly remember the "Festival of the Midnight Sun" in Sweden. The night sun was huge and luminous, and thousands of people cheered us after our young Swedish devotee, Lilashakti, gave a great talk in Swedish and English. We ended the whole festival by sweetly chanting the maha-mantra as the large, golden sun shone down on us throughout the night. After the show, dozens of people stood in line to get our autographs!

Die Reperbahn

As we rode through Hamburg's red-light district, Die Reperbahn, I tried to cover my eyes, my senses, my lust, as we passed by the garish and brightly illuminated sex signs. Girls and women—maya in all forms—dressed in flimsy lingerie, displayed their bodies in bay windows, a small door and a bed just visible behind them.

I closed my eyes and sank deep inside myself. With the Holy Name on my lips, I withdrew into a peaceful reverie. The sound of a loud horn and a near accident pulled me into the world of illusion again.

We arrived at our venue, the Star Club, where the Beatles had appeared early in their careers. George once told me that the Star Club gigs had enabled them to come together as a musical group.

The Star Club was a dark and dingy hole of a place. The stage was small. The audience was comatose for a long while, but gradually, since they were there anyway, they warmed up to our chanting. It was like a rathskeller— German beerhouse—chant, but that was fine with us.

We did two shows and were supposed to collect 1,000 marks, but they paid us only 250. They gave us a small, ratty room, and we found it impossible to sleep. Mukunda and I had the address of the promoter, so we decided to go there to try and get our money, as we were leaving for Kiel the next day.

We trundled through the Reperbahn and found the address. The apartment was on the fifth floor, so we trudged up the stairs. We were slightly out of breath when we arrived at the apartment door. Though it was late at night, we knocked on the door; it was slowly opened by a curvaceous woman wearing only a thin slip, who blocked the doorway.

"Is Gunther here?" I asked her.

As she was telling us he wasn't there, we saw a rifle barrel through the slit between the wall and the door. I didn't know which was worse, the girl in the slip or the gun.

Again she said, "Gunther is not here, ja!"

We left the message with her that he owed us 750 marks and quickly left.

We did not receive our money from Gunther until we returned to Britain, and then Red Door collected for us.

The rest of our German tour was less eventful, but much more successful. We went to universities and clubs, and we held sankirtan on the streets of Munich, Frankfurt, Kiel, and several other towns in Germany. The club owners paid us concert fees of 500 pounds, or about $1,000, per night.

Royalties from sales of our two hit singles, the money from concerts and club gigs, and collections by the sankirtan party on the streets of central London financed our ever-growing UK yatra. And all this publicity was attracting more and more new, fresh, bright, and enthusiastic young devotees to join us every day.

A letter from Srila Prabhupada was like fuel for the fire of our devotional service:

> Los Angeles
> 21 January, 1969
>
> My Dear Gurudas and Yamuna,
>
> Please accept my blessings. I beg to acknowledge both of your letters dated 14, January 1969, as well as one letter from Gurudas dated 16, January 1969 with an enclosed picture and newspaper cuttings. This picture is undoubtedly very unique because perhaps in the history of the world it is for the first time that Western boys and girls in the dress of pure Vaishnavas are chanting on the street of a very important quarter of the greatest city in the world, London. So by the Grace of Krishna you are all six together doing very nice Krishna Conscious activities, and I am so much pleased. In your letter I can understand that people from many important cities of Europe and Africa are taking part in our sankirtan movement, and you have got continuous engagements almost every night. This is very much encouraging.
>
> I am so glad to understand that as soon as your finances are almost depleted, Krishna sees to everything. This is the process of Krishna consciousness. If we are sincere, Krishna will supply us with all necessities of life. When we serve some mundane master, he gives us sufficient salary, so when we serve the Supreme Master, how it is possible that He will keep us fasting? Actually due to our lack of Krishna consciousness sometimes we become disturbed with shortage of funds. But we should be confident that our necessities will certainly be fulfilled by the Supreme Lord. The same incident sometimes happens in New York temple. When there is a shortage of funds, sometimes they find money accidentally without knowing the source.
>
> I have received report from Mr. Parikh and others that they are enamored by your behavior, your character, and your devotion. In the newspaper cuttings also they gave such hints. In other words, everyone is appreciating your presentation. Please keep up this standard of behavior. Do not make any artificial discrepancies amongst yourselves because you are acting on a very responsible business. Perhaps you know that there are many political parties in a country, but when the country's total responsibility has to be executed, they become combined. To have some little disagreements amongst yourselves is not very unnatural because we are all individual beings. But

as we are all working on behalf of Krishna we should always forget our personal interests and see to the prime cause.

I have noted with great satisfaction the list of foodstuffs offered on the meeting day, and they were so much appreciated. I have not as yet received any letter from Mr. Fakirchand who is interested in starting a temple. I hope this meets you both in very good health.

Your ever well-wisher,
A. C. Bhaktivedanta Swami

Finding 7 Bury Place

By the spring of 1969, about thirty devotees were regularly attending our meetings or were living with us, and we were outgrowing the Betterton Street quarters. Most were young British boys and girls, but, London being an international hub, some devotees came from France, some came from America—veterans of the Vietnam war—and another came from Armenia. Germans, Indians, even Arabians came and took part in our devotional activities. We definitely required a larger headquarters.

We looked at various options for a new temple, including a World War II morgue. This building consisted of two floors of dull and dreary rooms at the end of a hidden alley in East London. We could feel the ghosts of slain soldiers, and when we saw the metal tables with holes to allow blood and body parts to pass through them, we knew this building was not suitable.

George Harrison was very kindly willing to be our guarantor on a new property. Prabhupada wrote regarding this.

> But for the time being all of you should concentrate your energies to occupy the house mortuary by all means. It is understood that Mr. George Harrison has given a letter of guarantee for payment of rent, but if they want further guarantee, I can ask Bank of America or any other bank to give the necessary guarantee of payment. Somehow or other, you must satisfy them and occupy the house. That is the immediate program, and as soon as this is done, I shall go there to adjust things in right order. If some way or other you miss to occupy the house, then you can arrange for me some place with someone who can receive me as guest at least for one month. That also will help me in organizing things there.

We looked at many places in central London, all of them far too expensive for our limited means. Then one day I was standing in queue at the bank, in dhoti and sikha, and an English fellow came up to me and asked if I knew an American bloke from San Francisco named Shyamasundar. I said yes, that in fact he was in London, and then told him our whole story. It turned out that this guy was formerly Shyamasundar's neighbor in Haight-Ashbury, but now he was an estate agent in London. Furthermore, the man had a building, ideal for our purposes, which he was willing to lease at a very nominal rate. It was on Bury Place, not too far from Betterton Street.

Shyamasundar, Mukunda, and I walked the two blocks over to 7 Bury Place and looked at a narrow, five-story building that was once used as a Bible distributing office. How appropriate, as the building was already zoned for religious activities. The location was perfect. The charter allowed two caretakers. We were now about forty devotees, but we reckoned we would figure that out later. Shyamasundar had shipped a load of redwood lumber from Northern California for the purposes of building the interior of our new temple.

We wanted to get started, but we would still have to find living quarters during the rebuilding of the interior of the 7 Bury Place building.

TITTENHURST PARK

John Lennon had just purchased a vast estate in Buckinghamshire, near Windsor Castle, about an hour's drive south of London. One day he mentioned to George that the place needed lots of work on the house and the 35 acres of grounds. George knew our plight so he said to John, "Well, why don't you let the Hare Krishnas live out there in return for a bit of work?" John agreed and asked us to come out. He would provide room and board, and in exchange we would do repair and grounds work while we lived there.

Tittenhurst Park was named after its original owner. Mr. Tittenhurst was a horticulturist who erected greenhouses and nurseries, and he planted virtually every type of tree and shrub that would grow in the British climate. Many plants were imported from other parts of the world.

Tittenhurst Park was laid out with a large main house in the center, surrounded by greenhouses, lawns, and a lotus-pond fountain on one side of a long arbor of sculpted trees. There was a large building called the Gallery, very ornate with white marble columns, where we set up our temple room, and two-story blocks of servants' quarters, where we lived. The estate included a forest and fenced-in pasture grounds, bordered by trails and footpaths. One of the pastures was the habitat for a donkey, which Derek Taylor had brought over to Tittenhurst. The main house, where John and Yoko lived, sat on a raised hillock overlooking the grounds. It was large but very simple inside. The bare living room, furnished only with a piano and an old confessional booth, looked down wide cement steps to the beautiful sloping grounds below.

All the devotees except Shyamasundar and Tirthapada, who were remodeling the 7 Bury Place Temple, moved to Tittenhurst Estate. Soon we settled into a daily routine, attending early morning and evening kirtan services and helping the Lennons restore the buildings and grounds during the days. We led an almost monastic life during our stay at Tittenhurst Park, although I was required to travel to London quite often.

Then Prabhupada said he was coming to join us in London. We were all very excited as we received the good news: Prabhupada would be coming to England!

New Vrindaban
21 June, 1969

My Dear Gurudas,

Please accept my blessings. I have received your note about the new house, and I have arranged to send the money as requested by Mukunda. I hope the money is already received by you and the transaction is nicely executed. After hard labor, you are getting a nice house just suitable for your purposes. Now decorate it nicely, and go ahead with new vigor and energy to push on the Krishna consciousness Movement in London. You have already created an impression in the greatest city in the world, and I hope in the future there will be even greater hope for this movement. I am glad to learn that the Beatles have showed guarantee for payment of the rent. It is a nice, friendly gesture. Recently Mr. John Lennon had an interview with one of our disciples, Vibhavati, and it appears that he is also sympathetic with our movement. Another point is that in BTG we shall now publish as many pictures of our Sankirtan Movement in different cities as possible. So get good snaps of your kirtans and engagement in London, and send the photos on to NewYork.

Regarding my going to London, I have now finished my engagements on this side, and I can go to London at any time you may call.

Please convey my blessings to the others. I hope this will meet you in good health.

Your ever well-wisher,
A. C. Bhaktivedanta Swami

Prabhupada's London Arrival

September 11, 1969: Prabhupada was finally coming to London! We made first-class arrangements for him. John Lennon provided a limousine to drive Prabhupada from the airport to Tittenhurst Park, where he would live with us until the renovations at Bury Place were completed. Because of our records and exposure, the press were interested in the person who had started this Hare Krishna phenomenon, so we arranged a press conference in the VIP lounge at Heathrow Airport.

The chairs were arranged in a circle, with Srila Prabhupada seated at the head. The media asked the usual questions about the meaning of tilak markings, etc. Then they asked Prabhupada why he rode in a huge Rolls Royce limo. Prabhupada answered, "I am God's servant; what He gives me for His service, I will accept."

Then one gentleman asked, "Why have you come here?"

Prabhupada answered immediately, "I have come here to teach you what you have forgotten: Love of God."

Prabhupada at John and Yoko's

About eighteen of us, including Srila Prabhupada, lived in the smallish servants' quarters about 100 feet away from the main house at Tittenhurst. We were sheltered, and we were near Prabhupada as well. I was elected President of our London yatra, so I would walk around the vast estate checking on how everyone was doing. I tried to emulate Prabhupada in my management techniques. If encouragement was needed, I supplied it as best I could. If discipline was required, I also tried to be both firm and kind.

Behind the great house was a "gallery," which was formerly used for chamber music recitals. The gallery hall was huge and had a large fireplace. We made a makeshift altar with pictures of Prabhupada, Bhaktisiddhanta Saraswati, Bhaktivinode Thakur, and Gaura Kishore das Babaji on one level. We placed paintings of Lord Chaitanya and Sri Sri Radha Krishna on the altar as well. Then Lord Chaitanya, Adwaita Acharya, Sri Nityananda, and Srivas were added. We also built a vyasasana, a seat, for Prabhupada.

After walking behind the gallery and living quarters, I arrived at an enclosed, isolated pasture where the Apple mule munched peacefully. I put my foot up on the lower fence rail. The mule reminded me of Eeyore, Winnie the Pooh's friend. I was staring at the mule, he was staring at me; as I was chanting, he was listening.

Prabhupada lived with his assistant Purushottam in one of the cottages, which had a small kitchen and sleeping area downstairs and a room for

Prabhupada's office and darshan upstairs. It was simple and sparse, but Prabhupada was happy. He could continue writing and chanting and be near his beloved disciples. He walked the grounds of the estate and talked to me of nature being the highest reflection of Krishna and how by studying nature one could feel closer to Lord Krishna. He led the services both mornings and evenings, lecturing publicly in the Gallery temple.

I wish to thank John Lennon and Yoko Ono for the great kindness they bestowed, letting us stay there while we built the Bury Place Radha Krishna Temple.

John and Yoko

The famous conversation between John Lennon, Yoko Ono, George Harrison, and Srila Prabhupada—which is transcribed in the booklet *Chant and Be Happy: The Power of Mantra Meditation*—occurred in the small front room of the servants' cottage at Tittenhurst Park. Mukunda, Shyamasundar, and I also crowded in. As always, Prabhupada was gracious and could make everyone feel so welcome and special.

Yoko Ono: "If all mantras are just the name of God, then whether it's a secret mantra or an open mantra, it's all the name of God. So it doesn't really make much difference, does it, which one you sing?"

Srila Prabhupada: "It does make a difference. For instance, in a drug shop they sell all types of medicines for curing different diseases. But you still have to get a doctor's prescription in order to get a particular type of medicine. Otherwise the druggist won't supply you. You might go to the drug shop and say 'I'm diseased. Please give me any medicine you have.' But the druggist will ask you, 'Where is your prescription?' Similarly, in this age of Kali, the Hare Krishna mantra is prescribed in the shastras, or scriptures. And the great teacher Chaitanya Mahaprabhu, whom we consider to be an incarnation of God, also prescribed it."

Something remarkable about this meeting is Prabhupada's reference to druggists and prescriptions as an analogy for receiving the right mantra from the right source. At the time, John and Yoko were having their own battles with addictions, so Prabhupada's reference was especially relevant and potent. Prabhupada gave an example of being "addicted to Krishna." I never heard Prabhupada use that analogy before. Prabhupada's point was that we can love Krishna similar to the way addicts love their substances. The addict feels separation from—is always longing for, waiting, and thinking about—gratification. But the difference is, while material relief is temporary, spiritual addiction is eternal bliss. Prabhupada offered an eternal solution to one's corporeal problems: love of Krishna, or God.

John asked how to recognize the right spiritual master. Prabhupada said that finding the right guru is very special and that the guru should be tested just like the disciple.

After the meeting ended, John and Yoko went down the narrow stairs. At the foot of the stairs, I overheard Yoko admiring how honest Prabhupada was and how simply he was living. She said to John, "I don't think we could live so simply; do you think we could live that way?" John answered, "No, I don't think we could be so renounced as the Swami."

Walking on Air

The expansive grounds of Tittenhurst Park were shrouded in morning mist. From the gallery and old servants' quarters where we lived, Srila Prabhupada, Purushottam, Yamuna, and I strolled past the main house. There was a manicured, grass yard that sloped onto a long, open field area where Prabhupada liked to walk. The early morning air was wintry and cold, and our breath made smokelike patterns in the frosty air. As we walked, I saw a worm heading right for Prabhupada's feet. No one else in our group saw the worm. It was on a direct collision course with His Divine Grace's lotus feet! I thought maybe I should say something and save the worm's life, but then again, if the worm went under Srila Prabhupada's boots it would be liberated, just as those who fall under the wheels of Lord Jagannath's cart are liberated.

As I was philosophizing, and before I could make a decision, the worm was under Prabhupada. Then I saw that there was no impression in the tall, wet grass where Prabhupada walked, whereas our sneakers made deep depressions in the grass. I looked back and saw that the worm was still going merrily on his way, as we walked on with Prabhupada leading.

Ghost Story

On the morning walks, Prabhupada would often greet Tittenhurst's gardener, Frank. He and Frank had respect for each other, as they were about the same age. Frank was living in a small, cozy Tudor cottage, and he had reported to John Lennon that strange sounds kept him up in the night. He thought the cottage was occupied by ghosts. John consulted with Srila Prabhupada and asked him if he could do something to remedy this situation. Prabhupada replied that he could.

He gathered us together, and we marched in a great procession across the low, grassy hills down to the cottage. Prabhupada led a dynamic kirtan and told us to "blow the conch shell very often and very loudly, as ghosts don't like that sound." After awhile he said, "They have gone."

Frank later confirmed that the strange sounds he heard in the night were, indeed, gone.

Best Perch

After the morning program in the gallery, I made sure all the devotees were eating prasadam. Then I made my morning tour to see that everyone was engaged and that everything was going on all right. I finished my rounds on a brief but invigorating morning japa walk and then, feeling refreshed, proceeded to Prabhupada's quarters to report to him.

When I entered, Prabhupada smiled and said, "I was just thinking of you, and you have come. In India that means you shall live for two hundred years."

I sat down, and as Prabhupada seemed to be in a meditative mood, I also sat silently, content just to be with him.

A butterfly was circling the room and fluttering towards Srila Prabhupada. Prabhupada put out his finger and motioned slightly with it. In easy flight, the butterfly jumped onto His Divine Grace's finger. "This butterfly must be a great devotee," I thought.

I had my camera with me, and thought of taking a photo as Prabhupada raised his hand slowly to show me the perching butterfly. I really wanted to photograph this scene, but I didn't want to disturb the moment with movement or loud camera shutters. Then the butterfly lazily flew up to a corner of the room. Prabhupada immediately changed expressions and started talking to me about the day's activities and an upcoming program. "I have accepted Mr. such-and-such's invitation," he said.

I replied, "We went to his house one night and only a few neighborhood people showed up. They talked during our kirtan. I think it is a waste of our time to go there."

Prabhupada agreed and said, "I must accept, that is my duty; now you must think of a way to not go, that is your duty." We laughed together.

The butterfly began to fly around the room again. Srila Prabhupada noticed it and pointed towards the window, silently indicating: open the window so the butterfly can go out, otherwise he will not have anything to eat.

His face and mood had changed again, so completely and so easily. I felt like I was in a scene in Krishna-loka.

Early Arrival

David and Donna were street vendors in downtown London. One day they saw our sankirtan party pass by on Oxford Street. Spontaneously they folded up their barrow (portable table), packed up their incense, crystals, tarot cards, and a very young baby, and followed our sankirtan party back to Tittenhurst Park. They were interviewed by a television crew 20 minutes after they were with us. They had decided to join our group and never left. They were living together but not married, so we asked them to get married, and they agreed.

They were fortunate to join us when His Divine Grace was present. Prabhupada presided over their combined wedding and initiation ceremony at Tittenhurst Park. The ceremony was held in the huge gallery that was serving as a temple on John Lennon's estate. The spacious room, with a fireplace and stone floors, enabled us to surround Prabhupada and the fire ceremony. The mood was festive and cozy—intimate, as only the small band of London devotees attended. Srila Prabhupada was expert and wonderful as always, and I learned so much simply by watching and listening to him. After the fire sacrifice, His Holiness gave the new disciples the names Draupadi and Devadhatta.

A moment later someone asked, "What is the baby's spiritual name?"

Prabhupada replied, "Baby comes out after wedding, not before." Then, as he had done so many times before, Prabhupada relented to the will of his spiritual children and said, "The baby's name is Dhruva."

BUILDING 7 BURY PLACE

While most of the devotees were renovating John and Yoko's estate (doing righteous work, chanting, and residing in the refreshing English countryside), Shyamasundar and Tirthapada were busy converting the Bury Place building into a dazzling Vaishnava temple right in the heart of London. Our new temple was completely unique, as the workers shaped the room from ceiling to floor with massive redwood and cedar planks imported from California. Modeled after a famous Buddhist shrine in India, the room resembled a ship's hull turned upside down.

Mukunda and I traveled from John's place to central London almost daily to conduct various business matters, including charity registration, processing paperwork for 7 Bury Place, and arranging preaching engagements and our recording sessions with Apple Records. We also had to maintain the lines of communication between Prabhupada and his other temples in Europe and the United States.

Since our overall devotional activities, including morning and evening programs, were going along smoothly at Tittenhurst Park—as was our interaction with John and Yoko—I could now concentrate on Bury Place for awhile. I would meet almost daily with Shyamasundar, Mukunda, Yamuna, Tirthapada and Dhananjaya to discuss plans for rebuilding and organizing the Bury Place property and make decisions how to properly and effectively utilize the five available stories.

We planned like this. In the basement was a small kitchen, which we enlarged. There was also a room for eating prasadam next to the kitchen. This was not big enough for many guests but had sufficient space for the resident devotees to eat or to meet at night and have warm milk before retiring. The entire first floor would be the entryway and temple room. Our love feasts would also be served in the temple room. The second floor would be Prabhupada's quarters.

The third floor would be the brahmacharini (female devotees) ashram. The fourth floor would be for brahmacharis (celibate male devotees), and the fifth floor would be an office and living quarters for grihasthas (married couples). The attic was to be used for storage.

The 7 Bury Place building, one-half block off Oxford Street—London's most important thoroughfare—was perfectly situated for our preaching work, as it was located in Bloomsbury, traditionally a neighborhood for scholars, artists, and mystics. We were just two blocks from the British Museum and around the corner from the Swedenborg Society and Annie Besant's Theosophical Society. Our building was also near High Holborn, an important confluence of streets. The British Broadcasting Corporation and the Indian Consulate were along nearby King's Way, and after that came "the Strand," famous for its large hotels and restaurants. We were close to Fleet Street (the media row) and the "Old Bailey" courthouses and Lincoln's Inn and the Temple district where London's great solicitors (lawyers) practiced. Parks like Russell Square, Holborn, and St. Giles surrounded our street. We were also close to Shaftesbury Avenue and the theater district, Piccadilly Circus, Oxford Street, Regent Street, Tottenham Court Road, and Trafalgar Square. In short, we had a great location, right in the heart of central London!

Zoning

The quiet street wasn't zoned for a temple, nor was the building itself. The building was formerly a Bible distribution warehouse. In reality, only two caretakers were allowed to reside on the premises, yet we had plans to house at least thirty devotees. With so many guests coming and going, along with our chanting, we would certainly provide a contrast to the normal activities of the otherwise sedate street.

As always and with the grace of Srila Prabhupada, we went ahead with our plans. The temple construction was proceeding at a slow pace. Mukunda and I worked on obtaining our ISKCON charity status, on getting zoning for the temple, and other organizational duties. Tom Driberg, a Member of Parliament, helped enormously in our project. He was shy the night I visited him in the darkened rooms of his church-like domicile near the House of Commons. Another time, when all seven of us visited Mr. Driberg in the hospital, Yamuna profusely shook a patient's hand and said, "We are so happy to meet you Mr. Driberg!" The sick man started shaking violently. From another bed across the room we heard a dry British voice say, "But I am Mr. Driberg." The seven of us left the confused patient, settling at the correct bedside.

"We are happy to finally meet you Mr. Driberg!" We all laughed. This was a good sign. Mr. Driberg smiled wanly. He was undergoing an eye operation, and we had brought along tapes and books for him to read.

A year or so later, Tom Driberg, M.P., the tenderhearted soul, saw us chanting in Piccadilly. I held out my contribution container, and he began to empty out his pockets. Shillings and pence clanged to the street, followed by some pound notes, until he had given us all the money he had in his pockets! He was fortunate to have run into us on this particular evening, because he happened to be very drunk. We carefully guided him to our Krishna van. He slept as we took him home. Later, we found out that Mr. Driberg led a double life. Authorities discovered he was a double agent, a spy, working with both the KGB and the British CID (Central Intelligence Department).

Tom Driberg wrote many letters on our behalf, but the process of procuring official permits for Bury Place was slow. We had also engaged the firm of Lord Goodman, the Prime Minister's solicitor, so we were holding our own. Obtaining our ISKCON charity status was another time-consuming business, and moreover all of us foreigners had to frequently go down to Lamb's Conduit Street to renew our tourist visas.

Despite the zoning restriction governing how many people could live on the premises, the clerk in the Greater London Council office threw the opposition's complaints in the rubbish bin when he saw George Harrison's and Tom Driberg's names on our documents. With the help of these well-known men we were able to procure permits for 7 Bury Place as a place for public meetings.

Mr. French

Gradually we moved in with all the paraphernalia we had accumulated and, despite the clutter of ongoing construction work, we set up a makeshift temple, kitchen, and living quarters. As always, we held our morning kirtans at four in the morning. Apparently, when we danced and chanted with drums and kartals, the sound went through the brick walls into the next building where lived a wholesale flower merchant named Mr. French, along with his wife and their frenetic, small poodle.

Mr. French complained, and he contacted the Greater London Council, the same Council that had granted us the zoning change. A meeting was arranged between the involved parties at 7 Bury Place to try to resolve the matter. On the appointed day, we borrowed chairs from the Swedenborg Society, and Mr. French, two solicitors, two representatives from the Greater London Council, Dhananjaya, Mukunda, Shyamasundar, and I met in the upstairs office, as a *quiet* kirtan was going on downstairs in the temple room.

As Mr. French launched into his attack, our solicitor fielded his complaints. French was furious about the noise from the kirtans. Tom Driberg had come along to help defend our cause. At the appropriate time we invited everyone to proceed downstairs.

About a half-dozen devotees were carrying on what appeared to be a full-on kirtan, but nothing could be heard through the soundproofed door! Normally the noise would have penetrated the door, the wall, and through to Mr. French's apartment, but today we had organized ourselves so that as we opened the door the devotees would sing very loud, and when we closed the door they would sing very quietly. The soundproofing appeared therefore to be working. Mr. French suspected a trick and became very irate.

We went back upstairs to the office, and all the while Mr. French was yelling, "It's a bloody trick!" Mr. French's solicitor, an Olympic fencing hopeful, tried to parry, but Mr. French blew up and went storming for the door. He pulled on the door with such fury the knob came off in his hand, and he went flying backwards and fell. He turned beet red, got up sputtering, and went back to the door, pried it open with his fingers, and exited abruptly. The Council decided in our favor, and we got our zoning ordinance to hold temple services at 7 Bury Place.

Except for Srila Prabhupada's living quarters, most of the temple construction was complete by now, and Prabhupada, impatient with the quiet country life at John Lennon's place, wanted to move to London. So until his rooms could be finished, we rented a temporary apartment for Prabhupada on Baker Street near Madame Tussaud's Wax Museum in downtown London.

Our departure from Tittenhurst Park was timely, as Yoko Ono's behavior was becoming more and more erratic. She essentially asked us to leave one day but then rescinded, saying, "The only people I trust have shaved heads." Leaving the property for London, I rode with Prabhupada in his car. As we were driving away, a freak storm was brewing, and only minutes after we exited, many of the prize trees of Tittenhurst were ripped out of the ground by an angry wind.

"I CAN DO MORE THAN ONE THING AT A TIME"

I coordinated some slides of Rathayatra and other subjects in London and showed them to Prabhupada at his Baker Street apartment. The handheld individual slide viewer enabled him to view each slide in a leisurely way. I would hand him a slide and put away the one he had just viewed. Soon it was time for lunch prasadam, and his assistants started bringing in the plates.

I started to excuse, myself but Prabhupada bade me to stay. "I want to see more," he said. I continued handing him slides and then holding the viewer up to his eye as he ate. Enjoying the images, he said confidentially, "I can do more than one thing at a time."

> Once when describing a problem:
> *"What can I do, it is like washing coal."*
> —A. C. Bhaktivedanta Swami

BHAKTIVINODA THAKUR

Prabhupada and I were walking, just the two of us, in the misty, morning fog in Regent's Park, near the Baker Street apartment in London. We were discussing transcendental literature. I mentioned that Bhaktivinoda Thakur was my second-favorite author.

Prabhupada questioned, "Second?"

Bhaktivinoda Thakur was a great devotee of the Lord and also a very inspiring and prolific writer. Perhaps Prabhupada read my mind as I told him this little fib, because sometimes I actually enjoyed the language and poetry of Bhaktivinoda Thakur's writings even more than Prabhupada's.

We were silent for a while; then Prabhupada said, "If I had one tenth the . . . [he was sobbing] of Bhaktivinode Thakur, I would be a great devotee."

Although I couldn't understand the word he used, our mood was one of mutual transcendental love and respect for his Grandfather Guru.

KINDNESS

Finally Prabhupada's quarters at 7 Bury Place were complete, and he moved in, just as the autumn weather began to grow cold in London. Many of my fondest memories are my walks with Srila Prabhupada on those frosty mornings. As I was a leader of the London Temple, I made sure that each devotee got an opportunity to share a morning walk with Prabhupada and, of course, I frequently scheduled myself as well. However, one morning I thought I should stay behind and give one other devotee a chance to walk with Prabhupada.

As Prabhupada was coming down the stairs from the second floor of Bury Place, I was vacillating in my mind whether to go with him or stay. As if reading my mind, Srila Prabhupada paused and asked me, "Are you not going on the walk?"

I quickly changed my mind, timidly answering, "Yes."

Then he said, "Thank you very much."

Economy Lesson

On a walk in London's Russell Square, Prabhupada saw a high-rise apartment with X's on the windows. He pointed out other places on the building, indicating that the apartments were still being built. There were also large FOR RENT signs.

Bury Place is ready!

Prabhupada turned to me and said, "They are renting out apartments when the building is not yet finished; this is a sign of a poor economy."

Once while we were riding in the car together, I pointed out the building called Centrepoint, a modern skyscraper right in the center of London at the top of Oxford Street. It had been vacant and empty for many years. Later, when we were talking about Britain, Prabhupada remarked, "England is just coal and potatoes, when she once was a glorious empire." "Coal and potatoes" was Prabhupada's way of describing the economically depleted culture.

Flexibility

After a morning walk, we were standing in front of the Bury Place temple. Prabhupada pointed to an iron fence between the sidewalk and a service entrance to the basement. "We can put a banner sign here," he said.

I answered, "I have inquired from the Greater London Council, and they informed us that no signs or banners can be put outside, in the front.

Pointing with his cane over the top of the iron fence, Prabhupada said, "But this is inside." He then pointed to the window and said, "Put a large sign up there."

Unfortunately I had to say, "I also inquired about a sign inside, and the GLC did not give permission."

"But this is outside," he answered immediately.

Mistake

After returning from a cold, winter, morning walk in London, Srila Prabhupada said as he walked up the stairs, "Just see, how I make a mistake." He still had his mittens on instead of putting them neatly at the base of the stairs like he did every other morning. To Prabhupada, that was a great mistake.

Bonding

Many times while I was riding or walking with Prabhupada, he would look at a building or a plot of land and inquire as to its use. "What is that building?" he would ask, pointing with his cane. It was if Prabhupada wanted to slowly offer a whole city to Krishna, piece by piece.

One day, in his usual manner, he pointed to a large building with a FOR HIRE OR SALE sign in front. The building was five stories high and took up two corners in central London, right on Shaftsbury Avenue. Prabhupada asked me to inquire further into its zoning and usage.

The real estate agent informed me that the building was once used by the YMCA before they moved to their present headquarters on Great Russell Street. I procured the keys, and Srila Prabhupada and I walked back over from the Bury Street temple to see the inside of the building.

I felt good, basking in the golden glow of my mentor, as we strolled past the public baths and the Shaftsbury Theater (which was showing the play *Hair*) and crossed over to Endell Street where the main door was located. The lock was old and rusty, and it took some strength to turn the key. Prabhupada patiently stood by my side. By Krishna's grace the lock opened, and the double-door parted. We looked at the large main foyer, and I could feel Prabhupada's mind making plans. We walked into a basketball court/gymnasium, and we both knew that this would be the temple room. I could just imagine an altar replacing the hoop at the far end of the gym.

We examined the lockers and bathrooms. The fixtures were old, and as I pointed out some cracks in the wall, Prabhupada acknowledged them. We had been through this before. In San Francisco, while looking at an old church on 14th Street, Prabhupada had showed me how to look for cracks, leaks, termites, and so on. By now I knew what to look for while inspecting buildings.

There was a decaying kitchen that could be repaired. We walked up one of the wide stairways and surveyed the second floor. The rooms were large. There was plenty of room here for a magnificent temple.

I ran up the stairs to the third and fourth floors and saw that they basically were the same design as the second. I ran back down the stairs to report this to Prabhupada so that he would not have to climb the stairs himself.

Prabhupada wanted to inspect the basement. Debris that had gathered around the bottom of the basement door was loosened, and bit by bit the rusty door swung open. Slowly, I descended the stairs, with Prabhupada following close behind me. As we alighted onto the basement floor, he stuck even closer to my side. I felt like we were two kids exploring an empty house. The basement was one huge room with many pillars supporting the ceiling.

Suddenly, the few light bulbs sputtered, dimmed, and extinguished, leaving Prabhupada and me in total darkness. I felt his hand clutch the cloth of my kurta, and I reached out to him. I was simultaneously scared and elated by this intimate proximity to my spiritual master. I then felt his hand touch mine. He took my hand, and we held hands as we groped around in the dark. My nose was filled with his pleasant, comforting sandalwood scent. I knew that for us to separate would be futile. We were standing together and were safe in each other's presence. I heard him chanting, "Hare Krishna, Hare Krishna, Krishna Krishna, Hare Hare . . ."

I felt the strong desire to protect my Guru Maharaja. He was always protecting me, maybe I could repay him! With my other hand I felt for the wall, but felt nothing but air. We took small, slow steps towards the stairs. Finally, my hand felt the rough surface of the wall.

We inched our way along the wall, walking a razor's edge between standing and falling. I whispered to Srila Prabhupada, "We are coming closer to the stairs." I felt calm, even with electricity coming from Srila Prabhupada's lotus hand into mine.

My foot hit the base of the stairs and said, "We are at the stairs." Very carefully, I lifted my foot and found the first step. I took each step slowly. Prabhupada was still holding onto me, and he followed as I ascended. As we got closer to the top of the stairs, we could see light filtering in through the doorway.

When we reached the ground floor, we saw that the lights were also out on that floor. Prabhupada was smiling and calm but still holding my hand. I wanted to remain that way forever. Then Prabhupada looked around and said, "This building is not suitable. There is too much to repair." Then, almost imperceptibly, he let go of my hand. I didn't wash my hand for a week and basked in the afterglow of our bonding experience.

Equality for Women and Men

One time, Srila Prabhupada was considering Yamuna for a position as Governing Body Commissioner, and some devotees complained, "A woman is not capable of being a GBC."

Prabhupada replied, "Men and women are the same on the spiritual platform."

Although Prabhupada suggested this job to Yamuna, she was more inclined towards Deity worship and singing bhajans, so she declined. Prabhupada treated his female disciples like daughters. They could approach him for advice and stand wherever they wanted in the temple during worship.

> *"The dogs will bark as the elephant caravan passes."*
> —A. C. Bhaktivedanta Swami

LAZY INTELLIGENCE

More than once I heard Prabhupada say, "An intelligent man can do more by sitting than an unintelligent person can do moving all about."

Prabhupada taught me that there are two types of intelligence: lazy and active. Of the two, lazy is the best, for the very intelligent only move when they have to. No unnecessary actions are made. Active intelligent people, however, sometimes act unnecessarily.

There are two types of foolishness also. If one is a fool, it is better that he be a lazy, rather than active, fool. Prabhupada told a story to illustrate this.

The king's ministers were complaining: "The chief minister gets more money than we do. Why?"

The king answered, "Because he is lazy intelligent."

"What do you mean?" asked the ministers.

"Go out and weigh my elephant," the king challenged, and the ministers left to complete the task. They searched for a scale big enough to weigh an elephant, they tried to invent mathematical formulas, and after so many attempts they returned to the king and told of their failure to weigh the elephant.

The king turned to the Chief Minister and requested that he weigh the elephant. The Chief Minister led the elephant to a barge, put the elephant on it and when the barge sank down, he marked the water line outside the hull. He then took the elephant off the barge, and it rose again. Next, he put fifty-pound sacks of rice on the barge until it reached the line he had drawn on the side of the boat. Counting the sacks, he was able to weigh the elephant. He returned to the king and gave him the answer.

The king turned to the other ministers and said, "That is lazy intelligence."

"Accounting means putting down every expenditure immediately."
—A. C. Bhaktivedanta Swami

Unending Compassion

One afternoon, as I was walking through the streets of London, I noticed the struggle and squalor and started reflecting on injustice, wars, starvation, and prejudice in the material world—and became sad. I went to Prabhupada's room and remarked to him, "Sometimes I feel sad for humanity."
Prabhupada replied, "Why sometimes?"

"Karma is like touching fire; it burns whether we recognize it or not."
—A. C. Bhaktivedanta Swami

Dr. Joe Burke

Dr. Joe Burke was a well-known psychiatrist in London, a colleague of Dr. Ronnie Lainge, who gained notoriety for his work with schizophrenics. He became a friend of mine, and one day when I mentioned that he might enjoy meeting Prabhupada, he readily agreed.

I picked him up at his office in the Krishna Van. When one of his staff asked him where are he was going, Dr. Burke answered, "I am going to see my psychiatrist."

Dr. Mishra

In 1965, shortly after arriving in New York, Bhaktivedanta Swami had stayed a few weeks with Dr. Mishra at his Sanskrit and Yoga Institute. Haridasa (Harvey Cohen) was a student there but soon joined Swamiji in his service. Dr. Mishra and the Swami were friends even though Dr. Mishra was an impersonalist in his philosophical understandings, which differed from the Swami's personalist point of view.

Once, when Dr. Mishra got sick, Swamiji moved into his room to take care of his friend from India. Prabhupada nursed Dr. Mishra back to health both with his kindness and special prasadam. Doctor Mishra credits the Swami with "saving my life." Dr. Mishra later opened an ashram in San Francisco, and I met him there briefly. Our Dharma-dyaksha and Rashanghi prabhus also came to us from Dr. Mishra's ashram.

In London, Dr. Mishra and I met again and shared the stage at a Hindu Centre program. Because Prabhupada had treated him as a friend, I did too. Prabhupada was also in England, so I arranged a reunion at 7 Bury Place.

Shyamasundar and I arranged for a meeting between the Abbott and Srila Prabhupada at Westminster Abbey.

During this meeting, Dr. Mishra showed great respect for Srila Prabhupada, and they laughed and talked like old buddies. Prabhupada usually preached a little to everyone he met, but this time they talked about India and writing. Prabhupada also expressed how proud he was of his disciples. Dr. Mishra was philosophically an impersonalist, and Prabhupada was a staunch personalist in the Vaishnava tradition. The two approaches to spiritual understanding are diametrically opposed, yet Prabhupada and Dr. Mishra had transcended these differences and remained friends through the years.

THE ABBOT OF WESTMINSTER

The Abbot of Westminster had a reputation for being open-minded towards other religions. Shyamasundar and I arranged for a meeting between the Abbott and Srila Prabhupada at Westminster Abbey.

At the prearranged time, the three of us passed through a side entrance adjacent to the beautiful gardens of the Abbey and were met by a novice who guided us to a comfortable, wood-lined room decorated with centuries of tradition. The churches in England are graveyards as well as church halls. Popes, cardinals, bishops, and kings—even poets and statesmen—are buried inside the church buildings. Prabhupada strode in, regally but humbly, and was offered a large, plush seat. Prabhupada appeared confident, as if Westminster Abbey was any ordinary place, nothing special. Lord Sorenson, our friend and a well-known skeptic, was also present.

Prabhupada asked for a glass of water, and the abbott brought it himself and offered it to him with a smile. Lord Sorenson got fidgety, especially when there was silence in the room. He was embarrassed by the lack of conversation. Both Prabhupada and the abbott were elders and great religious leaders; they sat together quietly, as elderly men who were friends. A serene word or two was spoken now and then, but most of the time they seemed content just to be silent in each other's presence, two men of God.

Calm in a Storm

The Dutch version of the "Top of the Pops" program invited our Radha Krishna Temple to Amsterdam to do a television show. With the widespread fame of the "Hare Krishna" and "Govinda" hit singles, we had already appeared live on TV in Britain, Germany, Scotland, and Sweden. However, this time Prabhupada was with us in London, so I called the Dutch television people back and arranged for more air time so that, after our chanting performance, Prabhupada could speak for a few minutes. I was able to convey to them that Prabhupada was special.

Prabhupada and eight other devotees flew to Amsterdam, and we were picked up at the airport and driven to a TV studio in the countryside. We came upon a long, deceptively arranged complex of buildings that seemed to sometimes snake underground and rise up again. Once we entered the television studio, we were given two dressing rooms and some fresh fruit. We had many hours to wait for the show to begin. Prabhupada rested as we chanted japa. Eventually they summoned us, and we went into a large open studio.

The director of the show wanted the usual go-go dancers to dance to our song, but I told them we would walk out if the miniskirted dancers gyrated around us. Remembering our previous experience on the "Top of the Pops" show in England, I offered the same alternative and suggested that the dancing girls get some material to wear as saris. Then the devotee girls would show them how to wrap the fabric, and they could do the "trance dance" to the mantra. This suggestion proved satisfactory to everyone.

During the show, they put dry ice in front of the stage to make us look mystical, and the smoke became so thick we all had to stand up to perform!

Despite this, the show turned out splendidly, and after our performance of "Hare Krishna Mantra" Prabhupada spoke to a large segment of the people of Holland for about five minutes.

Subsequently, I have met some souls who saw that show and became devotees as a result. Prabhupada distributed his saintly teachings in so many ways, and his glory expands and grows eternally.

The whole television complex was underground, and to get from one place to another we had to walk through long, windowless corridors. Prabhupada commented on this aspect of life when we reassembled in his dressing room after the show. "In the future, some people will live their whole life underground. They will never see sunlight."

After we left the underground television complex for our return to London, everything was disrupted at the airport. The plane was late; the party had to separate and go on different flights; there wasn't enough money; and there was some bureaucratic, paper mix-up. In the middle of this turmoil sat Srila Prabhupada, with his head on his cane, looking so peaceful.

"An empty bowl makes the most sound; a full bowl is silent."
—A. C. Bhaktivedanta Swami

Sri Sri Radha-London Ishwara

Srila Prabhupada, Yamuna, Mukunda, Radharaman, and I went in the van to the Hindu Centre. Mr. Goyal, the Hindu Centre president, had indicated that they would donate their large, white-marble Radha and Krishna Deities to our temple, because one of Radharani's fingers was damaged. When Prabhupada arrived Mr. Goyal stalled. He wanted to sell the beautiful, marble murtis rather than donate them as previously indicated. Mr. Goyal said he would deliver the Deities in a fortnight (two weeks). Srila Prabhupada said, "We can take them with us now in our van," and so we did.

Meanwhile, at 7 Bury Place, the temple room and altar were nearly complete as we frantically added the finishing touches. Prabhupada had set December 14, 1969 as the date for installation of the Deities, and we were preparing to open our doors with a grand inauguration, complete with dignitaries and the press. Mukunda and I handled the announcements, invitations, and press releases. Shyamasundar was building a lotus-shaped Vyasasana out of redwood and copper metal strips. He was still building the sacred seat, which looked much like the caterpillar's seat in *Alice in Wonderland*, the night before the ceremonies. There was so much to do, and Shyamasundar couldn't possibly do it all by himself. He finished the Vyasasana and began assembling the altar, working far into the night.

The next morning, at our opening ceremony, the turnout was large. Contingents from the Hindu Centre and the East Indian community came. Some prominent politicians, such as Tom Driberg and the Indian Consul General, attended as well. Many newspaper reporters arrived, along with a BBC television crew. The London hip community showed up in full, and the temple was completely packed from front to back. Prabhupada began chanting for the inauguration ceremony. Sri Sri Radha-London Ishwara (Radha and Krishna) were already in place. Lord Jagannath, Subhadra, and Lord Balarama were brought behind the altar curtains and placed above Them on a platform about eight feet high.

Like a Lion

Prabhupada went behind the curtains to begin the *abhishek*, the ceremonial bathing of the Deities. He asked me to assist him.

Outside in the temple room, the ceremonial fire was filling the room with smoke, and we could scarcely see. I yelled out from behind the curtains to please open the front door for ventilation and asked that more wood be put on the fire to counteract the smoke.

Suddenly, I heard a cracking sound from above us: the entire altar was falling! I looked over at Prabhupada: his eyes were blazing like a lion's! He held up one side of the altar, I held the other side, and between us we kept it from falling. Out front the loud chanting overpowered all other sounds, so the guests were unaware of what was going on. While holding up my side of the altar with one hand, I put my head through the curtain and, as softly as I could, asked Dhananjaya for help. He and Tamal Krishna came behind the curtain and relieved Srila Prabhupada, whose expression was one of resolute, determined strength. Shyamasundar was quickly called in; he made some repairs. and after about ten minutes of hammering and sawing, we opened the curtain and went on with the ceremony.

With his fatherly demeanor and sweet voice, as if nothing had happened, Prabhupada delivered his welcoming words, calmly inviting everyone to enjoy the peaceful, dynamic, and infinitely rewarding opening ceremony of the London temple. But what I remember most was seeing Prabhupada behind that curtain. Prabhupada was so strong and sturdy: his eyes were blazing brightly, his hands were like talons, his feet like pillars, and he appeared like a lion!

A few days later, with the Bury Place temple officially opened and Sri Sri Radha-London Ishwara installed, his mission accomplished, Srila Prabhupada left us to fly back to his devotees in Los Angeles.

Busted in Piccadilly!

After Prabhupada's departure we were all now going out on sankirtan in the streets of London three times a day, so we were becoming quite visible. We wove our way down Oxford Street in robes every morning and afternoon. Shoppers would stop in their tracks to watch and listen. A lot goes on on Oxford Street. It's almost like Times Square in some places, but people still watched us. We offered our books, and they would ask, "What's this in aid of?"

I would say, "These are the names of God, and we are suggesting that everyone love God." Many people purchased Srila Prabhupada's books.

Each night we would go to the Eros fountain in Piccadilly Circus. We would proceed there, singing in double files all the way from our temple in Bury Place, down Shaftsbury Avenue with its many theaters, and on through Cambridge Circus to Piccadilly. At Piccadilly Circus, people could come to the middle of the circle and gather around us without obstructing traffic. Still, the police claimed that we were obstructing foot traffic, even though there was plenty of room for pedestrians to move around the base of the fountain, as it was fenced off from traffic like a steel oasis. The curious surrounded us when we sat on the pavement and chanted, but there was still plenty of room for people and pigeons to stroll by.

One night, returning to the temple, the police followed us down Shaftsbury Avenue with a paddy wagon. I led the party of devotees through Soho instead, down one-way streets impossible for the paddy wagon to traverse. We lost them, but this indicated to me that the police around Piccadilly "had it in for" us. The next night we were issued a warning: if we came back and chanted we would be arrested.

We consulted together and came up with a plan. We would go out dressed very nicely, in two rows of two, eighteen of us, so a length of nine altogether. Mondakini, who was always staring at the sky and looking saintly, and Jyotirmayee, her godsister from Paris, would lead the party because they looked particularly innocent. I would disguise myself in "karmi" clothes, e.g., trousers, a London Fog coat, and Tamal's plastic businessman's hat. My plan was to photograph the police arresting us. Derek Taylor from Apple was prepared to help release the photos to the press. After I took the photos, as many devotees as possible would disperse and meet back at the temple.

As we commenced our procession, I lurked close by. A policeman approached the robed group, and this particular "bobby" was huge and hulking—perfect for our plan. I was in a position to photograph and signaled the devotees. The constable faced the front of the line, just as Mondakini and Jyotirmayee folded their hands in supplication and went down to their knees. The whole line followed. The constable towered angrily over them as I snapped off four photos. Another constable saw me take the photos. Then, as the first constable issued another warning, the second constable blew his whistle and started to approach me.

I flashed the prearranged signal for the devotees to disappear, and the ensuing mayhem allowed me to cross the street and blend into the back alleys. I heard running footsteps and whistles in the fog-shrouded night, sometimes close by, then distant, then gone. I crossed Lincolns Inn Fields and took the roll of film to my friend at a Fleet Street newspaper to develop and print. In one of the photos, you could see the hulking constable's back, his hands on his hips facing Mondakini, who gazed innocently at the sky.

The next night we returned to our usual spot in Piccadilly. A couple of times that night I had to calm down Jai Hari and another devotee, both former Muslims, who wanted to fight the police. On our way back to the temple, crossing Shaftsbury Avenue, we were again approached by a constable. Yogeshwara and I were in the front. They informed us that we were under arrest. I quietly motioned for the others to leave quickly. Sixteen devotees faded into the night. The officer, now joined by another, took us away to Central Station, where we spent the night in jail. The next morning we were released.

At the Bow Street Court, the magistrate looked over his half-crescent bifocals and asked what we were doing. First of all I said we were peacefully singing the names of God. I asked when, where, and at what time we were arrested, according to the report. The bailiff read out Shaftsbury Avenue. I pointed out that our temple was in Bury Place, and that we go to sleep at night at 10:00. Being that the arrest took place shortly after 9:00 P.M., then clearly we were returning to the temple. Yet the police claim that we were obstructing the walkways in Piccadilly Circus, many streets away. This is a false report, for a false arrest.

The Judge *harrumphed;* the policeman coughed.

"Surely," I added, "there are more important arrests to be made. Besides, how is it that the constable allowed sixteen of us to escape?"

The magistrate looked over the rims of his spectacles at the officer and asked, "Is this true?"

The officer sheepishly admitted that it was true.

The magistrate then said, "Based on this evidence, the case is dismissed." But the judge had to have one last word: "Must you parade in the public thoroughfares, in those costumes?"

I countered: "These so-called costumes are our traditional robes, and they represent that we are devotees of God, just as your robes and powdered wigs signify that you represent the law."

"Quite, quite," said the judge in agreement, "case dismissed."

Ratha-Yatra in London

There are many important celebratory events in the Gaudiya Vaishnava calendar, such as those commemorating a saint's birth or death or those that celebrate a pastime of the Lord. However, the most important Vaishnava holidays are Janmastami (Krishna's appearance day), Vyasa-puja (the spiritual master's appearance day), Lord Chaitanya's appearance day, and Lord Jagannath's day, which is venerated by pulling three huge carts, or *raths*, through the city streets. It is customary at ISKCON centers all over the world to celebrate this Ratha-yatra festival in a very big way. I have already described the first Jagannath Ratha-yatra festival in the Western world, in the San Francisco chapter.

In London, our Jagannath festivals were huge in scope and were very well attended. The first year, 1969, the cart was so bulky that it collapsed in Bayswater Road near Marble Arch on the way to Trafalgar Square. In one letter, I wrote to Prabhupada that I thought the cart collapsed because of my poor devotion. On July 31, 1969, Srila Prabhupada replied:

> ... But I could understand that you were immersed in great confusion on account of the wheels giving way just after starting. I have received one letter from Shyamasundar dated July 25, in which it is stated that the magnitude of the rath was double than the one you had in San Francisco. I think it was a mistake of engineering calculation. The load was heavier than the wheels could carry. So there is no question of being disappointed.

The next year, 1970, municipal officials joined with the police to ban us from having a rath-cart in our festival. They would allow a parade, but not a cart. We pleaded with them to test our cart, for this time Shyamasundar and Nara-Narayan were trying very hard to make the cart safe and sound. In the British spirit of fair play, we asked, "Why not give the cart a sporting chance?"

They answered, "All right, Mr. Grant." (The officials called all of us "Mr. Grant," which was actually Mukunda's given surname. I accepted that we must all, with our shaved heads, look alike to outsiders.)

They laid out an almost impossible test course, with a ninety-degree angle at the end of the parking lot where we were building the cart. The police pushed and even helped steer the cart. Lord Jagannath's chariot passed the test. One of the devotees jumped from the cart and stated loudly for the police, "Isn't God great?" The police and other officials had no choice but to agree, because the fact that the cart passed their grueling test was indeed a miracle!

The day of the Ratha-Yatra was sunny. Devotees arrived from all parts of England and from Germany, France, and Holland. That day, thousands took part in the chanting and dancing, marching through the streets of London. From Marble Arch, down Park Avenue, Piccadilly, and Haymarket, the festival culminated at Trafalgar Square, where it seemed the whole world had gathered at the base of Nelson's Column. Prabhupada's movement was growing by leaps and bounds in London, so much so that we were quickly outgrowing our 7 Bury Place headquarters.

Bhaktivedanta Manor

Due to the sheer numbers of initiated devotees, guests, and visitors, we were again forced to start looking for a bigger place. With the help of George Harrison's real estate agent, we eventually found a place in Letchmore Heath, near Radlett, Hertfordshire. The names of the towns, streets, lanes, and houses are so quaint and so different and personal in England. This estate, "Piggott's Manor," was a name you might find in a book like Kenneth Graham's *Wind In the Willows*.

The 17-acre estate was dominated by a large manor house with two floors, plenty of space for a temple, rooms for Prabhupada, and living quarters for all the men, women, and children who were now part of our community. There was also enough space for our Life Members to stay in specially designated guest rooms. There was space for a gurukula (school), a small auditorium, offices, kitchens and dining rooms, sewing rooms, reception, and bookstore. The Manor was surrounded by spacious grounds, including a lake, greenhouses, paths, and gardens. We, of course, liked it.

The Manor was surrounded by spacious grounds, including a lake, greenhouses, paths and gardens.

George purchased the entire Manor and grounds, with the proviso that we maintain and improve the property and utilize it for spreading Krishna consciousness.

Since things were going well in Britain, Prabhupada requested that I go to India. I was to lead the second wave of devotees going into India. This seemed to fit a pattern developing in my devotional service: I was sent by His Divine Grace to pioneer some new place, such as San Francisco and London, and now I was being sent to India for yet again another new start.

Los Angeles
15 March, 1970

My Dear Gurudas,

Please accept my blessings. I beg to acknowledge receipt of your letter dated 8th March, 1970.

At first, I must thank you very much for your slides and the viewer, which I enjoy whenever I find some time. The pictures of London Temple immediately get me there, and I enjoy your company. So I can understand that everything is going on well in London Temple. The service of the Lord should be so nicely executed that Radharani will bestow upon you blessings, raising Her right hand palm. You have got a very nice wife, a devotee and intelligent. So both husband and wife combined together please see that the temple service is being executed regularly and nicely, and thus make your lives happy and successful.

Side by side, both of you should train your junior brothers and sisters in the service of the Lord, so that in case both of you go for preaching work, the scheduled program of the temple may not be hampered. We should follow two important lines, namely the Pancharatriki-vidhi as well as Bhagavata-vidhi. The Bhagavata-vidhi is preaching work, and sankirtan, and Pancaratriki-vidhi is temple worship of the Deities. The temple worship will keep us sanctified, and when we shall preach in sanctified, pure heart, the preaching will be immediately effective. So we have to follow the two parallel lines simultaneously for successful execution of devotional service.

Regarding George Harrison, I am sure he will improve now in Krishna consciousness. Krishna consciousness is developed only by service. So he has very willingly and gladly served Krishna in many ways. The recent "Govinda" record, which your good wife has sung along with you, is certainly super-excellent, and it has become so nice because of George's attention upon it. So whenever this nice boy comes to our temple, please receive him very nicely. Give him prasadam and if possible talk with him about Krishna, and thus he will advance more and more in Krishna consciousness.

When I remember all of you in London, as well as George Harrison, I become very happy because the combination is very much hopeful. I am so glad to learn that George has said, "I don't want to make nonsense records any more." This version of George I consider very valuable. His popularity and his great talent can be very nicely utilized by producing such nice records as "Govinda," instead of producing something nonsense. In our Vaishnava literature there are hundreds and thousands of nice purposeful songs, and if those songs, under George's supervision, are recorded, I think it will bring a great revolution in the record making business.

So when he says that he does not wish to produce nonsense this does not mean that he has to close his business. On the other hand, he will get greater opportunity for producing the finest transcendental records, songs which are still unknown to the world. When you meet him again, you can talk with him what I am speaking to you in this letter. My special thanks are due to your good wife, Srimati Yamuna devi. Her singing songs of Krishna consciousness, and Krishna will certainly bless her and you all.

Please offer my blessings to all the boys and girls, and be happy. You will be pleased to know that Acyutananda is also doing very nicely in Calcutta. He is moving in very enlightened circles of Calcutta, and somebody is giving us a plot of land worth Rs. 80,000 for constructing a temple there. When the temple is constructed, I shall ask you to go there with your wife and preach Krishna consciousness amongst the Indian community. Sometimes you desired to go to India, and Krishna will fulfill your desire to a greater extent. Krishna's service is so nice. Keep this faith always in mind and serve regularly your life will be sublime.

Hope this will meet you in good health.

Your ever well-wisher,
A. C. Bhaktivedanta Swami

P. S. Please send more beautiful slides in plain cardboard frames.

INDIA

"Going to India is not a matter of buying a ticket, it is a matter of being spiritually pure."
—A.C. Bhaktivedanta Swami

BACK IN 1967, IN SAN FRANCISCO, I had requested permission from Prabhupada to make a pilgrimage to Vrindavan, the birthplace of Lord Krishna in India. At the time I didn't consciously know why I wanted to visit this holy place. Subsequently, Krishna's service had taken me to Montreal, New York, London, Amsterdam, New Vrindavan, and many other destinations in the West, and during these years I was so absorbed in moment-to-moment devotional revelations and service that thoughts of going to Vrindavan had receded to the back of my mind. Srila Prabhupada, however, had never forgotten my request, and three years later he empowered me to go to the holiest of holy tirthas.

From the time I was a young boy I was allured by the enchantment of India. Books and magazines displayed cartoon versions of skinny, turban-headed men levitating or raising a rope into thin air. Cobras, tigers, maharajas, and Kipling's stories intrigued me and captured my mind. Behind her mysterious gossamer veils, Mother India beckoned and enticed me to come to her. Little did I know that Krishna, standing in His three-fold stance, with one lotus foot placed over the other, smiling his beauteous, shy glance, was attracting me to come closer, into His sheltering arms.

Now, in the early autumn of 1970, not a romantic child anymore, I was actually going to India. Not knowing what to expect, I would be coached by the best: Srila Prabhupada. By now I had received some training from him in ways to pierce through the wall of material nature, into the deep spiritual core that is India's essence. Problems such as nescience, bacteria, noise, lack of privacy, mechanical breakdowns—all part of daily life in India—would disappear, erased by the playful innocence and humility of many of India's people, by peaceful sunsets on sacred river banks, musical strains of holy names heard from all ten directions, in all languages and creeds, and by a genuine love of philosophy, humor, and spirituality in the hearts of most Indian citizens. Srila Prabhupada remembered my subconscious plea to be united with my inner self in Vrindavan. I would be allowed to experience firsthand the essence of village life and my Vaishnava traditions in a place where the majority of people were chanting, offering food, and studying the *Vedas* just as I was. I would no longer be the outsider, the freak, the cult member, because I was returning to my actual spiritual home.

Airship in a Storm

For our first thrust into the land of Bharat, I was to lead a party made up of "strong" devotees from various parts of the world. Profits from the sales of our Apple Record's *Radha Krishna Temple* album would help finance the trip. Prabhupada requested that we take equipment to India to help with the preaching work. We loaded up with film and slide projectors, movie cameras, tape recorders, blank film and tapes, irons for pressing clothes, and many other small appliances to facilitate our activities in India, where much of the machinery was primitive compared to the West.

We arranged our journey through a newly initiated Indian godbrother who resided both in London and Belgium and who was an executive for an Arabian airlines named Brothers Airlines Service Company (BASCO). The India-bound group was to gather in Brussels. We stayed at the godbrother's apartment. Shyamasundar and I met the devotees as they trickled in from all parts of the world. Dinanath came from Seattle, Kausalya came from L.A., Giriraj came from Boston, and so on.

At the airport in Brussels we saw that the airplane had only two prop engines and it closely resembled the plane used in the old Bogart film *Casablanca*. It turned out to be a surplus World War DC-3, though which World War, I wasn't so sure!

We boarded the plane, which was scheduled to stop first in Cairo for refueling, then in Aden, then Saudi Arabia, and then on to Bombay, India. The few other passengers inside were wearing jellabahs and chadors, and we felt like we were in the Casbah. Piles of makeshift cabin luggage resembled an Arabian marketplace. The cockpit was separated by only a waving piece of cloth, and we could see inside. The lazy-looking pilots didn't exactly bolster my confidence! "Hare Krishna Hare Krishna, Hare Rama Hare Rama," I chanted, and soon, exchanging worried glances, the other devotees began chanting also.

I contrived to sit next to Giriraj, because I liked his intelligence, his humility, and his philosophical curiosity. The Boston temple was famed for its austerities and conservative thinking—and lack of humor. Somehow I sensed that Giriraj had a natural sense of humor that he was suppressing. There seemed to be some hint of irony in that stoic frame. I tried to loosen him up with a little humor about our "airship," but he was resolute at first and remained rigid like an impersonalist. (This is the same determined soul who, a year later, when his father offered him one million dollars to leave Krishna consciousness, refused.) As we left the ground, he chanted and wouldn't look out the window or around the cabin. I eventually questioned him about this. He answered, "Maya is out the window."

"Maya can also be in our heart," I answered. "The fact that someone is vomiting in the aisle shows that Maya can be inside this airplane also."

Slowly he relaxed a bit, especially when we entered a turbulent storm. The plane started shaking, fixtures were falling from the cabin, and people were vomiting in the aisles. To me it was absurd theater, very funny, but Giriraj remained reserved. Finally, I talked to him about the austerity of the Boston temple. I joked about one of their legendary *ishtagosthis* (group meetings). "I heard that the Boston temple devotees met to decide how to split up the garbanzo bean into three: Giriraj would get the left part, Yadurani the middle, and Satsvarupa, the right part." Giriraj finally broke out laughing, but he soon regained his stoic demeanor.

After some time, I continued, "If Krishna gives you the natural talent of a sense of humor, then it is a disservice to submerge your tendency and not utilize it. Prabhupada has a great sense of humor."

He was thinking about what I said and I persevered: "Prabhupada once told me that someone without a sense of humor is like a dead man, and that being jolly is a sign of spiritual advancement."

Finally Giriraj relented, and it was like a burden had been lifted from his shoulders. After that, he smiled, relaxed, and joked with me.

> *"They cannot fly the 747 unless Krishna*
> *has told the wind and air to become like that."*
> —A. C. Bhaktivedanta Swami

Chaitya Guru

The BASCO airship landed in Cairo, Egypt. We were told we must change to another airplane that flew to Bombay. We happened to land the day after President Nasser died; the country was in turmoil. Black bunting draped the airport. As I oversaw the transfer of our luggage, the rest of the devotees went right out onto the tarmac and started chanting. They jumped up and down, passing the time between planes in the best way they knew how: chanting.

Returning from securing the safe transfer of our luggage and tickets, I saw the devotees chanting. I took out my 8mm camera and started filming them. Through the lens of the camera I noticed Egyptian soldiers with guns and fixed bayonets charging towards my godbrothers and sisters! Abruptly, I stopped filming and wondered, What would Prabhupada do in this situation? *Chaitya-guru* means Krishna's instruction from within. Suddenly I knew what to do, and I ran out between the army and the chanting devotees.

"We are singing the praises of President Nasser," I said. "We are singing the glories of President Nasser." I pointed to a large, hanging picture of President Nasser and *pranamed* respectfully. They smiled, put down their guns, and stood listening to the holy names. They left us unharmed. Soon a large crowd of people from the airport ventured closer to bask in the maha-mantra's healing rays.

Recently, Yadhubara prabhu sent me a copy of this 8mm film.

Bombay Arrival

Flying over the Arabian Sea, we watched the sun and sea meet in a spray of colors and light. We swooped down through some thin, cirrus clouds and onto the parched, white clay of India. I led the party of seventeen out of the rickety airplane. Overwhelming even the relief at being out of the airplane was the feeling of welcome I received from Bharata, from India, this Motherland.

A gust of warm air hit me right in the face. This felt good, and I breathed more easily as I walked down the metal stairs onto the ancient soil. I felt at home. The airport was in the middle of empty, barren fields. There was no sign of people or activity except our flight coming in. There were no taxis or buses to meet us, no police. A few skinny dogs looked up lazily from their sleep. An old sign pointing to customs brought us to a small hall with three long tables and two customs men moving slowly, surprised to see eighteen shining, white Vaishnavas wearing dhotis, saris, sikhas, japa malas, and tilak. They marked our bags with X's without even looking inside. A calm stillness pervaded the air, a dreamy sense of timelessness. The feminine bosom of Mother India welcomed and embraced me completely. To me the United States seems masculine, but here in India I sensed a motherly woman overseeing all, pervading the atmosphere. The strong, shy consort of Krishna, Srimati Radharani, was present in my soul.

We zipped through the nonformalities and were met by a man in a brown fedora who looked like a detective. He identified himself as Kailash Seksaria. Since he looked like a detective, I asked to see his identification, which surprised him. He took out a telegram from Prabhupada addressed to "Gurudas Adhikari (American-in-charge)." The telegram instructed me to take the party of seventeen and go with Mr. Seksaria to the place we would stay while we waited for Prabhupada to join us from Calcutta in a week's time.

Despite a few pieces of lost luggage, our arrival went smoothly. Mr. Seksaria had three Ambassador cars waiting outside the small terminal, and he invited me to ride with him. He was actually quite jolly, and he inquired nicely how was our trip. I decided not to talk badly about BASCO Airlines and replied, "Fine." I was still feeling the relaxed glow of being in India. Kailash asked what we would need in the way of comforts, and I said we required only a few rooms for our party to sleep in. We all carried our own bedding or sleeping bags with us.

The cars left the airport and turned left towards Bombay. Soon the countryside of India unfurled before us. The hot air became cooler, and I stuck my head out of the open window. I saw dried-up rivers, cows, farmers, and women carrying water on their heads. Water buffalo cooled off in small muddy pools, their eyes rising out of the water like surfacing submarines. Small villages of perhaps six huts dotted the countryside, usually with a white, arched temple nearby.

I noticed that as soon as the driver of our car saw a person beside the road, or came close to another car, he honked the horn and honked again and again. Then he slammed on the brakes. I soon understood that in India the brakes and horn of a car are much more important than the engine. The horn was loud, but so was India at times. The smells were stronger, the sights fuller, the food more spicy and pungent, but to me it was all a divine symphony. (After talking to many world travelers, I have learned that people either hate or love the magic of India. There don't seem to be any in-between or neutral feelings about India.) The small shops of spice merchants and bicycle repairs, roadside tea stalls, a dentist sitting on his mat with a drill run by a foot pedal and a large sign of a mouth with teeth—all flashed by my vision as we drove into the outskirts of Bombay.

Crowded suburbs and traffic soon made our trip stop-and-go. The driver of the car also shut off the car's motor at stoplights. Then, as he started again, of course he honked, and others honked too: it was a honk-a-thon! Soon, however, the road widened and we were speeding along. The balmy shore of the bay appeared on the right. Then we rode inland, and I kept my eye on the water. The bay reappeared between buildings, and then again we were driving along next to the wide ocean. A small palace with the word "Shalimar" in lights reflected against the sky and water. Large boulevards continued, and soon we were turning onto Marine Drive, circling a lovely bay bordered by a rocky, public beach.

Large, six-story apartment buildings lined the left side of the road. The cars turned into a side street and then into the garage of one of these large buildings on Marine Drive. Mr. Seksaria ushered us out of the cars and said,

"Welcome to my house." This building, taking up half the block, was all his. The rest of his family was waiting, and they greeted us with warmth, smiles, benign epithets, and fruit on silver serving plates. "Would you like to wash up and rest first before we eat?" Kailash inquired.

I said, "That would be nice." He led us to some cool, dark rooms with hemp cots. I washed my face and hands and settled into a joyful rest, nestled in the warm embrace of Mother India.

Ram Navami Blessings

The day we arrived in India coincided with the celebration of Ram Navami. Ram Navami is the anniversary of Lord Rama's defeat of the demon Ravana. Many interpret the story of Lord Rama's jump across the ocean to retrieve his consort, Sita, in the *Ramayana*, as the power of good over evil. Examples of hope, spiritual perseverance, great loyalty (in the person of Hanuman), and great courage (in the person of Jatayu) are also found in the *Ramayana*.

As we entered India I felt as if the swaying trees, lapping water, the laughter in the children's eyes, and the clothes flapping in the wind were banners heralding our arrival. The breezy air felt auspicious. Good omens appeared unexpectedly, and then routinely: omens such as full containers of water, elephants, waving flags, swooping hawks, and silent owls. I was realizing that, to me, India was much more than an interesting travel destination—I was on a mission here, one blessed by my spiritual master. I did not want to make the mistake of drawing too many comparisons between this foreign land and my own culture or take advantage of her as many men had done in the past. Because India's culture had now been adopted as my own culture, I felt totally at home here.

However, Maya often tests those who feel spiritually secure.

Mr. Kailash Seksaria and his house staff were being so kind to us. It is the custom in India for most families to show expansive hospitality and special care for sadhus (holy people). And visitors from overseas have always been treated especially well, a subtlety left over from the times of the British Raj. The Seksarias cooked lavishly, provided laundry service, and took care of many things that we were used to doing for ourselves. I was the leader of the party, so in order to maintain our integrity and practices as devotees, I suggested that we hold morning and evening services and that we also go out in the streets for kirtan, this being the heart and soul of Lord Chaitanya's movement.

Our host seemed quite impressed with this idea, but it was possibly more than he had bargained for. Most Indian sadhus arrive, sit, read, do some sedentary sadhana, and speak a little. Here we were, eighteen mostly college-age youths, strong and enthusiastic, ready to throw ourselves headlong into the streets, into the interactions of huge, unfamiliar crowds—crowds that included thieves, con men and numerous pickpockets!

I could see that Kailash was reluctant to let us practice kirtan. Although he agreed in words, he shook his head from side to side. And rather than chant in front of his house on Marine Drive, Seksaria thought it would be better to transport us to Kalbadevi, a teeming market area of Bombay.

Dinanath, with his great stamina, heart, and voice, was an exceptional kirtan leader, and he had brought along his medina drum. I motioned to him to begin, and we gathered in a circle around him. He sang out beautifully and loudly in the ancient Sanskrit language that very few natives still spoke. Then, as we completed Bengali prayers to our spiritual masters and began to chant the Hare Krishna mantra, a huge crowd formed around us. I was oblivious to everything but the Holy Names. I was connected eternally someplace in Gokula, another universe. The hot (more than 120° F) afternoon sun beat down, and sweat poured from us in streams. Suddenly, without our asking, uniformed servants from Kailash's house came up to us with towels to dry our tender, western brows! We reluctantly received these kindnesses; as simple devotees we felt that this pampering was unwarranted. We were used to doing everything for ourselves, including wiping our own heads. Previously we had chanted in blinding snow, to uncaring crowds in foreign lands, and we were quite used to being mocked, laughed at, spit on, or harassed. No wonder we felt that this show of servants catering to us was uncalled for!

To add to the embarrassment, in front of the watching crowd of rickshaw drivers, skinny beggars, and hungry children, Kailash's servants brought us large, silver urns of ice-cold *nimbu pani* (lemonade). All the devotees felt uncomfortable and looked to me for instruction. I indicated that we should drink the offering anyway, because it would be an insult not to accept the gift—and we were very thirsty.

Through the years, I saw Prabhupada accept many kindnesses that he didn't require or request. All acts come from Krishna, so perhaps this was Krishna's grace, His prasadam on His devotees. So I handed out stainless steel glasses of lemonade to some of the onlookers, much to the chagrin of Kailash, who was overseeing his staff. (He made sure his glasses were returned!) I spoke to the surrounding crowd: "How happy we are to be here in the land of Bharat!" A man started translating my words into Hindi: "We are here by the mercy of his Divine Grace A.C. Bhaktivedanta Prabhupada." Then: "We will be chanting the Holy Names of Rama and Krishna, as Lord Chaitanya did when he traveled throughout India."

The human circle pressed closer and became more intimate, more quiet. Then I said, "By the grace of Lord Krishna everyone can chant. All people, even a child, can do it." I was gesturing as I spoke, and my Seiko watch gleamed in the sun. When I finished I asked, "Are there any questions?"

A man asked, "How much does that watch cost, sir, and will you sell it to me?"

Though I laughed internally, outside I remained aloof and calm. I answered, "I don't know how much it costs. This watch was a gift to me. Just like everything we have on Earth, this life is a gift from Krishna." I went on, "We are caretakers for Him, we are renting, for a lifetime; but everything, all things, come from God, from Lord Krishna, even time itself." Many in the crowd liked my answer and nodded their heads approvingly yes, and made loud sounds like "*Ahh ahh ha*," and clicked their teeth, sounds that I had heard at gatherings in London, sounds that conveyed support.

Then I signaled, and Rebatinandan led a kirtan. After about three hours we stopped, and I went over to Kailash, who was smiling but also restless. I waved to the people. We entered the waiting Ambassador cars and rode contented through the streets of Bombay, onto the sweeping beachfront Marine Drive, for a nap and some prasadam.

The next day, after our morning program, Kailash told me about a seminar of holy people called the "Sadhu Sammelan." He told me that the organizers of this conference of gurus and yogis were excited to hear of our arrival and that they had warmly invited our group to attend. I accepted the invitation and informed the others. We prepared, gathering our instruments. Kailash led us out the side door, through a few streets, and into a large hall with a stage. The plain meeting place looked like many high school gyms or a summer-camp recreation hall without baskets or balls.

A well-dressed man named Haridas Agarwal greeted us. Lining all sides of the hall were four-legged, fold-up card tables with holy men sitting on them. Some were dressed in silks, others were hardly dressed at all; some had tridents, some had matted hair, and some had shaved heads; all had different tilak marks on their foreheads. We were led to some empty card tables and sat down. We could feel a change in the atmosphere: Lots of curiosity, some disbelief seeing Westerners in dhoti robes, shaved heads, tilak and sikhas.

A speaker was on the stage, so we sat quietly. Then another sadhu took the stage and spoke in Hindi for awhile. After some time, we were invited up to the stage. I said a few words about Prabhupada and his mission in the West and then opened the *Gita* randomly to Chapter 2, verse 61: "One who restrains his senses, keeping them under full control, and fixes his consciousness upon Me, is known as a man of steady intelligence."

I spoke about the meaning of the verse, yoga in general, and about our Gaudiya-sampradaya philosophy of loving God through bhakti-yoga. I differentiated between loving God and trying to become (merge with) God. We have a relationship with Krishna and can be loving children, servants, or friends to him. Again my words were translated into Hindi. Then, as prearranged, Dinanath Prabhu led a kirtan.

The singing charged a rather dry atmosphere, and many of the audience sitting in the middle of the hall joined in. When we left the stage, they honored Lord Krishna by clapping and cheering. Politely, I thanked the assembly and we left. The organizers were so enlivened that they invited us back to another large gathering—the main event—on Chowpatty Beach a few days hence.

Meanwhile, Kailash kept on treating us lavishly. Some devotees took advantage of his generosity, and I had to balance things out between accepting gifts and remaining renounced towards material temptations. Later on I heard that one of Kailash's friends from Delhi had criticized us as being "princes."

Prabhupada sent me a letter:

From Calcutta
5 October, 1970

To Bombay
My Dear Gurudas,

Please accept my blessings upon you all. You are welcome in India. Now my going to Bombay is postponed and my enclosed letter to Sri Bajoriaji will speak for itself.

Now if your preaching work in Bombay is going nicely, then you can stay there for some time and do preaching work as they are doing here in Calcutta. Otherwise, you can immediately come here and work jointly. We are expecting to have our own place by the end of this month. When you come, you should send a telegram with the details of your arrival.

If you are interested to open a branch in Bombay, you can see the following gentleman and he will help you.

Dr. Ram Chandra Pal
62, Keluskar Road
Sivaji Park, Dadar
Bombay 28

Your ever well-wisher,
A. C. Bhaktivedanta Swami

Prabhupada Reunion

I missed Prabhupada, but I continued doing what I could to please him from afar. Then one day Krishna granted my wishes. I received a telegram: Prabhupada was coming to Bombay!

Shyamasundar and Kailash Seksaria went to meet him at the airport, while I helped arrange a rooftop press conference atop the Seksaria residence on Marine Drive. I had not been up to Kailash's roof before: The view of the ocean was magnificent, and the rooftop's high, stone walls provided a feeling of safety. The marble floor was covered in rugs; large palm trees swayed in their round ceramic pots. Many floral decorations and garlands festooned a small stage. Much of the area was covered by a colorful, cloth canopy, and the seats were laid out in neat rows. Long tables covered by white linen tablecloths offered liquids and other succulent prasadam refreshments.

I was doing a sound check with the microphone when I received word that Prabhupada had arrived. I ran downstairs to the ground floor where he had just settled in. He saw me and smiled. I bowed down. "Gurudas Prabhu, you didn't come to meet me at the airport." A question and comment simultaneously.

"I am helping to arrange a press conference."

"When will that be?"

"Tonight."

"Very good."

I sat in the middle of the room on the ground floor, between devotees and guests. Someone was motioning me closer to Prabhupada, who was sitting behind a small desk, but I didn't want to receive preferential treatment, knowing that I would see him later. Some young children came to one of the open, barred windows of the room and talked loudly, interrupting the discussions so much that we couldn't hear Prabhupada speaking. He looked at them and handed them some prasadam through the bars of the window. They accepted it and became quiet. Many more people crowded outside the open windows, looking in and talking animatedly. Again Prabhupada turned to the curious crowd at the windows and, with golden fingers, distributed sweets to everyone, aristocrats and beggars alike. My compassionate spiritual master was back.

"The cloud pours rain on both
the ocean and the rocks—this is Krishna's mercy."
—A. C. Bhaktivedanta Swami

That night a grand press conference was held. I sat and listened to my guru as he glorified Krishna and requested that the Indian people embrace their traditional culture, as these Westerners had.

Many well-dressed guests arrived, and the whole meeting was very genteel, very polite. Sometimes I was called away to take care of something or other, but I preferred to stay by my mentor's feet. Whenever I returned to the scene, there he was, holding court, answering questions and making jokes. I am reunited with Swamiji again, and I find that I feel protected, contented, and immensely joyful in this faraway land.

Intimate Time

After the press conference at Seksaria's, Prabhupada was alone in his room. He summoned me, and as I entered his quarters he said quietly, "The table can come here." I set the small coffee table in front of him. He leaned forward on it and beckoned me closer. I rested my elbows on the table; our faces were only inches apart. "There is trouble in London. You may have to return there and manage." After a pause he continued, "But you are here now, and there is work here, too. So stay here for now, and if you have to go back to London, then you will." I was ready to do anything. Prabhupada made me feel so important, so welcome, so needed.

We sat quietly together and chatted about Bombay. Just as in Vrindavan where the rocks, trees, and rivers are personalities, Prabhupada also saw the personality in seemingly inanimate objects like the table when he said, "The table can come here." Prabhupada saw everything as Krishna-ized, and so to be honored. In this way, all things, even a table, could have personality.

These intimate times were my favorite moments with Srila Prabhupada. He was relaxed with me when the everyday, administrative decisions were set aside for a few moments. We spoke softly, sometimes communicating nonverbally. We moved slowly or not at all. I felt that I would do anything for Prabhupada and that Prabhupada had already given me so much.

I thank you, Srila Prabhupada, for granting me so many of your precious moments, so much time, your presence, your wisdom, and empowerment.

"Who Is Acharya?"

Prabhupada was going ahead with plans to establish our Bombay temple. At his behest, Rishi Kumara dasa and I were looking for a temple location. In the meantime Prabhupada gave me the additional service of writing the Legal Charter and registering ISKCON in India, just like we had in London. We formed a board of directors and had one meeting. The Charter stated that we would propagate Krishna consciousness, and there were some clauses allowing us to purchase property in India and be tax-exempt.

I studied the manuscript for any signs of legal irrelevance or impersonalism. But this was a legal document after all, not a philosophical one. Some amendments were added where needed, such as: "The stationery shall read Founder-Acharya His Divine Grace Tridandi Swami A.C. Bhaktivedanta." Next I wrote: "The Founder-Acharya shall have full veto power." I took the document down to the court, had it registered in ISKCON's name, and brought the official copy back to Prabhupada.

He carefully went through the document, then stopped. "Where it says the Founder-Acharya has complete veto power," he said, "who is the Founder-Acharya, where is the name?"

I told him, "Your name is mentioned as Founder-Acharya in the stationery amendment." When I'd gone over the document, I'd assumed that the mention in one clause would include this clause as well.

"That is another category," Prabhupada continued. "With no name, this is impersonal. Who is Acharya? You?"

I was devastated. He had struck me deeply. At first I could only remain silent. Finally I protested that "I just overlooked that clause, it was a mistake." I pleaded, "I don't want to be Acharya." But he was detached and noncommittal until I was silent again.

"Have this corrected," he said.

I went down to the same office where I had originally registered the document. The clerk acted like he didn't know me and took a long time to locate the file. He examined the papers slowly. I indicated where I wanted the changes. "You have to get your board to amend this," he said.

I went away, called a board meeting, personally took the amended document to the different board members to get their signatures, and then brought it back to the clerk, who was acting like a king. "Oh, we can't do anything about this now, it will take a few weeks."

I knew this petty man wanted some bribe to do what he was paid to do. I persevered, "I have brought the proper signatures and amendment as you requested. You either don't know the law, you want a bribe, or you are just incompetent," I said, slamming my hand down hard on his desk.

I was venting my frustration from Prabhupada's disapproval. I continued, "There is a press conference tonight. What do you want me to say about how you are handling this matter? Incompetence, bribery, or ignorance?"

Stunned and shaking, he signed the document's amendment immediately.

Three days had passed since Prabhupada instructed me to correct the document, and in those three days he wouldn't see me, speak to me, or look at me. I brought him the revised version. He looked it over, found no mistakes, and put it down. I cried, "I don't want to be Acharya! I just overlooked it!"

He finally ended the silent treatment and said, "I do not think that you wanted to become Acharya, or were devious, but since my name was left out, I could think like that."

I was crying. He beckoned me towards him. I put my head on his lap, and he petted my head and comforted me.

This was a lesson on how to think and execute duties with care. This was an instruction in how impersonalism can come up in subtle ways. When we forget Krishna as a personality, that is impersonalism. When we treat a godbrother or godsister without respect or take them for granted, that is impersonalism. If we take shortcuts or are inattentive when chanting, these are all pitfalls on our spiritual path.

It made me sad when Prabhupada was forced by us to display his anger. I wanted to avoid being either the cause of his displeasure or the object of his ire. I shall never forget these instructions regarding treating anyone's name lightly, especially Srila Prabhupada's.

> *"If you do something that I don't forgive,*
> *Krishna will forgive you,*
> *and if He doesn't forgive you, Radharani will."*
> —A. C. Bhaktivedanta Swami

Akash Ganga

Prabhupada very much wanted to open an ISKCON center in Bombay. An adequate space was going to be difficult to find in this crowded city. Meanwhile, about ten devotees were temporarily living at the Sea Palace Hotel in Colaba, a downtown borough of Bombay. Mr. Chaabria, a friend from London, owned the hotel and kindly provided three rooms for us. Rishi Kumara, several other devotees, and I went out daily to look at places suitable for a temple. One day, driving along near the sea, the sight of many towering apartments offered hope. We saw an APARTMENTS TO LET sign on a newly constructed highrise on Nepean Sea Road, facing the Arabian Sea. The name of the building was Akash Ganga, which means "Milky Way" in Hindi.

One apartment was available on the seventh floor. We informed Srila Prabhupada about the apartment, and he told us to rent it. Of the four-and-a half rooms, the large living room would serve as the temple room, and Prabhupada's quarters would be adjacent to it. Three balconies overlooked the ocean.

At Prabhupada's request we moved in, even before the final negotiations had been completed. Madhudvisa, Rebatinandan, and Shyamasundar were in Bombay and helped with the move. Dinanath, Kausalya, and Durlabh soon joined us.

We made separate brahmachari and brahmacharini quarters. Yamuna and I lived separately, even though we were married. Gradually many devotees moved in, and I personally carried a Deity up the seven flights of stairs when the elevator was broken. Prabhupada presided over everything and stayed amongst us. It was so spiritually intense, fun, and exciting to live with Prabhupada in the same apartment!

One day a man came to challenge Srila Prabhupada. At first he was just slightly disrespectful, but he became more and more abusive. Prabhupada was rather silent and noncommittal. The man continued abrasively. Then Prabhupada's eyes flashed! Suddenly the man collapsed to the floor and lay in a shivering heap. Prabhupada said, "Attend to him." We had to carry the man out of Prabhupada's room. He shook for some time, then got up dizzily. We carried the stunned man to the foyer hall and sat him up against a wall. An hour or so passed before the man regained his movement, color, and composure. He stood up and left without saying a word.

> *"It is not wise to pick a quarrel
> with a crocodile while in the jurisdiction of the water."*
> —Bengali proverb

EYES BLAZING

One time at Akash Ganga, Prabhupada's servant was not present, so Prabhupada asked me to fill in as his personal secretary and assistant. He would ring his bell, and I would attend to the needful. At night I rolled out my sleeping mat and lay down right in front of Prabhupada's door, in case he wanted me. One night, light was coming out from a crack in the door. I slowly put my eye to the crack to see if His Divine Grace was all right. I peeked in. His eyes were blazing!

He was writing something, then thinking, then writing. Seeing his glowing eyes reminded me of the story of how the viceroy of India couldn't understand how my grandfather guru, Bhaktivinode Thakur, could dispense with his court cases so rapidly. The viceroy thought that Bhaktivinode Thakur must be shirking his duties. When the viceroy snuck up to the Thakur's house and looked in the window, he expected to see a lazy man sleeping. Instead he saw Bhaktivinode Thakur, his eyes ablaze, writing vigorously. Like Bhaktivinode, Prabhupada was absorbed in Krishna at every moment.

Thrift

Prabhupada and I were standing on the balcony of the Akash Ganga apartment in Bombay, and we saw a taxi pull up with one Western devotee in it. Less than a minute later, we saw the same thing again with another white devotee getting out of a cab. Prabhupada pointed out the waste. "Why can't they go together, two, three in one taxi?" Then he told how he would walk all the way across Delhi to sell his *Back to Godhead* magazines and thus save five paisa by not taking the bus. This was also confirmed by Hans Raj Gupta, the mayor of Delhi, who knew Prabhupada at that time.

No Hiding

In Bombay, Prabhupada and I were discussing the new life membership drive. Tamal Krishna prabhu came in with some money for Prabhupada, and put it on the table. Then we heard that a very rich man was coming in. We had been trying to solicit a donation from this particular man for some time. Before the man entered, Tamal started pushing the money underneath the desk blotter. Prabhupada watched this with amusement. Tamal's idea was that if the rich man saw the money, he would be less inclined to give a donation. Prabhupada told Tamal, "Leave it," and the money was left in plain sight. Prabhupada went on to convince the man of his spiritual sincerity, and the man gave a nice donation. Prabhupada was always straightforward, relying on Lord Krishna. This was another invaluable lesson His Divine Grace showed me by his example. Also, Prabhupada said more than once, "Money makes money." So the man, seeing the money on the table, thought, "I shall also give money to Prabhupada."

Small World, or Did You Ever Ride With a Saint in an Elevator?

In London I had arranged for Srila Prabhupada to appear on an important BBC television interview show. The host asked good questions with interest and respect. The show had been widely viewed in England and greatly enhanced our public acceptance there.

In Bombay I met an Indian doctor from London who was now living in Bombay and managing a medical clinic. The good doctor had seen the BBC show in London and told me how much he had appreciated Prabhupada's message. He invited Prabhupada to visit his clinic. The doctor gave us a personal tour of his three-story facility, and as the doctor showed Prabhupada around he mentioned having seen the television show in London.

As we continued the tour, the doctor said, "Now we are all together in Bombay." He gushed, "Now you are here in my clinic. You were there in London, and now you are here. Isn't this a small world?!"

Prabhupada answered, "Yes, it is insignificant," and walked into the waiting elevator.

Spiritual Distinction

Before Yadubara got his spiritual name, his birth name was John. Young John came to the Sea Palace Hotel in Bombay where we were temporarily residing. John had with him a copy of an underground magazine that had accepted a photo-article he had submitted, which he wanted to show Srila Prabhupada. The magazine also contained several photos of naked women and some rather risqué advertisements. John opened the magazine to the article, hoping Prabhupada would not look at the rest of the magazine. I was watching intently with amusement. As I suspected, Prabhupada did just the opposite of what John was hoping for. Prabhupada opened the magazine to the beginning and turned each page carefully with his lotus hands.

John, soon to be Yadubara, was starting to get embarrassed. I was waiting for Prabhupada's reaction to the naked women. His face remained the same. As John got more and more embarrassingly red, Prabhupada finally reached the Krishna-conscious article. His eyes lit up, and he calmed John by saying, "This is very nice," and then, "When you find gold in a filthy place, pick it out."

Prayag Kumbha Mela

When planets and gods line up in perfect confluence, that is the time of the Kumbha Mela near Allahbad (Prayag) in Uttar Pradesh State, India. Here, on a large plain at the confluence of the Ganges, Yamuna, and Saraswati rivers, Lord Narayan's effulgence rains down. Millions of holy people come from all over the world to attend this variegated spiritual event. The Kumbha Mela is very special and is only celebrated once in every four years. The 1971 Kumbha Mela was to be even more special, because this particular astrological confluence happens only once in every twelve years.

Prabhupada had gone on to Kumbha Mela from Bombay, taking all the devotees with him, leaving only Rishi Kumar and me behind to complete the rental negotiations for the Akash Ganga apartment. We felt abandoned, even though we had been left behind for important service.

Mr. Chaabria came over to see the new temple, and he told us that he was leaving the next day for Kumbha Mela himself. I sent a note to Prabhupada in Mr. Chaabria's hand, stating that the negotiations were now finalized and asking him if we could please join him at Allahabad. Soon a telegram came from Prabhupada that said, "Please join me immediately." We were overjoyed. It felt so good to anticipate being with my spiritual master again—and attending Kumbha Mela.

Prabhupada had sent Bhanu dasa, a very nice devotee from Japan, to greet Rishi Kumar and me at the train station in Allahabad and take us to the ISKCON site. The area was vast, bordered by the Ganges and Yamuna rivers, and at its center was the Tribeni, a giant whirlpool where the underground Saraswati river wells up to meet the other two great streams. We walked past many sadhus performing austerities (tapasaya), such as standing on one leg, or keeping the body in one position only, or staring incessantly at the sun. Clusters of tent cities had been erected. All the various sampradayas, sects, and yogis coexisted side by side on the huge mud flats and sand dunes. Followers of Ramanujacharya nestled next to those of Shankara and Nimbarka, and these guys were bordered by Maharishi's and Guru Maharaji's camps. Satya Sai Baba sat next to Swami Satchitananda, and Ramakrishna followers edged out some Sri Aurobindo disciples for a corner piece of the mela grounds.

The conditions afforded mere survival, and sometimes the groups would share food and materials and visit each other's camps. But the real closeness came during the bathing times. The first one would start at Brahmamuhurta, one-and-a-half hours before sunrise, or about three-thirty in the morning. It was cold and dark, but I would go every morning, and then again around ten A.M. The early bathing had a scattering of pilgrims, but at the other times tens of thousands flocked to the river. The Shaivites, carrying their tridents, had a separate bathing area because they ran into the river, splashed each other, and were generally too wild for the mass of stationary pilgrims saying Gayatri prayers on their sacred threads.

Besides the chanting and speaking programs at our ISKCON site, we would go out on harinama sankirtan in large groups led by Srila Prabhupada. Another time, on a morning walk, His Divine Grace gave out paisa (small coins) to rows of beggars lined up by the pathways. At one point we saw a sadhu riding an elephant. Someone said to Prabhupada, "You should ride an elephant."

Prabhupada replied, "I would rather walk with all of you."

> *"You cannot directly take shelter of Krishna, but you can take shelter of the person who has taken shelter of Krishna."*
> —A. C. Bhaktivedanta Swami

How Do We Know Krishna Is God?

At the Kumbha Mela we nonchalantly strolled past century-old sadhus; we saw holy men buried alive with just one arm jutting out of the ground, their fingernails so long they curved and wrapped around their arm. Decorated elephants; naga (snake) babas; thousands of pilgrims with horns, drums, kartalas, and tridents, wearing every type of tilak and representing every kind of spiritual line—it was all there at this Kumbha Mela gathering.

Prabhupada was stationed in a great tent resembling the tent of a Bedouin nomad. The tent had a large, high, square interior and was comfortable. Inviting cushions were spread around for the many ISKCON leaders who came from all over the globe to sit in a crescent circle at Prabhupada's lotus feet. His golden fingers plucked out a letter from Hansadutta. He announced, "There is trouble in Germany. I have informed you of this yesterday. Why is no one going to help him?"

I thought, "Our godbrother is in trouble, and that is all that's important to Prabhupada." I volunteered to go, but Prabhupada said it was necessary for me to remain in India.

Srila Prabhupada then changed the subject. "How do we know Krishna is God?" he asked us.

"Because Krishna says so in the *Bhagavad-gita*," a devotee said.

"Anyone can say that," Prabhupada countered.

I piped up, "You told us so, and you're a representative of Krishna, a spiritual master . . ."

"Someone will say I am just an old man."

Not knowing what else to say, we were silent. After a few moments, Prabhupada said, "You know Krishna is God because you feel His presence when you chant, as well as when you serve. You feel the ecstasy: this is the proof."

Someone said, "The proof of the pudding is in the eating."

"Yes," Prabhupada said.

Years later, on a morning walk in Philadelphia, again Prabhupada phrased the question: "How do we know Krishna is God?"

I waited to see if someone would answer, but there was only silence. I spoke up confidently, "You know Krishna is God because you feel Him when you chant and when you serve. You feel the ecstasy. That is the proof."

Prabhupada said no, and answered instead, "Because the *Bhagavad-gita* states it . . ." and he quoted a verse.

I said quietly, "But Prabhupada, you said at the Kumbha . . ."

But he and the group were already walking on.

Here we see that Prabhupada might say two different things on two different occasions. Both were transcendental instructions. Prabhupada would give one instruction to one person and a different instruction to another. Both messages apply according to time and circumstance. Both instructions are transcendentally correct.

Afterthought: Many devotees get entangled in what "Prabhupada says." I have witnessed devotees making such statements to support their own arguments or endeavors. This phenomenon of "Prabhupada says" is like the game Simon Says. A leader may say "Prabhupada said," taking an instruction out of context to get the devotee sheep to follow. The "Prabhupada says" prefix may even be used to goad or force other devotees into doing something unjust. Vaishnavas should not misinterpret the instruction of guru or shastra to advance their own agendas to gain power. Wrangling and politics get in the way of spiritual advancement and naturally lead to Vaishnava-aparadha or spiritual violations.

Rather than engaging in political debates, we must first realize the instructions of Prabhupada and shastra, discuss them jointly, and then unite and cooperate with one another to continue Prabhupada's offering to the world, i.e., Krishna consciousness. One must not take Prabhupada's instructions piecemeal in order to justify one's own angle of vision. The idea of Bhakti-yoga is to serve Radha and Krishna and our godbrothers and godsisters, and not to fight with each other. Instead let us use our intelligence and energy to give what Prabhupada gave us, his lovely family of devotees. Together, united as a family, we can feed his spiritual message to the whole world.

GOLDEN TEMPLE, AMRITSAR

A gathering of mostly Mayavadi impersonalists was convening in the city of Amritsar, in Punjab State, northern India. Srila Prabhupada was invited to speak there, so all together Prabhupada and many of the India devotees—including me—traveled from Bombay to Amritsar by train. Traveling with Prabhupada to the Golden Temple of Amritsar (the holiest shrine of the Sikh religion) was a special treat. I was always so happy and enthusiastic when I got to go places with Prabhupada. Only Krishna knew what adventures would occur, what encouraging words would be spoken, or what jokes might be shared between us!

Side by side we walked between two long, man-made lakes. We strolled past gardens and passed the Samadhi (tomb) of Guru Gobind Singh, the great Sikh hero who died fighting, literally holding his own head in his hands. We were taken into the many rooms of the Golden Temple. It seemed there were not as many altars or as much decoration as in Hindu temples. At the top of the cathedrallike Golden Temple was a room from which we could see in all directions, a vista of three-hundred-sixty degrees. In this room a man was reading from the original manuscript of the Guru Grantha Sahib, the sacred scripture that is divine revelation for the Sikhs. This reading is performed nonstop, just like the twenty-four-hour kirtans performed in Vrindavan. We descended and walked past another water pond into the dining area, a part of every Sikh Gurdwara (temple).

As we walked around in the kitchen area, Prabhupada especially liked the huge wok that was the size of a large room. People were stirring dahl with long, wooden paddles for the thousands of pilgrims to eat. As we were leaving the compound Prabhupada indicated that he was impressed with the organization of the Golden Temple.

"Spiritual communism," he commented.

Banned from Speaking

As part of the week-long mela, or conference, at Amritsar, one day I was scheduled to give a talk and lead kirtan. Thousands of people sat in the audience. Because they were mostly impersonalists I talked about our Vaishnava choice to love the person God, or Krishna. I put forth the doctrine of acintya-bheda-bheda-tattva, or simultaneous oneness and difference. I preached about each individual's personal relationship with Krishna. "We do not merge with Krishna," I continued, "we can have loving relationships with Him. *Sat chid ananda vigraha.*" I elaborated on the idea of choice and distinction, as opposed to oneness, by saying: "We are naturally attracted to some things over others. Just like the swan chooses a clean pond, and a crow chooses garbage. Therefore, as we purify ourselves, we can also choose the highest platform, love for Krishna."

I persisted, "We can choose to love God, rather than trying to become Him, because there is variety in the spiritual realm, not oneness. That is why we marry a certain friend, a partner, rather than going in the street blindfolded to pick our companion; that is why we pick a sweet we like to eat, rather than eating the stool in the street. . . ."

I heard gasps from the audience. This was too much. Inside I thought that the threat to their philosophical underpinnings was more intimidating than the so-called vulgarity. They had an excuse to object. Soon they asked me to cut my talk short. Giriraj replaced me, and I heard him continue where I left off, but more tactfully.

After the event ended some angry mela officials went to see Prabhupada, complaining about me as I sat silently in his presence. They loudly accused me in Hindi and English and kept repeating the phrase "eating stool in the street instead of sweets." Over and over they said, "Going in the street blindfolded to pick your marriage." They had taken my words out of context and forgotten the logical aspects of my talk, but I had faith that Prabhupada knew my intentions.

Prabhupada remained calm as they put their case before him. He looked at me. I said, "I wanted to express the idea of acintya-bheda bheda-tattva and our personal relationship with Krishna. I illustrated the idea of variety and distinction and our choice to love Krishna with the example of picking a marriage partner, rather than accepting anyone blindly."

I continued, "Then I said that we choose to eat sweets, rather than eating stool from the street, which exemplifies variety and choice to love Krishna."

Prabhupada absorbed what I told him and a moment later turned to the agitators and said, "My American and European disciples sometimes give graphic examples." He quietly laughed. He calmed them some more, changed the subject, and they left satisfied. They probably thought that I would be strongly reprimanded by my stern father.

When they were gone Prabhupada turned to me like a coconspirator and in a childlike way asked, "What was that example, 'stool in the street, instead of sweets?' Good example!"

We both laughed heartily.

Impersonalism

At another gathering in Amritsar, the hall was full of sadhus espousing the idea of merging with God, the impersonalist point of view. Though our speaking was controversial because of our philosophy of a personal relationship with Krishna, someone from our ISKCON group would be speaking at some point in the proceedings. We waited our turn in the large hall while the impersonalist sadhus droned on and on. As I had been banned from speaking publicly anyway, I decided to go over to Prabhupada's quarters, which were adjacent to the meeting hall. As we sat in Prabhupada's room we were subjected to the impersonalist diatribe next door through the loud and raucous public address system which blared out all over the compound.

An argument was going on regarding the meaning of "*aham brahmasmi*," the same tired, old, overworked argument that has been going on since the beginning of Eastern philosophical thinking.

Someone brought Srila Prabhupada some prasadam. He smiled and said, indicating the loud arguments, "They are laboring so hard without reaching a conclusion—and we will reach God by eating." He popped the prasadam into his mouth and continued smiling, almost prankishly.

> *"You can buy a sacred thread for a penny, but love of God is not so cheap."*
> —A. C. Bhaktivedanta Swami

Quality, Not Quantity

At the mela in Amritsar I made sure all the assembled devotees had a place to sleep. All the sleeping space in one room was taken, so Giriraj and I had to find another place to sleep. Across the compound we found a large dormitory-type room, and we lay down in a corner. A sadhu came over to me. Giriraj was already asleep.

The sadhu said to me, "We are all God, just like the spark of the fire and the fire are one."

I answered, "They are similar, and the spark has the quality of the fire, but not the quantity. Just like we have some of the qualities of God, but not the quantity that He has. We are qualitatively similar but not quantitatively equal to God. We can't cook a meal with a spark."

The sadhu wouldn't give up, and he pressed his point. He took a thread from his blanket and said, "See, this thread is the same as the blanket."

Krishna from within inspired me. I took away his blanket and gave him the thread. "If they are the same, then this thread should keep you as warm as the blanket." I rolled up his blanket and used it as a pillow. It was very cold and after an hour or so of shivering, the sadhu came back to me.

He said, "You have proven your point, the thread is not the same as the blanket. I prostrate myself before you—you have defeated me."

I replied, "Do not bow before me, bow before my Guru who has taught me."

The next morning the sadhu went to Prabhupada and bowed before him.

Liars Without Law Books

I received word that the Amritsar solicitors (lawyers) were having their weekly meeting and they wanted Srila Prabhupada to address them. I confirmed the time, and we attended the lawyers' meeting. However, it was Srila Prabhupada who held court. I asked many of the barristers if they had read the Manu-samhita (Law of Manu), and they all said no. Prabhupada whispered to me, "Lawyers without law books." He pronounced "lawyers" as "liars."

The gist of his talk was that, being lawyers, they were required to follow the law and the law books. In other words, they should follow God's laws as found in *Bhagavad-gita*, the greatest spiritual law book of all time. He then explained why: "Water the root of the tree," he said, "and all the leaves and branches are nourished." The lawyers were very appreciative after the talk, and they came up to him, asked questions, and offered respects by bowing down before Prabhupada.

Maharaja Baladeva Indra Singh

Deep in the Punjab, we drove further into farm country and away from Amritsar. Riding along in an automobile in such close association with my mentor, I did not know exactly where we were going, neither did I care. I was with Prabhupada, going to an engagement at a farm. I would have the opportunity to learn from my guru by getting a chance to see him interact with other souls. I learned by his example as he interacted with people from all walks of life; the man we were about to meet was supposedly a king.

We turned off the rural road and passed through some large gates onto many acres of farming land. We noticed barns, cows, water buffalo, men in livery costumes, and many servants. We passed planted fields of yellow mustard, cabbages, beans, and potatoes. Our cars pulled up to a huge, one-level ranch house. We were a party of about fourteen. The woman of the house was in front to greet us. She beckoned us inside, showing Prabhupada to a special seat, and then sat at his feet. Two boys and a young girl came in, and the mother introduced her children in Hindi language. They then touched Prabhupada's feet. On the walls were seven-foot-tall paintings of the ancestors of this royal family. Corpulent warriors, they sat atop horses in their ancient armor and kingly costumes with proud visages, jeweled crowns, swords encrusted with gems, silk sashes, feathers, and peacock fans. I have since seen similar paintings in other Maharajas' palaces in Alwar, Bharatpur, Jaipur, Barasat, Dongadra, and other places.

The regal Baladev Indra Singh entered the room with bold and confident strides. He was not a large man, but he walked and held himself as if he were huge. His mustache made him look fierce. His children and wife gave him room and seemed to be frightened of him. He sat across from Prabhupada on a special seat prepared for him. They talked in Hindi, and I could understand some of the conversation, which ranged in topic from books and temples around the world, to farming and philosophy. Baladev Indra Singh's children hung on his every word, and when he simply glanced in their direction they would spring to attention to do his bidding.

He invited us to have prasadam in the next room. We got up, and Prabhupada and the king went ahead of us into a large and spacious high-ceilinged room, where animal-head trophies were surrounding us instead of paintings of kings and warriors. Wildebeest, elephant, lion, tiger, and antelope heads stared straight ahead, lifeless and especially repulsive to us, who treat all living entities with respect and compassion. We bhakti-devotees were getting restless, unsure of what to do or say in this awkward situation. I saw a few devotees searching the food to see if there were any animal parts to be found there. I looked at Prabhupada for guidance, because I was interested to see how he would handle the situation. The food was heavy Punjabi cooking, prepared with buffalo milk, and quite spicy, abundant and tasty. Prabhupada started eating. Seeing the devotees' discomfort he stated, "Ksatriyas (kings) must hunt animals to practice how to kill people in battle. A ksatriya's dharma is to fight, so they must practice by hunting. This is described in the *Vedas*. We are in the house of a real ksatriya." Since Prabhupada remained calm, so did everyone else, and we were able to relax and eat with Prabhupada and the Maharaja Baladev Indra Singh.

TRANSIT TALES

What To Do?

Returning to Bombay from Amritsar by train, Prabhupada and I were in a first-class compartment together, just the two of us. Any time I could spend alone in the company of my spiritual master was very special and sacred to me. Our stay in Amritsar would be fondly remembered by me, I thought, as the fields of yellow mustard flowers drifted past outside the train window. Occasionally my glance would shift to Srila Prabhupada, and I would gaze entranced at his perfect movements. His every word, deed, and gesture was infused with divine purpose. I was in the presence of a saint, a yogi, a friend.

The train compartment contained four beds, actually two sets of bunk beds, two up and two down. I put most of our luggage on one top bunk while Prabhupada sat on the bed below it. Then I took my seat on the lower bed opposite him, along with a few of our handbags. The two men who were to share our compartment came in and left an abundance of luggage on their reserved upper bunk, above my head; they briefly greeted us and hurriedly left. Prabhupada sat cross-legged across from me, looking out the window. Finally he said, "There is enough land to farm, and if they just put water there it will turn green." He pointed to a stretch of desert. "I have seen."

At a stop, Kausaliya brought in prasadam from the second-class compartments, sat for awhile and left. Prabhupada took out another thali (stainless steel plate) and started putting his maha-maha prasadam on the plate. I watched while Prabhupada's golden fingers deftly placed morsels of mercy into his mouth—and then to my surprise he handed me the plate of his remnants! He did everything so gracefully, so assured. Whatever he did, whether it was walking, eating, or giving me his prasadam on a plate, he did it with such ease and confidence.

When Prabhupada had finished eating, I brought him a bowl of water and a towel to wash and dry his lotus hands. Relaxing, Prabhupada then lay down prone, stretched out on his bed with his hand behind his head. He looked over at me and motioned me towards his seat: "You take rest, too." I was stunned.

But where was I to go? Was I to lay by Prabhupada's side, or cradle his feet or his head in my lap? Should I sleep on the floor? Confused, I didn't move.

Then I bolted up, put our handbags up on the top bunk with the rest of our luggage, above Prabhupada's head, and lay down on the lower bunk opposite Prabhupada.

Prabhupada smiled as he watched me and soon fell into easy dreams. I lay there, my eyes wide open like a frog, still wondering where Prabhupada wanted me to sleep, worried that the men would return and claim their bed. Finally, I too fell asleep.

The men never returned to the compartment.

Curiosity

I was in the first-class train compartment with Srila Prabhupada. He was switching the light switch on and off, and then the fan. He raised and lowered the small table by the window. I wanted to serve him, so I said, "Prabhupada, can I find something for you? Do you want me to switch on the fan?"

"No, I am just seeing all the mechanics," he said, switching the lights and fan on and off and on again.

"I Love My Disciples"

From the train compartment window I was gazing out over Kurukshetra, the same fields where Lord Krishna spoke the *Bhagavad-gita* to Arjuna.

"Krishna gives mercy to everyone equally," Prabhupada said, shortly after we had left Kurukshetra Station. "Krishna pours rain on the stones and ocean even though they don't need it, Krishna is so merciful." He continued, "I also distribute my mercy equally. I love all my disciples.

"If some devotee thinks he is favored over another by me it is because he or she has done something, some good service, so I encourage them. However, I love all my disciples equally, even if they don't know it. I give credit where it is due, so again if some disciple does a wonderful service to Krishna, I reciprocate by pointing that out."

Prabhu

As we rode along on a train, Prabhupada showed me the proper perspective in regarding other devotees as "prabhu," or master. "The idea is to be humble and to serve others as if they are your prabhus. If someone calls you prabhu and you think, 'Yes, I am master,' that is not the idea." He imitated a puffed-up person with a puffed-up chest and a mock silly look on his face. "When I call you prabhu, it is in the spirit of service; in that way, you are my master."

> *"If you make a dog king and he is sitting on a throne,*
> *and you throw him a shoe, he will run off the throne and bite the shoe."*
> —A. C. Bhaktivedanta Swami

"Get Down and See What You Can Do."

Traveling with Srila Prabhupada was always a great adventure. I never knew what to expect! Returning to Bombay from Amritsar, we pulled into the New Delhi train-station platform.

I watched as the vendors scurried about the platform shouting, "Pani! Pani!" (water), "Burfi!" (sweets), "Chai! Chai! Chai!"(tea), "Dudh! Dudh! Dudh!" (milk). Other vendors offered toys, stationery, pharmaceuticals, and magazines. I watched porters board the train with food and stewards load precooked meals into the dining car's kitchen.

In the first-class compartment with Prabhupada, I was relaxed. We were on the way to Bombay, and the countryside of India rolling by my window relaxed me even more. I continued to watch the people and the activity, lazily observant. Kausalya came from the second-class compartment to see if Prabhupada needed anything. Prabhupada nodded "*tik hai*" with his head: "Everything is all right."

Suddenly a man came into our compartment to receive Prabhupada's darshan (blessings). I checked with Prabhupada to see if he wanted visitors. Prabhupada was gracious as usual.

The two men began talking in Hindi. At first I tried to pay attention, but my eyes kept wandering to the scene outside the window. The man, a Mr. D. D. Gupta, a lawyer in a faded, black lawyer's coat with tattered sleeves, offered some sweets to Prabhupada. The aged sweets crumbled in his hands. They must have been left over from the Battle of Kurukshetra, I thought. The decaying, powdery sweets were the first indication of how different this man was. They continued to talk for a while. D. D. Gupta was embellishing his words with exaggerated hand gestures and nodding of his head. I thought to myself: "Oh no, not another empty-headed, hollow-talking man—many promises without substance!"

Prabhupada then turned to me and said, "Mr. Gupta has invited us to start a temple in Delhi." Then, to my surprise Prabhupada said, "Get down and see what you can do." A moment later he asked, "Who will you take with you?" My wife, Yamuna, was in the second-class compartment. My ticket said Bombay. I regained my composure and said, "Yamuna . . . and Giriraj." Then I had an idea. Gopal prabhu was a strong but somewhat surly brahmachari. He had trouble getting along with many devotees at one time, so I thought in a smaller situation he could help out a lot. "I will take Gopal dasa." (My intuition turned out to be correct. Gopal dasa was helpful and energetic, and we all got along with him just fine.)

I continued, "Kausalya, and Durlabh—"

Prabhupada interrupted: "I have plans for Kausalya and Durlabh in Bombay."

"And Bhanu?" I asked. Prabhupada said okay.

When the others were informed that they were to get off with me in Delhi, they too were surprised. They also thought they were going to Bombay. But Vaishnava devotees throughout history have been flexible in many situations and have shown great courage. So did my valiant godbrothers and-sisters. Everyone was determined and ready to serve Prabhupada and Krishna with only a moment's notice. Spontaneous, abrupt reversals are commonplace in India: people are always changing their minds; traffic darts between pedestrians and weaves around cows sitting on the road; birds fly inside houses; people in trades go stomping off and then return to break agreements. Mother India's flexibility gave us the motivation to be flexible also. We had no chance to become jaded or fall into a rut in our service. Every day was different, every moment new.

Somewhat apprehensive and with heavy hearts, we all assembled in the first-class compartment. I didn't want to leave Prabhupada. Mr. Gupta looked on. "Mr. Gupta says he has a place for you to stay, and he knows of a temple where you can have programs." From some place in his robe Prabhupada handed me fifty rupees. "Try and start a temple in Delhi—it is the capital of India and very important." We all bowed down, and Prabhupada patted my head. I took the dust from his feet, and we left.

ISKCON NEW DELHI

The First Days

Shocked and silent at our new situation, we followed Mr. D. D. Gupta to his Vespa motor scooter. He was actually trying to fit all of our luggage, sparse as it was, onto his motor scooter! He indicated that we should all try to sit on his motor scooter too! Then he gestured for the two women to sit. We watched him rearrange luggage and sleeping rolls. We started laughing to ourselves; I could see the amusement on all of our faces, but not until I actually said something did he stop his histrionics and hail a cab.

In the taxi there was scarcely room for the five of us and our few belongings. Mr. Gupta then bargained with the man in Hindi for the fare for our passage to Delhi Gate. They jabbered back and forth and settled on a fee, off the meter. The taxi followed D. D. on his Vespa. At one point D. D. stopped by an empty field, locked his scooter, and walked to the back of the field. We looked at each other with questioning countenances. We stopped watching him when we realized that, with his back to us, Mr. Gupta was urinating in the field.

When we arrived at Delhi Gate he looked at us to pay for the taxi. We sat silent, detached and inscrutable. He nearly had a nervous breakdown when he realized he would have to pay. After all, he was the person who invited us to New Delhi. Thus far, everyone else who had invited us anywhere took care of everything. Were we his guests? What had he told Prabhupada? We weren't sure what lay ahead.

Mr. Gupta then took us through a doorway leading to a courtyard and small temple. The rooms upstairs were like monk's cells. Each room was dark with bars on the windows to keep monkeys and people out. A small sink and small cot waited inside each cell—really everything that anyone needs.

Mr. Gupta came in to see if we were all right. Then he informed us that weasels sometimes visited the rooms—holy cow! Yamuna and I lived in one of these cells with the weasels, monkeys, and sparrows that came in and out. Giriraj and Bhanu lived in another room, and Gopal das in another. My Lower East Side, cold-water flat was a palace in comparison.

Delhi Gate is an arch that covers the road between New and Old Delhi. The New Delhi side was elegantly planned, with wide boulevards, trees, open areas, and government offices. The other side of Delhi Gate was a crowded street with teeming traffic, people, animals, and small shops—a noisy existence. The entrance doors to our temple were almost hidden on a street in New Delhi, while the interior and windows overlooked and faced Old Delhi. Busy car, coach, and rickshaw traffic flowed beneath the arch of Delhi Gate, and thousands of shuffling footsteps and muffled conversations could be heard passing by outside, ignoring our unassuming front entrance. Inside, a dark hall opened onto a large, sunlit courtyard. The tiny upstairs rooms we inhabited looked over the open inner courtyard.

Mr. Gupta then invited us to his house around the corner in old Delhi. His two-story walkup was simple and adequate. A law degree hung tilted on his wall. His wife brought us more sweets that also crumbled in our hands. As we sat in his house we saw Mr. D. D. Gupta, the lawyer in faded black coat with tattered sleeves, unlock his desk drawer. The attorney took out some dead batteries. Then he placed the batteries on his altar and started praying. He intoned prayers that would bring his dead batteries back to life. Then he said he would be able to play his transistor radio. I remember thinking to myself that perhaps he was one of the most frugal men in the world.

Prabhupada sent two letters guiding my actions in this new country, this new city, this fresh start:

From Bombay
1 November, 1970

To Delhi
My Dear Gurudas,
Please accept my blessings. I have safely reached Bombay and there was a nice reception. I am now staying at Chembur at the above address. I hope everything is progressing well with you in Delhi. Please let me know how things are going on there.

I am enclosing herewith one letter from Atma Ram and Sons, Booksellers; please take it with you to see them and show them our books and literatures and make some arrangement for their taking some of them for distribution.

When you inform me what is your estimation of Delhi and how people are reacting to our Movement, I shall instruct you how to proceed.
Hope this will meet you in good health. Please offer my blessings to Srimati Yamuna Devi and all the other devotees. Enclosed also please find one letter for Sriman Bruce.

Your ever well-wisher,
A. C. Bhaktivedanta Swami

From Bombay
7 November, 1970

To Delhi
My Dear Gurudas,
Please accept my blessings. I beg to acknowledge receipt of your letter dated November 2nd, 1970. Perhaps you have received my letter sent to you earlier.

Please see Atma Ram & Sons book distributors on Kashmiri Gate, New Delhi (Isha Kumar, proprietor). Isha Kumar has always been very respectful towards me. You can show him all our books and if he is interested, he may become the sole selling agent in India for my books and he will get a 40% discount, but he must order at least 200 copies of each book.

Instead of engaging in Sankirtan if you, husband and wife, try to see so many government members and ministers and other important men, that will be nice. You may try and see Indira Gandhi. And perhaps you can meet with this President Giri, shown in the enclosed news clipping. I think because your pictures are shown together with his, he will meet you.

There is an old friend of mine named D. R. Gupta on 4 University Rd. You should make arrangements to see him by telephoning him. If he is favorably impressed, he will certainly become a life member. That is what I want you to do while you are there to try to make as many life members as you can.

You should certainly see J. Dalmia at Scindia House, New Delhi. He will become a life member and he can suggest others who may also become life members. He is a relative and very close to Ram dasa Dandaria. Also you can see his big brother Ram Krishna Dalmia and make him a life member. His daughter came to London, Ascot to see me. If there is any difficulty in staying where you are, you can ask J. Dalmia to provide accommodation in Birla's dharmasala. That dharmasala is a very good place with lecture hall. You can speak in the lecture hall in English and you can advertise for members and they will appreciate it very much.

I've received a letter from Bali Mardan and he is very eager to carry on with his GBC activities. So he will not be resigning from his post and will continue in his position.

Also I've received some other letters and things in London are not as they should be. It seems that Murari has now become president of London temple. This is all right for a while but you will have to go back to the London temple. London temple is one of the most important centers in our society and it should not suffer for lack of good management. Under you and your wife's good care, things have gone very nicely there. So I want you and Yamuna to both be prepared to go back to London in the near future. You have come all the way to India, so for the time being you should remain here and see what can be done in Delhi.

I just received one letter from Radha Madhava Sharan and he has informed me that a big temple and compound belonging to the Maharaja of Bharatapur on the bank of the Yamuna at Kesighat is for sale. Therefore I would like you to go immediately to see Radha Madhava Sharan in Vrindaban (Address: 2/157, Radha Raman; Vrindaban; U.P.). You can go and see the sight and find out exactly from him the terms of negotiation of purchasing the temple and property. When you have understood the terms, you can go to Bharatapur along with Radha Madhava Sharan, taking him at our expense, and find out the exact person with whom the negotiations should be finalized. If everything is in order and the property can be purchased, then remain in Bharatapur. If the transaction is to be done there, you stay in Bharatapur and telegram me immediately. I will come myself and complete the purchase. We would like to get this temple and land at all costs, as it is very nicely situated on the Yamuna River. I know of this temple. I used to live next to it before living in the Radha Damodara temple. It is a very palatial building. The remainder of your party, including your wife, may remain in Delhi under the leadership of Giriraja dasa Brahmachari and see the men whom I've mentioned above.

Hope this will meet you in good health.

Your ever well-wisher,
A. C. Bhaktivedanta Swami

Patrons in Delhi

Prabhupada's letters showed the way by suggesting that I visit two men, a Mr. Dalmia and a Mr. Ish Kumar of Atma Ram Press. Prabhupada had established his new ISKCON Life Membership idea, where a life member who paid 1,111 rupees would in turn receive a complete set of the Society's books and be entitled to stay free in any ISKCON center in the world for the rest of his life.

So Giriraj and I went to many houses and offices and met some of Srila Prabhupada's influential friends. As we climbed the marble stairs of Mr. Dalmia's office building we noticed the absence of paan (betel nut) stains on the wall; instead there were pictures of Mr. Dalmia's different industries, such as cement factories, cashew plantations, etc. Mr. Dalmia canceled all other business and came immediately out of his office to greet us: Prabhupada's name had that much effect on him. For such a rich man he was very humble. He was slight of build and wore a simple, immaculately clean, khadi suit. He spoke kindly and softly, with an ingratiating smile. Mr. Dalmia became a life member immediately and eventually became an advisor. A Dr. Lokesh Chandra, M.P., was also in Mr. Dalmia's office, and he also helped out by becoming a life member, and, later on, a host and confidant. We are still friends to this day.

We were starting to meet people in Delhi, perform morning kirtans in the temple at Delhi Gate, and sign up life members, but I wanted to go to Vrindavan. I hadn't mentioned to anyone my desire to visit Vrindavan, but I kept thinking that Krishna's birthplace was only eighty kilometers from me! I was going through devotional motions in Delhi, but at heart I really wanted to be in Vrindavan. After some time things were going along smoothly in Delhi, so I prepared to go to the holy dhama. Prabhupada read my mind from afar, and with his letters he sanctioned my wishes.

According to Prabhupada's instructions, I was to go to Vrindavan to find the Maharaja of Bharatpur, who apparently had a palace called Laxmi Rani Kunj for sale. "Get that palace," Prabhupada had said. "I know this building, I used to live right nearby. It could be our temple."

VRINDABAN

"My dear Lord, what can I say about the opulence of Your Vrindavan? Simply the ornaments on the legs of the damsels of Vrindavan are more than Chintamani, and their dresses are as good as the heavenly parijata flowers. The cows exactly resemble the surabhi cows in the transcendental abode. Therefore, Your opulence is just like an ocean that no one can measure.
—Nectar of Devotion, p. 186

"Go Get a Palace"

Prabhupada was sending me to Vrindaban!

As always, Prabhupada instructed me so clearly, and I wanted so much to please him. I knew how important establishing an ISKCON Vrindavan temple was to him. Vrindavan is, after all, the center of the Vaishnava faith, a spiritual place on Earth, as Jerusalem, Bethlehem, and Mecca are to others. I left the other devotees in Delhi, and with a light heart I took the Taj Express train 80 kilometers to beloved Vrindavan.

Since 1967 I had dreamed of experiencing Vrindavan, the abode of 5,000 temples, the place where singing goes on twenty-four hours a day, the realm of grazing cows, dancing peacocks, and scampering monkeys. Braja Bhumi: the place of music, theater festivals, and daily processions through the streets.

When the train stopped at Mathura Station, eight miles from Vrindaban, I felt sheltered and welcomed. Mathura is the birthplace of Lord Krishna on this Earth. I bowed down to the magic place as I left the train. Locals were accustomed to others bowing at this place of pilgrimage, though some looked on with curiosity to see this Westerner bowing down.

Coming out of the Mathura Station, I was surrounded by ricksha drivers and horse-cart (tonga) drivers. I knew that Vrindavan was about twelve kilometers from Mathura, and as there were no bicycle rickshas available, only those pulled by hand, I thought that it would be too far for a ricksha driver to pull. But when I said I must go to Vrindavan, the ricksha drivers insisted vehemently that they could carry me. Yet I still thought twelve kilometers was too tough for a thin man to pull a ricksha.

I compared prices too, and the horse-drawn tonga was less expensive, especially if you shared. I chose the six-seated tonga.

We left Mathura Station at a slow trot, winding through some large, tree-lined streets, then through some smaller streets, around some turns, past some small factories, and out onto the country road going to Vrindavan.

Two men and a woman, clad in simple, homespun, cotton cloth, rode with me. They were born here, I thought to myself. They wrapped a strip of the cloth around their heads to protect them from the blazing sun. The tonga had a canvas covering, and a breeze came in through the side and roof slats. I was singing "Jaya Radha Madhava" to myself. This was a song about the glories of Vrindavan.

A large, white, modern temple loomed up on the left side. "Birla Mandir," the driver said, and I looked through the open gates into the clean courtyard. I could see at least three separate altars to Lord Radha Krishna, Laxmi Narayan, and Lord Shiva.

An easy reverie came over me: I was here in the holiest of places, and I had a chance to drink it in, at my pace, without having to think about schedules or life memberships or crowded, capital-city streets. Instead, thoughts of Radha and Krishna and their rasas (pastimes) filled my head—I was riding in the very places, the tirthas, where these inspiring, celestial diversions took place. I felt a charisma emanating from every rock and tree. I was not the only one being seduced by Braja Bhumi. Thousands of other pilgrims come to Vrindavan daily to circumambulate, visit temples, and to receive from sadhus sacred blessings, inspiration, and purification. Many elderly people come to Vrindavan, some by foot, to live for the rest of their days and then leave their bodies in this holy place.

Akrura Ghat appeared on the right-hand side of the road. Although I didn't know Akrura Ghat by name, I could feel it was a special spot. Every inch further took me deeper into Krishna country. All around me were places where Prabhupada, or one of the six Goswamis, or Lord Chaitanya, or Lord Balarama had walked or dwelled.

As I entered Kosi Kolan, the county boundary of outer Vrindavan, I felt a change inside me as well as in the scenery. (Ever since that time, whenever I cross the border at Kosi Kolan, by walking, train, car, or bus, I sense the same emotional phenomenon; my eyes can be closed, yet I will feel the border of Vrindavan, and open them, see the same, old palace parapets of Kosi Kolan in the distance, and feel secure.)

As I had requested, the tonga took me to the home of Mr. Radha Madhava Sharan, 2/157 Radha Raman, in Vrindaban village. No one was there, so I instructed the driver to take me to the Laxmi Rani Kunj Palace. Ancient wooden doors that stood twelve feet high confronted me. I knocked and waited. There was no answer. I knocked again louder, and again there was no answer. I walked around the corner of the high palace walls, saw an open area, turned left, and came upon the Yamuna River, the very river where Lord Krishna used to sport!

White and red sandstone steps embellished by sculpted designs led down to the river. At the water's edge, cavelike shelters appeared under ghats and buildings. These steps also bordered the six-mile-long parikrama path that encircles Vrindavan. Since over time the Yamuna's channel has moved away from parts of the village, many of the steps of former bathing ghats that once led down to water were now covered, dried up, and overgrown with weeds. Fortunately, the water had remained deep at the base of the steps at Kesi Ghat, adjacent to Laxmi Rani Kunj Palace.

I went down the palace steps to the edge of the water. A few people were bathing or sitting. The river came right up to the stairs and was about five feet deep. I splashed the sacred waters on my face and head. I took my kurta (shirt) off and splashed the train dust away with eternal elixir. The liquid spirituality refreshed and energized me, as did the thought that these were the same waters in which Krishna sported and bathed. Large turtles swam near the steps. I watched them swim onto the steps, dive off in slow motion, and swim out of sight. I turned around and viewed the palace I had been asked to acquire. It loomed three stories above me, with beautiful, hand-carved, sandstone balconies jutting out from each floor. Between pillars, artists had chiseled out from a single piece of stone the beautiful *jali* windows—a lost art. "This would be a nice temple for Krishna," I thought, "right here on the Yamuna River in the heart of Vrindavan!" I resolved to do my best to get this palace for Srila Prabhupada.

I walked back to the high front doors of Laxmi Rani Kunj Palace and knocked very loudly this time. But they remained closed and immovable. Some intuition or chaitya guru (internal direction) led me to go across the lane. I am sure that Prabhupada was also guiding me at this time. I looked into a large, open courtyard, big as a parade ground, surrounded by a four-storied building. The yard was now empty, but from written signs and the sight of books, small slates, and chalk I could tell that it was a schoolyard. A sign said "Maharaja Pratap, Padma Shri (National Medal of Honor), Headmaster." I looked to the right of the gateway and saw a small office with its door open and a man sitting inside. I knocked softly, and the man looked up and saw me. The well-groomed man visibly brightened and said in English, "Come in, come in. My name is Nirmal." He was the principal of the school and the assistant to the Maharaja Pratap.

Maharaja Pratap Singh was famous and had worked in politics alongside Nehru, Subash Chandra Bose, Gandhi, Stalin, and many others. He had inherited this former palace from his father. Maharaja Praptap, now a lonely, aging man, had decided to turn his palace into a school. The courtyard that had once supported processions of marching soldiers was now a playground for screaming children, scampering in all directions.

As the principal related this history, I interrupted him: "Speaking of palaces, my guru has received word that Laxmi Rani Kunj is for sale. I am interested in meeting the Maharaja of Bharatpur to discuss this with him."

"Very good," said Nirmal. I couldn't tell if he was favorable to the idea or not. I had been in India long enough to see that often people say one thing and mean another. The intrigue in India is subtle, and sometimes being non-confrontational is the best way to achieve one's goals. India has absorbed many invaders by smiling and offering water, food, and shelter. The intruders then get dysentery from the water—and retreat. Kindness is often used as a weapon to disarm the enemy. In ancient times, attractive women were given small amounts of snake venom. In this way they would slowly develop immunity to the poison, but their kiss was a deadly weapon to an enemy. However, this man seemed genuine, and I asked him for information to assist me in meeting the Maharaja of Bharatpur.

"The Maharaja of Bharatpur rarely comes here," Nirmal added. "Maybe once a year on an anniversary celebration. He lives in Bharatpur. There is a pujari (caretaker) living in the palace across the way. I will talk to him and tell him of your arrival. Come back here on the day after tomorrow and see me—I will arrange it."

I thanked him very much, pranamed, and left. I went down to the banks of the Yamuna River and prayed and chanted a few rounds on my japa beads. I thought I would look up my old friend Shyama devi from London, as perhaps she had some shelter and advice for me. I found a ricksha and said to the driver, "Shyama devi Ashram." The driver recognized my words and gestured warmly for me to sit in his vehicle.

The ricksha wound through the streets of Vrindavan village, past Vamsi Vhat, Radha Gopinath Temple and Radha Raman Temple. Every turn of the wheel, every foot we traversed was holy ground. We passed the monkeys on the steps at Nidhavan, rode through Loi Bazaar, and went out into the more suburban areas, past ashrams, dharmshalas, and open fields, into Raman Reti ("Enjoyable Sands"). I passed a large building. It was Swami Bon's—Prabhupada's godbrother's—College. The ricksha took me down a lane to the doors of Shyama devi's Ashram. I went inside. The courtyard was empty, and the doors to the rooms were closed. A man came out.

I inquired, "Shyama devi?"

He shook his head in acknowledgement, motioned me to wait and disappeared into one of the rooms. I paid the ricksha driver and waited. Soon I was beckoned inside. A different man, with shaved head, appeared wearing a sikha. Shyama devi was in an adjoining room, and when she saw me she greeted me heartily. I bowed. She laughed and told the others who were gathering around us how I had helped her with her Deities in London, and she told them about the kirtans we shared in Leicester. She tried to say San Francisco but said, "Sas frasisco, ha ha." We laughed together.

"Prasadam?" She asked. I shook my head "Yes." They brought simple rice, dahl, chapattis, and vegetables. The brahmachari, Gopal, spoke a little English, and he asked if I wanted to stay with them. "Yes, that would be nice."

Shyama devi took her leave and instructed me to go with her disciple. We went out of the ashram, around the corner, and across the main Raman Reti road to her goshalla (cow-protection area). There was a small meeting room surrounded by gardens. Nearby were six cows in a corral.

The brahmachari and I walked to the cows and petted and fed them.

Then Gopal took me to a long, comfortable room over the gate. Six windows looked out onto the main road. I heard the sound of kirtan wafting through the fields and growing louder as the kirtan party approached. Gopal asked if I wanted a tour of Vrindavan on the next day, and I enthusiastically agreed.

As the sun was setting, I felt at home and protected. But I could not sleep very well that night because the moon was full, and bullock carts sporadically passed below the windows of my room all night long, their drivers singing bhajans (devotional songs) softly to Radharani, delivering their sacks of cargo under the bright moonlight. My heart filled with ecstasy and joy as the holy names of Krishna were chanted across the landscape.

I took a moment to thank Prabhupada for remembering my request to come to Vrindavan.

The next morning I heard a sound emanating from a small hut nearby. As a man was sweeping out his hut, he was chanting a mantralike work song between the whooshes of his broom. I swooned in ecstasy, falling backwards onto a soft sandbank on the parikrama path. I recovered from my faint, stood up, and then returned to the goshalla ashram. Later that morning Gopal joined up with me, and we walked the same path I had explored earlier. The magic distracted me again: the very ground we walked upon was obviously Chintamani, or spiritual touchstone.

Bon Behar (Forest Wanderer)

I sat by the banks of the Yamuna River and watched turtles swim near my feet. My duties were finished, and I sat there simply praying and bathing. There were no water buffalo wallowing in the river today, with kids riding their backs, because the river was flowing faster then usual and had shifted its banks because of a flood. The usual riverbank was under water now. The bottom steps of the bathing ghat were also hidden. I sat higher up than usual, with my feet immersed in water. The flood had stripped and carried away whole fields. Mother Yamuna looked like a moving field. Greenery, strands of grasses, vines, and melons floated by. I was soon joined by my companion, Gunarnava.

Feeling carefree and protected, we made a game of spying a moving watermelon, swimming out to it, catching it, and seeing whether it was decomposed or still good for eating. We came up with one or two good melons.

Nearby was a small alley wide enough only for one person to pass. The alley looked like a dead end, a narrow passage between two buildings. However, when we explored the alley we found an entrance to a small, three-story temple. As we entered there was an altar, upon which was a large, flat rock, a grinding stone, with a footprint of Lord Krishna in it. This was situated at the base of a large tree. The rest of the temple was built around the tree, much like the Swiss Family Robinson's famous tree house. The footprint is said to have been made by Krishna when He tried to prevent His mother Yasoda from grinding wheat early in the morning while He was sleeping. The stone melted by the touch of the Lord's foot. Throughout Vrindavan the hand- and footprints of Sri Sri Radha Krishna and Lord Chaitanya still exist on rocks, trees, and in caves, and most of all they are imprinted upon the devotees' hearts.

Stairs wound around the tree up to the second floor, revealing more of the tree. The priests of the temple told us that Radharani was so in love with Krishna that She blissfully fainted against the trunk of the tree and left Her handprints there. The living quarters of the family that cares for the temple were situated on the third floor. These rooms wrap around the upper parts of the tree, and the Yamuna River can be seen through the windows.

One can then wander down an alley with doorways leading to houses on both sides. Many of these houses are also temples. In one of these houses we found a painting of Lord Shiva arriving at his wedding reception accompanied by some of his weird friends—like goblins, owls, and troll-like people—all heading for the buffet. Lord Shiva looks resplendent, dressed in tiger skin and carrying his trident. His bride, Parvati, also looks beautiful in a red-and-gold wedding sari. Her family and friends, however, are fainting at the sight of Lord Shiva's unusual friends, and they are depicted in the painting in their falling poses. Coming out of the alley, we saw the Ashta Sakhi Temple, with the eight main Gopis on the altar, and then we again came upon the Yamuna River.

Striped birds dove from on high, straight into the bosom of Kalindi. An elephant bathed nearby. The spires of Madan Mohan Temple were silhouetted against the sky. As I wandered, intoxicated and happy, back towards the enjoyable sands of Raman Reti, I felt the total bliss of being in Vrindavan.

Laxmi Rani Kunj

The next day, at the appointed hour, I went to meet with Nirmal, the principal of the school, who was again helpful and friendly. We walked across the street to the doors of Laxmi Rani Kunj Palace. We knocked, and waited for about three minutes. Then the huge doors opened slowly, and a grizzled, old man in a soiled dhoti looked up at me and then at the principal. They talked in Hindi for some time, sometimes pointing towards me and gesturing.

The man, who was the caretaker of the now-deserted palace, beckoned us inside. To the right of the enormous, open-air courtyard stood a large tree encircled by a bench at its base. The courtyard was surrounded on three sides by the sandstone verandahs of living quarters, inhabited at the time only by bats. The immense altar room rose up from marble floors to a high ceiling on the fourth side of the courtyard. The caretaker pujari led me to some windows carved in Rajhastani *jali* style, interlaced with delicate designs fashioned from a single slab of sandstone. He opened the windows with a flourish, and light flooded into the room. The floor-to-ceiling windows opened onto an exterior, sandstone balcony overlooking the Yamuna River. The view was glorious!

After absorbing the view I went back inside to the courtyard. The pujari swung open another door near the indoor tree and showed us a hidden, overgrown garden; this lush little park was the perfect place for a king to stroll or a devotee to chant japa. We then went up some dark, narrow stairs to look at the second floor. Bat sounds bounced off the musty walls at our approach. Vegetation covered the walls and floors.

We went back down the narrow stairs into the courtyard. The pujari went to the altar stage and opened the curtain so we could have darshan of the Deities, Laxmi and Narayan. Their clothes were old and dusty. The paraphernalia was unclean and dingy. Everything was run down and neglected by this lone caretaker-pujari.

After our tour I inquired as to the whereabouts of the Maharaja of Bharatpur. The pujari told us that the Maharaja was presently at his palace in Bharatpur, about fifty miles west of Vrindaban!

I thanked the pujari. Nirmal gave me directions to the Bharatpur Palace and helped arrange a car. I found Mr. Radha Saran, the gentleman Prabhupada wrote to me about, and he agreed to accompany me to Bharatpur.

The next day we left for Bharatpur by car, together with an agent for the Maharaja. As we traveled through the countryside I felt as if I were in an age past. We passed many ancient buildings, some with moats, and at last we spotted the lakes in the famous Bharatpur bird sanctuary.

When we arrived at the Bharatpur Palace, we were greeted in a very cold manner by a man with greasy, slicked-back hair. He twirled his handlebar mustache as his cronies gathered around him. He identified himself as the Maharaja of Bharatpur's secretary. After my very soft-spoken inquiries, the secretary reluctantly told us that the Maharaja was in Delhi. I returned with Mr. Saran to Vrindavan and immediately took the train back to Delhi.

I was reunited in Delhi with Yamuna, but there was little time to share personal news. I asked her to accompany me to visit the Maharaja, and we grabbed a taxi to the address on Malcha Marg.

Like many of the modern, ranch-style houses occupied by affluent people in New Delhi, the Maharaja's compound was very spacious, with large trees, and a porch that bordered two sides of the house. We asked to see the Maharaja of Bharatpur and were asked in return if we had an appointment. We told them who we were and that we were interested in purchasing Laxmi Rani Kunj in Vrindavan. We did not get to see the Maharaja then and there. He must have been busy with important duties. We did however receive an invitation to have lunch with the Maharaja in a week's time. At last we were making some progress!

A week later, Yamuna and I arrived in our best dhoti and sari. The mustache-twirler was there, but as we were now invited guests he led us more respectfully into a large room. Three royally dressed figures sat on three separate couches. The agent introduced us to the Maharani of Nabwah, the Maharaja of Bharatpur, and the Raj Kumar (princely son) of Bharatpur.

The Maharaja's bulk seemed to cover an entire couch. He was of medium height and chunky from good living. The despot had mischievously moving eyes, a large mustache, a turban on his head, and wore a silk lounging suit. I didn't bow, but I folded my hands together and *pranamed*, and Yamuna followed suit.

He lazily waved a hand in recognition. The Bharatpur Raj looked at us and asked, "Do you have any connection to the Peace Corps?"

I answered, "No, we do not have any connection to the Peace Corps . . ."

The Maharaja interrupted, "The head of the Peace Corps ran away with my wife. See if you can get my wife back."

He rambled on, changing moods at an instant, and was generally flitting about and making bad jokes. He turned to the Maharani (Queen) of Nabwah next to him. "Will you run away with me?" he joked. She smiled sweetly and just laughed. The Maharani was chubby, wore white makeup all over her face, and resembled a Japanese Kabuki dancer. She turned out to be a very amiable and contented person who didn't say much.

Next to the Maharani of Nabwah was the Raj Kumar (Prince) of Bharatpur, a cherubic eleven year-old with a high voice. The youth came over and sat at his father's side. The Maharaja, who seemed to be a little schizoid as well as spoiled, tried to discipline his son. "Don't sit here," he said. Then, "Oh, it's all right."

"His mother ran off with the head of the Peace Corps," the Maharaja repeated.

I felt a refreshing breeze from a fan that hung suspended from the ceiling and ran from wall to wall. The long fan was operated by a turbaned servant in livery costume pulling on a cord. The man was a human engine.

"Come, let us eat," the Maharaja gestured, and he led us into a large dining room. The plates were of rare china with the Royal Bharatpur crest, and the silverware was genuine silver. The meal was vegetarian of course: pakoras, samosas, subjis, puris, and saffron rice all delicately prepared. The uniformed servants brought large, silver finger bowls for everyone to wash their hands as we sat at the table. What luxury, I thought.

Throughout the meal the young prince was asking childlike questions, and his father answered them in a more tender way than when he talked to non-family members. The prince's high voice and angelic looks were charming, and I hoped that he would be a good and kind king someday.

After lunch we all went out onto the front porch and sat in high wicker chairs. I got down to business: "We are interested in Laxmi Rani Kunj Palace, in Vrindavan . . ."

"Not now," he interrupted. "You will be my guest for dinner and a parikrama, in Govardhan. We will discuss it then. See my secretary to arrange it." He continued, "You may go now; see if you can get my wife back."

As we left we heard him trumpeting, "The head of the Peace Corps ran off with my wife." As he blathered on, he seemed more like a caricature of himself than the real thing.

Govardhan Hill

A few days hence, before sunrise, with a group of about thirty people, we began our walk around the sacred Govardhan Hill. The entourage included the Maharaja of Bharatpur, two queens, the prince, various relatives, zamindhars (landowners loyal to the king), agents, a doctor, and eight soldiers dressed in Jat military uniforms, part of the Maharaja's private army. Twelve servants carried the supplies and the largest incense sticks I have ever seen. These incense sticks were twelve feet high and thick as a python. Servants, beautifully dressed in long, silk robes, carried large torches ahead of the party so we could see. Other servants carried food, fruit, lemon water, and bedding for this overnight excursion. Most pilgrims, including myself, walking in a leisurely fashion, could circle the hill in about four to five hours. The Maharaja took three days to encircle the sacred hill.

The Maharaja and I walked side by side. Occasionally as I looked in his direction I would notice that he had lagged behind me, so I would wait for him to catch up. Then later, again, I found myself ahead of him. Again I waited. This time when the Maharaja reached me he said, "Kings don't walk like men, they stride like elephants." Now I understood why it took the Maharaja and his party three days to go around Govardhan Hill!

After some time our group came upon a small temple. The Maharaja told me that his family had been owners and caretakers of this holy site for generations. The Deity, Who was an actual stone embedded in Govardhan Hill, was protected by an iron railing. Marble pathways allowed worshipers to offer fruit and flowers. While we were there the Maharaja and his pujari performed an abhishek (Deity bathing) ceremony. I was fortunate to participate in this ancient ceremony in the ancient temple. As we sang the maha-mantra, we offered many items to the stone Deity: milk, yogurt, rosewater, saffron powder, champa and kadamba flowers, several varieties of incense, a peacock fan, and a chamara (yak-tail fan). The Maharaja ordered one of his men to unlock and open a large trunk. He took out two huge, gold earrings about one foot long and six inches thick and a genuine pearl necklace and handed them to the King, who placed them on the brown, rock manifestation of the Lord.

After the bathing ceremony the whole party continued ambling along the base of the low hill. We overtook many pilgrims who were bowing down flat to the ground like a stick. They would chant a prayer, prostrate themselves, place a rock at their head to mark the spot, rise up, and with their feet beside the rock, repeat the process until they had completely circumambulated the sacred hill—six feet at a time! Some pilgrims repeat the process many times and it may take them several years. Some do it for life, never stopping, and they sleep right on the parikrama path!

One pandit (spiritual guide) who was out in front pointed to the hill, and the whole entourage stopped. The man walked up to a rock on the hill and struck it with a smaller rock, a piece of Govardhan Hill. The rock rang like a bell, to the delight of everyone. The king watched my reaction. When asked to ring the rock, I didn't move. As Govardhan is no different from the Lord, Gaudiya Vaishnavas do not walk on Govardhan. He respected me for my convictions.

The Maharaja and I developed an interesting friendship. The Maharaja saw that his roguish ways did not shock me. I refused to react to him—*nada*; I was detached—which seemed to diffuse his antics for a while. When he realized that his mischief seemed droll to me, he reduced his showing off like a child for my benefit. That night the Maharaja showed me how to tie my dhoti like a Jat warrior: each leg was wrapped separately, allowing freedom of movement, which was especially good for running and for sword fighting.

The next morning we were sitting near Manasa Ganga, a bathing ghat created out of the mind of Lord Krishna for His beloved Radharani. The sun was rising, and the Maharaja said to me, "Although I am King, I love the God." I believed him, for in his own eccentric way he was a devotee of Giriraj (Krishna as king of Vrindavan). Devotion, however bizarre, was a part of the King's life too—a small part, but a part nonetheless.

The Jat King reached into a painted treasure box and pulled out an old, rusty lock. It was about six inches tall and three-and-a-half inches wide. It was heavy and well built. A hand-made key was in the hole, but the key twisted around loosely and didn't open the lock. The King laughed and challenged me to open the lock. There was a cover over the hole and various mechanisms to press on the side of the heavy lock, but I couldn't figure it out. The King put it behind his back, and brought it out opened. He laughed, then put it behind him and closed it again. With a flourish he again presented me with the trick lock as a puzzle for me to unravel. His Majesty would check back every few minutes to see if I had figured it out yet and laughed when he saw that it remained locked. I showed the lock to others to see if they could figure it out, but no one could. A day later the Maharaja showed me the trick. One had only to pull down the keyhole cover, and the huge lock opened.

After the three-day circumambulation of Govardhan Hill, we were served a grand dinner in the sprawling Govardhan Palace. Great portraits of fighting ancestors looked down on us from huge horses. Billowing feathers, helmets, jewel-encrusted swords and their sheaths, falcons, spears, bows and arrows, and chariots embellished the walls. The Jats were famous for their expertise and fierceness in battle. Finally, at dinner, the Maharaja broached the topic of the Laxmi Rani Kunj Palace. He informed us that he was willing to "give us" Laxmi Rani Kunj Palace, plus thirty-three acres of farmland in Govardhan, as well as another palace on the banks of Manasa Ganga, the Deities within, and assorted Deity paraphernalia, for only three lakhs of rupees (Rs. 300,000) or about $38,000 then.

He took us to the other palace at Manasa Ganga. It was old and abandoned but beautifully situated on the lake that Krishna made for Radharani with his mind (Manasa). Though it was badly in need of repair, the palace was gorgeous underneath the dust. The King's offer was made on the condition that we would repair and maintain the properties. I told the Maharaja that I would inform Prabhupada about his offer and let him know Prabhupada's answer at once.

I wired Prabhupada immediately, listing the properties as well as the price. After some time Prabhupada wrote back, "He is King, we are Brahmins, therefore he should give us the palace. In turn, we shall fix up a first-class apartment reserved for the Maharaja of Bharatpur to visit any time he wants." In the Vedic system, Brahmins were the religious scholars and respected above Kings who were as much administrators as rulers. I could commiserate with the Maharaja of Bharatpur's desperation, as I knew the he needed money, not rooms. Over a period of several months, after exchanging telegrams, letters, offers, and counter-offers, the Maharaja lost his temper, and by that time the negotiations had broken down.

Before everything was finished we did have other adventures with the Maharaja. On one occasion the Maharaja invited Yamuna and me to a wedding in Delhi. The celebration took place in a sprawling backyard, gaily decorated with strings of colored lights, that led to a tent where the wedding couple sat. The Maharaja of Bharatpur was accompanied by the two queens we had met before. He sat close to and right behind the bride and groom and proceeded to get more and more intoxicated. He cracked jokes in their ears as the ceremony went on and was frankly obnoxious.

On another occasion the Maharaja invited us on a tour of the entire

Braja Bhumi Vrindavan area. He escorted us to many hidden and secret places with his fleet of Rolls Royce cars. We rode with him in the silver Rolls, imported from England. This vehicle had a wet bar in the back seat and a bubble-like protuberance on the roof to allow room for top hats. We arrived at one temple on a hill in the town of Dig, near the site where Conrad Rooks made his film *Siddhartha*. This temple also belonged to the Maharaja's family. The priest came out of the temple with a conciliatory, fawning demeanor. The Maharaja was chanting on his 108 pearl japa beads. Even though he refused to talk while he chanted, he still had to give orders. So he instructed his servants with gestures while he continued chanting. The priest then appealed to the king. The go-puja (cow worship) festival was coming soon, and would the Maharaja kindly donate some money for the festivities? Now that I had spent some time with the Maharaja I recognized the indications that he was about to erupt in anger.

His jaw became tight, his face red, and he folded his arms across his chest. With a spiteful look he held up one finger to indicate one rupee. His servant who dispensed money misunderstood and gave the priest a one-hundred rupee note instead. The Maharaja grew even angrier at this mistake. Because of his self-imposed silence, because he was chanting, the King refused to speak and was totally frustrated. His histrionics were actually humorous, but no one laughed out loud. When the Maharaja was finished with his chanting he abruptly ordered his soldiers to take the priest away, which they did, dragging him—his feet inscribing a path in the holy dust—down the hill, never to be seen again.

The King's entourage left the hill temple in the fleet of Rolls Royces to visit more holy spots. The monarch talked to us more about his family than about the spiritual significance of the place. "This temple has been in my family since 1894, and oh yes, by the bye, Krishna saved the town from Putana the witch here also." I didn't feel like talking, as I didn't know what to say. I have a hard time pretending to be content. I was also pretty concerned about what had happened to the pujari who had been dragged down the hill.

The rest of the tour was somewhat subdued. The despot tried to keep the small flames of conversation alive with his constant chatter, but the conversation flapped limply like a sail with no wind. The cherubic son, in his cute, high voice, asked his father, "Duddy, why did you take that man away?"

The King stuck out his chin and blurted, "I didn't like him."

"Krishna Will Provide"

As Prabhupada had promised more than one year before ("I will come myself and complete the purchase") in November 1971 he arrived in Vrindaban to try to save the situation. In the meantime I had arranged permission for up to sixty visiting ISKCON devotees to stay at Laxmi Rani Kunj Palace for our first annual Kartik pilgrimage. Shortly after some devotees had moved into the palace, the Maharaja of Bharatpur delivered a valuable silver-and-gold *jhulan* (swing) to Laxmi Rani Kunj, apparently as a gift for the Deities' enjoyment. The messenger, who arrived by jeep, presented a bill of sixty thousand rupees and wanted someone to sign for it. Achyutananda Swami met him and haughtily refused to sign anything. The agent of the King was perturbed and did not know what to do. Achyutananda forced him to take the swing back.

When Prabhupada, now in Vrindavan, heard of this, he became angry. He said to Achyutananda, "You have insulted the King, now he will not have anything to do with us." He went on, "It is considered a great dishonor to reject such a gift." Achyutananda was devastated and told Prabhupada that he would personally apologize to the Maharaja. Prabhupada replied, "It is too late." But Achyutananda was determined to rectify the situation. He tried to see the King, but the King's men refused his telephone calls.

Then Achyutananda asked me if I would talk with the Maharaja. He pleaded, "You have a nice rapport with him; please keep on trying." I agreed to try. But when the phone and telegraph messages did not go through, we decided to try to see him in Govardhan.

Achyutananda, Shyamasundar, Hayagriva, Yamuna, and I set out in a horse-drawn tonga to Mathura to find a taxi to take us to Govardhan. Suddenly, we found ourselves in the middle of a large crowd. The huge crowd was celebrating Durga Puja. I became caught up in the vortex of the festival, the fireworks, the pageantry, and the people. The intense humanity and atmosphere were so mesmerizing that I temporarily forgot our mission. When Shyamasundar discovered my interest in the event and noticed my hesitant gait, he guided me back to the group. Finally we found a turbaned Sikh driver to take us to Bharatpur Palace in Govardhan.

We arrived in front of the large palace gate and were met by the guards with fixed bayonets. Achyutananda said, "We want to see the Maharaja of Bharatpur."

They replied, "The Maharaja is not here, he is in Delhi." We didn't believe them, and they didn't believe themselves; they were bad liars, on purpose, to rub salt in our wounds.

Achyutananda said, "I am his guru, let me in!" That got us nowhere.

They finally let us into a large, outdoor compound, and the taxi went all of six feet before being stopped again by a gaggle of soldiers with guns. The Sikh driver got more and more nervous as Achyutananda, an American in sadhu's clothing, railed about the army. He didn't want to be caught in any crossfire and, for that matter, neither did I.

Just then, about fifty yards from us, we saw the silver Rolls Royce screeching out of another exit of the palace. The silver blur sped out onto the black line of the main road. We knew it was the Maharaja. We ran to the taxi and ordered the driver to follow that car: "Jaldi karo! [Hurry]". At first the driver didn't want to chase the King, but we offered him extra money. We told him we would take care of everything. The taxi was practically falling apart, but now that there were no guns around, the Sikh began to enjoy the adventure.

Just as we caught up to the Rolls and Hayagriva leaned out the window to yell to the Maharaja, the Rolls Royce sped ahead at comparative warp speed and left us in the dust. The silver car turned onto the main road to Delhi—and disappeared. Hayagriva (Professor Howard Wheeler) also wrote of this incident in his book *Vrindavan Days*.

The 1971 pilgrimage was over. We vacated the palace. The devotees dispersed to different parts of the world. Rejuvenated from the pilgrimage, they left with renewed excitement to continue their various transcendental activities. I felt bad though, that we were not able to get the palace for Krishna.

Prabhupada was right. Our good relations with the Maharaja of Bharatpur were over. Prabhupada quoted a proverb, "China dish once broken is hard to mend." Was I to blame for the breakdown in negotiations with the Maharaja? I tried my best, but our procurement of Laxmi Rani Kunj was not meant to be. I reasoned that Krishna did not want us to have Laxmi Rani Kunj Palace; as the Maharaja of Bharatpur was unstable, it might have been difficult to deal with him on a day-to-day basis.

I read from the *Bhagavad-gita* (3:19): "Without being attached to the fruits of activities, one should act as a matter of duty, for by working without attachment one attains the Supreme."

On this verse Prabhupada comments: "Action in Krishna consciousness is transcendental to the reactions of good and evil work. A Krishna conscious person has no attachment for the results but acts on the behalf of Krishna alone. He engages in all kinds of activities but is completely nonattached."

I went before Prabhupada and asked him if I could have done anything differently to obtain Laxmi Rani Kunj. Prabhupada looked kindly upon me and said, "You tried your best—who can ask for more?" He continued, "The Maharaja was a rascal, and he would not have been a reliable person to deal with. Also, there would have been so much repair work, so it is best for us to build our own temple in Vrindavan." He continued, "Krishna will provide."

Soon after, Krishna did provide.

> *"If you make a dog a king and then
> throw an old shoe, he will run and fetch it."*
> —A. C. Bhaktivedanta Swami

CIA

Untruths, rumors, and innuendoes sometimes arise when we make spiritual progress. During the early '70s, there were some popular rumors in India regarding the ISKCON devotees. People thought that the Western-born "Hare Krishnas" were drug-using hippies, and this untruth was perpetrated through a badly-made Hindi film called *Hare Krishna Hare Ram*. Children would mock us in the streets, singing the song from the film, "*Dum maro dum*, Hare Krishna Hare Ram." (This means, really, "smoke pot and chant Hare Krishna.")

One of the other rumors, also a lie, was that we were CIA agents. While traveling through many villages in India, I encountered so much hospitality, but one time I was met by pure hostility in a village near Govardhan. A group encircled my two companions and me, claiming that we were CIA agents. What a preposterous supposition this was, I thought. In all my previous underground activities and avant-garde thinking, I would never have imagined that someone would see me as a CIA agent!

In this village we were surrounded and angrily questioned. Some people came closer, prodding and jostling us, as if they were ready to attack. Others were shouting, "CIA! CIA!" The atmosphere was getting a little ugly.

I thought about Prabhupada in similar trying situations, as when he encountered crazy men in New York, San Francisco, and Bombay. He always remained calm and turned the situation into peace. I remembered "If you believe in something, try to convince others" and "Silence means affirmation—you must speak out if there is a misunderstanding" and "If you can teach someone a lesson by example, this is better than telling them."

I then stepped forward, and they gave me room. I held up my hand peacefully, with my palm turned out. I smiled at them and *pranamed* with folded hands. Speaking quietly I said, "We are bhaktas of Lord Krishna only. We only want to glorify your culture, not destroy it. I don't know any CIA men that chant sixteen rounds of japa each day. I do not hear of any CIA that get up during Brahma-muhurta (an hour and a half before sunrise). Besides," I continued, "if I were a CIA man, what would I want to steal from India—all of your machinery breaks!" They laughed with me. Then I held up and displayed an Indian-made pen that was leaking ink all over my hand.

I continued, "The only secret formula I want to steal from you is your wisdom about God consciousness—and your recipe for gulab jaman (rosewater sweets)."

They laughed again and began talking amongst themselves. The entire atmosphere changed. They pranamed, and some bowed.

Then the whole village came up to us, apologized, and slapped us on our backs. We led a group kirtan and retired to one of their houses as honored guests. They offered us prasadam and rest.

In Delhi I discussed this CIA issue with a high-ranking official in the Indian Government.

I had the good fortune to meet Umar Shankar Dixit, the Home Minister of India and chief advisor to Prime Minister Indira Gandhi. He was a wise, elderly gentleman who believed in getting to the matters at hand. We met at his house; the doves could be heard cooing in the bushes around his large yard. We sat on a screened verandah as the sun descended below the horizon. The lights were low, and so were our voices.

After some nice, philosophical discussions, I brought up the absurdity of the CIA rumors. I expressed how ridiculous these rumors were, for we were following tradition, living simply, chanting, and doing God's service. I also pointed out that we came from all backgrounds and that we are an international society, not just Americans.

Umar Shankar Dixit, being a frank man, laid his cards right on the table: "I know that you are not CIA agents, however the Government of India's stand is to neither dispel the rumors or encourage them. We have to remain a secular state." He continued, "We are afraid of you advancing too fast. Your food distribution program was so successful that it made our government look bad, but we will neither assist nor deter you."

I replied that I truly wished India would modify its secular state structure, as the great traditions were slowly being lost. He listened gravely. I continued, "I truly appreciate your honesty—your candor is very refreshing." We remained friends, and later he assisted me in importing ISKCON's books.

Covered in Flowers

Yamuna and I had been in Delhi and Vrindaban for nearly two months, and we were feeling great separation from our spiritual master, who was in Bombay. We heard that Prabhupada had been invited to Surat, in Gujarat State, for a week-long series of lectures and kirtans. By telegram Prabhupada confirmed that we should meet him there. Coincidentally, Tamal Krishna informed us from Calcutta that he was stopping in Vrindaban on his way to Surat and that after seeing the Holy Dham we could continue to Surat together.

When Tamal arrived at the goshalla we embraced warmly, as we had not seen each other for many months. "Show me Vrindavan," he said, soon after settling in at our rooms in Raman Reti.

We set out on the parikrama path. "This is where Krishna and Balarama played." We both bowed down in the white sands, covering our heads with the same sand touched by Krishna's lotus feet.

We turned right, following the wide path. "That is kusa grass," I informed Tamal, "the grass that sages make into mats to sit and meditate on." We saw the spires of Madana Mohan Temple in the distance, and I noticed that he was absorbed in the beauty of the five-hundred-year-old temple. "Madan Mohan was built at the request of Sanatan Goswami, one of the Six Goswamis, by a merchant named Krishna dasa Kapoor. This is the story: The Madan Mohan Deity, Krishna as a mischievous boy, requested from Sanatan Goswami an offering of bread and salt. Sanatan had neither of these items to offer, so he began to pray. Just then Krishna dasa Kapoor's boat, loaded with bread and salt, got stuck in a mud bank on the Yamuna River where the temple now stands. Sanatan requested the merchant to offer Madan Mohan some bread and salt, and as he did so the boat was freed from the mud. After selling the salt, the merchant came back and built this temple."

I took Tamal to the Darshan Mandap, another empty tabernacle. The caretaker recognized me, and he let us both pull water from the same well that Krishna had used as a boy, when he incarnated as a youth living with the devoted Sanatan Goswami. Tamal Krishna was in bliss. I showed him the Guru Granith Temple just behind the Radha Madana Mohan Temple, which contained sacred books and writings of the Six Goswamis and other great devotees. Two parrots perched near the entrance, making it even sweeter.

When we saw the Yamuna River we ran to it and swam and cooled off. There were some water buffaloes nearby, and, laughing, we watched children climb onto their backs and fall off, and then climb back on, holding onto their ears, and then fall off again into the holy water. Drying off on the riverbank, I applied twelve tilak markings to my body with Yamuna mud, and he did the same, following the custom of the local people. Tamal was beaming like a little kid. We sat back on our haunches, carefree, and watched the sacred waters flowing by.

A few days later we were in Surat. We took a ricksha from the train station to "Motorcycle Bhavan [Building]" and asked for our host, Mr. Jariwala. After a warm greeting, Mr. Jariwala guided us to the rooms where the other devotees were staying, and we had a joyful reunion with Shyamasundar, Kausalya, Giriraj, Dinanath, and the others. Prabhupada greeted us and asked for a report on our search for a temple site in Vrindavan. I relayed our progress.

The next day, we went out for street sankirtan. Banners and signs all over town announced our arrival. People rushed from their houses and threw garlands of flowers over us. There were about sixteen in the party, and we were garlanded up to our foreheads. I took some garlands off and threw them back to the crowd, but they offered more. People tossed flowers on us from balconies. It reminded me of demigods throwing rose petals on exalted beings. We were totally covered in flowers!

The Highest Transcendental Pleasure

After the breakdown of the Laxmi Rani Kunj Palace negotiations, in March of 1972 Prabhupada requested that I travel to Vrindavan with him to decide our next step in founding a temple there. A Mr. Saraf had expressed the possibility of donating a parcel of land to Prabhupada.

I was awaiting Prabhupada's arrival in New Delhi's Palam Airport. He had asked me to arrange a car to take us to Vrindavan. He had said, "Vrindavan doesn't mean buying a ticket. It is an attitude, a way of accepting the special mercy of the dhama." I had been to Vrindavan before, but this time Prabhupada was not only arranging the journey, he was taking me through the gate himself. I thought to myself that if I could choose the highest transcendental pleasure, of all the endless choices available, that highest transcendental wish would be to be with Prabhupada in Vrindavan. The purest devotee and the purest place were now combined, and my transcendental desire was fulfilled.

Only Tejiyas and I were there to greet Prabhupada. Still, he accepted our garlands, sandalwood, and rose water with a grace that made us bashful. The driver of the Ambassador car arrived. Prabhupada handed me his small, white satchel that held the basic documents of our Movement: important papers, bank books, current reports, letters, etc. Shyamasundar, who was traveling with him, opened the car door, and Prabhupada slid into the front seat slowly and rhythmically. Shyamasundar climbed into the back seat, and I sat beside him. We waved good-bye to Tejiyas and zoomed out of the airport onto the road to Kosi Kalan and Agra. I awaited Prabhupada's words; he said nothing.

Shyamasundar and I were like two school kids, exchanging whispered news of devotees and activities around the world. We talked in low, subdued voices so we wouldn't disturb Prabhupada. Minutes seemed like hours as I waited for transcendental words, some instruction, some acknowledgment; but Prabhupada was silent.

Actually, I didn't need acknowledgment. I was his disciple, and it was Prabhupada's mood that always determined our own. Even silence was comfortable. Whenever I came into his room, for example, I waited for Prabhupada to establish the mood. I didn't push myself. If Prabhupada wanted to joke, I joked; if he wanted to chastise, I bowed my head remorsefully; if he wanted to talk business, I talked business; if he wanted to talk philosophy, I listened and asked questions. "No questions?" he sometimes said. "Then you must know all the answers." Yet on the way to Vrindavan I anticipated some divine instruction, some words of wisdom, a sloka (spiritual verse), anything, as he sat relaxed in the front seat.

At a stoplight, an Indian version of a biker rolled up beside the car. Prabhupada turned his head slightly and said, "Hare Krishna." The young, greasy-haired youth responded with "Hare Krishna" and started talking animatedly to his friends in Hindi. They jabbered back and by Prabhupada's grace transformed into Gandharvas and innocents who gave us a royal motorcade escort for a few miles before speeding off. We still hoped for Prabhupada's words as he chanted quietly. We were in the country now. Suddenly Prabhupada's authoritative voice, a honey-like gravel sound, broke the silence.

"Cement," he said.

Everything I'd read in those romantic spiritual books about perfumed saints and do-nothing sadhus vanished like bubbles in the air. "Cement," he said again. "We need lots of cement to build something like that." He pointed to a large water tower by the side of the road. "We should build one like that in Vrindavan." I smiled; Prabhupada had taught me another lesson: the practical application of devotion.

The Ringmaster

By Srimati Radharani's grace, we were on the way to finalize arrangements to acquire a piece of land in Raman Reti, even though others were competing for the same piece of property. Prabhupada had persevered, even after promises were broken by kings and businessmen.

When we arrived in Vrindavan, his ever-bright eyes became brighter. We were staying at the home of Mr. Saraf, the donor of the land in Raman Reti. We set up camp on the top floor, which consisted of six small, side rooms off a large, central hall. Prabhupada took a middle room as would a field general. He had a foreknowledge of what was to occur the next day.

Prabhupada's godbrother Krishna dasa Babaji appeared, and they greeted each other warmly. Krishna dasa Babaji knew without notice when Prabhupada arrived in Vrindavan. More godbrothers, officials, and goswamis arrived to greet Prabhupada, summoned by some mysterious means like silent animals gliding out of jungle thickets.

Prabhupada requested Shyamasundar and me to invite Mr. Saraf into his room, and all together we arranged for the ground-breaking ceremony for the

Krishna-Balarama Temple. An agent for one Shyama devi, who wanted the same piece of land that we were planning to build on, waited in another room. He was accompanied by the police and a retired member of parliament he'd brought with him. After speaking with Mr. Saraf, Prabhupada went to speak to the agent, and as he appeased him he also convinced him that Shyama devi's hopes for getting the land were in vain.

They left just as the two goswamis Madan Mohan and Gourachand arrived simultaneously from the Radha Damodar Temple. Even though they lived a courtyard apart, they hadn't spoken to each other for years. Gourachand Goswami, who was practically blind, was led by his son Panchu. Prabhupada sprang up again. He greeted one Goswami and put him in a room and had me greet the other and put him in a separate room. One by one Prabhupada went in the rooms and finalized arrangements for his rooms at Radha Damodar.

Meanwhile, Shyamasundar drew up the final agreements for the Raman Reti property. Prabhupada went from room to room and signed two agreements with three parties within two minutes. Each now took Prabhupada to be an ally. More godbrothers and old friends arrived. He fed them prasadam in his room. He was like a great ringmaster in a celestial circus, with a dancing bear in one ring, a tightrope act in another, clowns in another, and lions in another. He tamed and charmed us all.

> *"You can buy a ticket to Vrindavan,*
> *but God is not loitering in Loi Bazaar."*
> —A. C. Bhaktivedanta Swami

"Guard These with Your Life!"

The Radha Damodar Temple was built in A.D.1542 under the direction of Rupa Goswami, who later asked Jiva Goswami to oversee the seva (service) to the Deities. In the *pravesh mandap* was a cowherd-boy's flute, an imprint of Krishna's foot and a cow's hoof in a flat rock, and a Govardhan sila (a rock Deity from Govardhan Hill). This sila was given to Sri Sanatan Goswami when he was elderly so he could worship in Vrindaban instead of having to go to Govardhan Hill. In the courtyard are the samadhis (tombs) of Rupa Goswami, Jiva Goswami, Krishna dasa Kaviraj, and Sri Bhugarbha Goswami. On the other side of the temple is the bhajan kutir of Rupa Goswami.

For many years prior to his going to the West, Srila Prabhupada had lived in two rooms at Radha Damodar Temple, and while he was abroad he never failed to send the goswamis who ran the temple his monthly rent to keep the rooms.

After settling the Raman Reti land with Mr. Saraf, Prabhupada was getting ready to leave Vrindavan. We were sitting together at the Radha Damodar Temple. He took out two large, copper-brown, hand-beaten metal keys on an old piece of string. "Guard these with your life—I shall tell you what to do with them later." I tied the keys inside my bead bag, where I knew they would always be with me.

A few months passed. Then Prabhupada gave me his instructions regarding the keys. "These are keys to my rooms in Radha Damodar Temple. Go into my rooms and clean them. Take all the items inside the rooms. Save the necessary and burn the rest. Look for the Gita Jnana in Bengali; they are hand-written in composition books. This is very important."

I did not want to undertake such an important assignment alone, so I asked my two trusted friends to cooperate with me on this matter. Yamuna and Giriraj watched as I very respectfully, very carefully, very much in ecstasy, put the old key into the large lock. A lot of time had elapsed since the lock had been opened. The key was stuck at first, but I persisted, and the key slowly turned, and the lock sprang open. We entered the room. Prabhupada's cot was there. I looked for and found the Gita Jnana in several school composition books, hand-written in Bengali and wrapped in cloth. I kept them safe. Among the other items were small account books, pens, spectacles (two pairs), a penknife, chemistry beakers, and test tubes. There were also some handwritten articles for *Back to Godhead*, *Truth or Beauty*, advertisements for the first three volumes of *Srimad-Bhagavatam*, blank typing paper (Indian-style double-page), advertisements for De's pain liniment, a one-by-three-foot, cardboard poster for De's pain liniment with a drawing of Prabhupada as Mr. De. There were also lists of all the maladies De's pain liniment could heal. More early *Back to Godheads* were piled up on one of the walls, as well as some subscription forms. The original charter plan for the League of Devotees was there, along with membership lists and bookstore addresses in Delhi. Also included were original letters to Mahatma Gandhi, Lal Bhadri Shastri, Pandit Nehru, and others. As you can imagine, the burning pile was very small and the keeping pile was huge!

Gaurachand Goswami

Prabhupada asked me to contractually secure his rooms at the Radha Damodar Temple and to negotiate with Madan Mohan Goswami to lease an additional two rooms and a patio upstairs. Madan Mohan Goswami was in the line of Jiva Goswami. He was nice and somewhat sensitive but a lonely man. Prabhupada suggested that I treat him like a father, which I did, and eventually he allowed us to live in the rooms.

The Gaurachand family was in the same line of Jiva Goswami, and they were caretakers of Radha Damodar Temple. Gaurachand, who did the basic job of puja with his two sons, was a loud, blustery jokester and a comic caricature of himself, the opposite of Madan Mohan Goswami. Pot-bellied and unself-conscious, he blatantly smoked bidi cigarettes on a woven-rope cot out on the small verandah of his rooms, adjacent to the main courtyard. He had very bad cataracts on his eyes, and as he could see only vague blurs, he would stare straight ahead with bulging frog-eyes and yell orders to his wife and sons. He was always friendly to me, and invited me to eat with his family regularly. When I invited them, they politely refused because any Westerner, including myself, was not a Brahmin in their eyes. Nevertheless, I would secretly feed the youngest boy, three years old, who enjoyed visiting me often. I would wipe his mouth clean before he returned to his house across the compound.

Once, in the course of his circumambulating the temple, one of my godbrothers took Gaurachand's pack of cigarettes and hid it from him. Gaurachand felt around for them under the blanket of his cot, thought a moment, then felt around the floor. No bidis. He yelled, "Pancu, Pancu!" and his eldest son appeared. A discussion in Bengali ensued so loudly all of Vrindavan could hear.

One day Prabhupada asked me what I thought of Gaurachand. I replied that he was a rascal, but he had a good heart, and I liked him. I said further, "He has always been kind to me, and I think he respects and likes you too."

Prabhupada said, "Yes, that is my feeling too. He has invited us to dinner—he specifically asked for you—and we can attend. You may arrange."

So I informed Gaurachand, who was so happy that we were accepting his invitation to dinner that he yelled it out loudly. Staring through his coke-bottle glasses in my direction, he again yelled out so loudly how happy he was that we were coming that all his neighbors behind and on either side could hear him, as could Jiva Goswami, Rupa Goswami, and all the monkeys, donkeys and parrots in Vrindaban!

Two days later, at around twelve thirty, Srila Prabhupada, Dr. Kapoor, Shyamasundar, and I arrived. The family was standing, waiting for us. They greeted us warmly. Animated laughter and Bengali conversations ensued, and Gaurachand motioned for us all to sit. There were banana leaves placed on the freshly swept and cleaned porch. Gaurachand's cot was brought into the house. Bengali delicacies were served, including some of Prabhupada's favorite preparations, like shukta, stuffed portals, and bitter melon fried in mustard oil. Prabhupada was relishing the food so much that he leaned on his left arm, which he did only when he really enjoyed the prasadam. I too was relishing it when suddenly a partially-eaten burfi (sweet) slid onto my plate, placed there by Prabhupada's divine lotus hand. I quickly scooped up the maha-mahaprasadam and ate it. Then another bit of maha mahaprasadam, an already-tasted pakora, slid onto my plate. I was ecstatic.

After he finished eating, the near-blind Gaurachand sneaked behind the wooden door to his rooms and lit up a bidi cigarette. That is, he thought he was behind the door—actually he was still on our side of the door. He was bent over with a sneaky look on his face, just like a child hiding. The look of stealth was so evident that it was comical. Smoke billowed. I tapped Srila Prabhupada, who was still engrossed in prasadam, and pointed to Gaurachand. Prabhupada and I couldn't help but laugh out loud. Shyamasundar and Dr. Kapoor noticed Gaurachand, and they started laughing too.

At that point Gaurachand realized he was being observed, went red with embarrassment, and blustered out, "Radhe Shyam!" He also yelled, "Govinda!" Pretending to be spiritual, he shouted out the holy names to cover his embarrassment. This is the power of the holy names. Not only can they take away our foibles, but they can wash away our offenses as well.

Prabhupada's Sacred Rooms

I had to go to the law courts in Mathura to legalize the renting of the two upstairs rooms and patio at Radha Damodar. The ride to Mathura could take an hour or more if I went by horse-drawn tonga, about two hours or so if I took a bicycle ricksha, and seven hours if I walked. Another option was the meter-gauge rail train that left from Vrindavan twice a day at 6:45 A.M. and 5:10 P.M. (thirty-five minutes).

The Mathura law courts did most of their actual business outside in a large, rectangular "courtyard" the size of a football field. There was an interior courtroom, but depositions and documents were all typed outdoors by clerks and solicitors dressed in trousers and black coats with shiny elbows. They worked at small desks with old Royal typewriters, and they stacked rocks on the documents to save them from flying away in the breeze.

Prabhupada enlightened me in two letters about the nuances and intrigues being crafted by the two Goswami families who controlled Radha Damodar Temple.

Los Angeles
11 May, 1973

My dear Gurudas,

    Please accept my blessings. Herewith please find the letter I have replied to Madana Mohan Goswami in response to his letter dated 4/5/73.

    He refers to your letter dated 26/3/73, which I do not possess. So you send me a copy of your letter as well as a copy of the letter which I issued to him in 1972 when I was in Vrindaban. This man is playing some trick, so we shall also play some trick. We shall take all the Shaivites to court and pray to the court to settle the matter.

He has mentioned that you are the licensee, but according to the present act the licensee shall be considered as tenant or owner if the licensee has occupied the building or land in February 1973. I think we shall keep this place at Radha Damodara Temple as tenant. As Madan Mohan Goswami is trying to play trick we shall not vacate any of the rooms upstairs or downstairs; this should be our policy.

The deposit money of Rs. 700/- with the other Shaivite has not yet been settled up. We shall file a petition to the rent controller court and fix up a standard rent for all the four rooms up and down. And the rent which will be fixed up for the upper two rooms, we will adjust for one years rent from the Rs. 700/- with interest. When you file the petition we shall bring in all their names. In this way we have to deal with these men.

Hoping this meets you in good health.

Your ever well wisher,
A. C. Bhaktivedanta Swami

Los Angeles
14 May, 1973

My Dear Gurudas,

Please accept my blessings. I am in due receipt of your letter dated 6/5/73. I have noted the contents carefully.

I have already sent you one letter dated May 11, 1973 as well as a copy of a letter sent to Madan Mohan Goswami by registered post that same day. I trust you have received that letter by now and you are proceeding as per my instructions therein.

First of all ask Gaurachand Goswami that he is taking the money on account of two rooms occupied by me, now Madan Mohan Goswami has asked us to vacate, so clearly understand from him what is our position. Whether he is going to accept the money continually or does not like to accept it. So on hearing this statement, if he says that he'll not accept and we must vacate, then it is to be understood that all the Shaivites have combined together to evict us. Then we'll have to take the matter to the rent controller court as I have already advised in my previous letter.

In India, we have got experience, there are so many cheaters. So be very carefully of them and do everything carefully, keeping in touch with all the senior members and do the needful.

I am advised by my Calcutta physician that I should go back to India. So I am returning and will reach in Calcutta sometime next week. Ananda Pandu wanted to stay with me, so if he likes he can come to Mayapur where I shall stay. Offer him my dandabats.

ACBS

As always, Prabhupada knew all the facets of the situation, and he taught me how to deal with them carefully and in a businesslike manner. Prabhupada's guidance through letters was essential, and we were able to meet the challenge together via the post from afar. One of the relationships with the guru is called vani, which is the awareness of your guru's presence even from afar. Vani is also the feeling of separation from one's guru. This longing to be with your guru in physical form is analogous to the gopis' feelings of separation from Krishna.

After presenting our case in many visits to the courtrooms of Mathura, the matter was settled out of court as Prabhupada had predicted. The two Goswamis did not want to go to court in Mathura, as they were already burdened by the litigation they were forcing on each other. Prabhupada thought that the filing of the case alone would prompt them to settle. Thus was I able, by Prabhupada's and Krishna's grace, to secure the rooms at Radha Damodar Temple for life.

All this litigation took some time, however, and meanwhile Prabhupada had arranged with Madana Mohan Goswami that some ISKCON devotees could live upstairs at Radha Damodar, overlooking the courtyard and Seva Kunj Road. In keeping with Prabhupada's courtroom strategy, I moved out of his original downstairs rooms, and these were locked and sealed. You could see in through cracks in the door or windows, but the rooms remained obviously dark and unused. Five other devotees from the United States and England joined me in living upstairs, and we bathed in the benedicting rays of Radha Damodar while preparing for Prabhupada's arrival in October of 1972, when he delivered his famous Nectar of Devotion lectures in the temple compound of Rupa and Jiva Goswami.

Years later, Prabhupada wrote some other ideas regarding the Radha Damodar rooms.

Mayapur
18 February, 1977

To Gurudas,

I have received your letter dated Feb. 12, and examined the contents. Please accept my blessings. About the locks on the door, ask Gaurachand to help. I have just arranged to send him Rs. 50 per month for his lifetime, and he will cooperate with us.

If you like to stay in my rooms at Radha Damodara then you may stay there. I allow it. Preaching also means reading and writing, or else what will you preach?

If I do go to Manipur I still plan to go to Vrindavan afterward. My schedule is being planned as leaving for Manipur on the 8th March and staying utmost a week say until the 15th. So as the festival program in Vrindavan runs through the 22nd March, I will still be there during the festival.

N.B. You say you are on good terms with Madan Mohan Goswami. Under the circumstances take the whole house on rent from him. Although he is appealing to the court it will not stand. Better while the litigation goes on let him take money from us and let out the whole house to us. That will be his own gain. Whatever the court decides for the time being he can rent from us for the whole house. If you can induce him it is gain for him. Rent should be at the same rent as present.

And in another letter Prabhupada wrote the following.

Bombay
25 March, 1977

My dear Gurudas,

Please accept my blessings. I beg to acknowledge receipt of your letter dated 18th March, 1977.

There is no need to pay Gaurachand. I have already advised the bank, and they will pay him directly. You need not. As you have described the placing of my photograph and offering to it prasadam, that is good. In my room at Radha Damodara Temple you should keep one photo of me and offer to it prasadam of Sri Radha Damodara.

In consultation with Aksayananda Maharaja, just find out some responsible men to stay there. Everything should be kept neat and clean as if I am staying there. It is very good if someone daily sells books from there.

Thank you, yes, I am feeling a little stronger now. On the 28th instant I shall be moving into my new quarters and then we have to organize Bombay as our world headquarters from every point of view,

culturally, scientifically, philosophically, etc.
I hope this meets you well.

Your ever well-wisher,
A. C. Bhaktivedanta Swami

BE INDEPENDENT

In the upper rooms of the Radha Damodar Temple I saw Prabhupada washing his dhoti in a bucket of water. I said, "Prabhupada, I would be happy to wash your cloth for you."

He replied: "I can wash my own cloth, and in that way I can remain independent." He continued, "I shall teach you to roll a chapati with a bottle—just bring me one bottle." I fetched a bottle, and Prabhupada taught me to roll a chapati with the bottle. Then he said, "But I don't even require the bottle," and he proceeded to teach me how to flatten the dough into a perfectly round chapati with only his hands.

Yet another time, I saw Srila Prabhupada down on his hands and knees washing the floor. When he looked up and saw me, he said, "Be as independent as possible."

THE MONKEYS OF VRINDAVAN

The trees, rocks, plants, and animals in Vrindavan are said to be great, devotional souls. Monkeys permeate life in Vrindavan in a very personal way. Living among the trees and rooftops in Vrindavan village, they cause merriment and excitement. They hang on the electricity wires until the lights go out. They take your food when you aren't looking. They kidnap passports and bead bags from devotees and ransom them for bananas or other food. During Krishna's earthly pastimes they lived at Seva Kunj and danced with Radha and Krishna on the full-moon night.

One day, a little baby monkey fell through the bars of Radha Damodar Temple's upstairs room where Srila Prabhupada was living. Screaming from the separation from her baby, the mother monkey was trying to get through the steel bars. Very carefully Prabhupada picked up the little monkey and, with his lotus palms, gave the baby back to the thankful mother. After that incident the mother came to the window every day looking for Prabhupada.

BRAHMINICAL ETIQUETTE

Besides general etiquette like washing hands, eating with the right hand, not stepping over people, and so forth, Prabhupada taught me the intricate nuances of brahminical ways. "Some do not consider you Brahmins, and some do. Invite Brahmins to dinner—and if they accept, they consider you a Brahmin; if they refuse, they do not." On another occasion, regarding real hospitality, he said, "You don't know you've been invited until you are washing your hands after the meal."

Preach to Devotees

I was asked by many of the traveling parties to preach outside of Vrindavan. But Srila Prabhupada wanted me to stay in Vrindavan, and I also wanted to stay there myself. However, one time I asked him, "They want me to preach outside, on tour. What should I do?"

"Preach to devotees," he said.

This was a strong realization for me. Too often after their initiation we take the new devotees for granted. Prabhupada added, "Devotees need to hear preaching." So I took my duties as president in Vrindavan more seriously and gave more attention to the precious devotees living inside the temples.

Kalpavriksha Trees

One day, as Srila Prabhupada was holding court in his rooms, someone was expressing frustration about not getting what they wanted. Prabhupada told this story.

One time, a woodcutter was walking to the forest to chop some wood. As the trees near his village were cut down, he had to walk a long distance to cut wood. When at last he reached the forest, he was tired from the long walk. He sat under a tree, mopped his brow, and said out loud, "I am so tired I wish the wood would chop itself." To the woodcutter's amazement and pleasure, the trees segmented into neatly chopped piles. The woodcutter looked at the piles, scratched the back of his head, and said out loud, "If only the wood would go to my house, so I wouldn't have to carry it so far." The cut wood began hopping towards the cutter's home. The woodcutter realized that he was sitting underneath a *kalpavriksha* tree. He thought, "I am so hungry from all my wishing, I will wish a feast." Anything that came into his mind thus manifested: sweets, savories, subjis, puris, rice, and so on. After gorging himself he thought, "Oh, it is now late at night, and I am lost in the forest. What if a tiger should come and eat me!"

"*GRRRRRR*," a tiger appeared and ate the woodcutter. Prabhupada growled and shook his fists in the air like two transcendental paws.

There are ten-thousand-times-ten-thousand kalpavriksha ("wish-giving" or "desire") trees in Vrindavan. Many of these kalpavriksha trees in Vrindavan gave me shelter and insight. I sometimes visited a special tree in Seva Kunj, a tamala tree where Radha and Krishna danced.

Whenever I had a hard administrative decision to make during the construction of the Krishna Balarama Temple and needed further help than I could glean from my own mind, I would go to a small temple down an alley near the Yamuna River. I would sit under the kalpavriksha tree where Krishna conversed with Radharani. When I opened myself up and listened carefully, wisdom came from within. I came away refreshed, my thoughts clear on how to serve my spiritual master.

Cow Dung

One beautiful morning in Vrindavan, Prabhupada, a few other devotees, and I were walking on the parikrama path in Raman Reti. We passed by two large, intertwined, black-and-white trees. These two trees are Radha and Krishna combined, according to the Brijbasis who live in Vrindavan. We continued walking along the beaten-down Vrindavan clay of the parikrama path, watching the swallows, chipmunks, and squirrels as they ate and played in harmony in Krishna and Balarama's playground.

Suddenly I spied some cow dung! In an attempt to impress Prabhupada, I recounted one of his purports and said, "There are less flies around cow dung than around human dung. Cow dung is pure—"

He cut me off and quipped, "Oh, you have done research?"

Everyone laughed, including me, especially when they saw Prabhupada's amused face and joking manner.

Krishna's Mercy

Another time, when I asked Prabhupada about Krishna's mercy, he imitated Krishna and poked me three times in the belly, saying, "Take my mercy, take, take."

> *"Lord Chaitanya says one must*
> *remain a fool before his spiritual master."*
> —A. C. Bhaktivedanta Swami

Transcendental Mood

One day Prabhupada appeared to be ill and was less communicative than usual. Other devotees noticed this too. By the third day we began to be concerned. Prabhupada called me in to discuss some Vrindavan program that had been arranged. I meekly asked, "How do you feel? Will you be attending?"

He said: "Yes. They think I am sick, but I am in transcendental mood."

Listen

"Have you had darshan of Govindaji?" Prabhupada asked Shyamasundar.

"Huh?" Shyamasundar answered.

"You have not heard this term, '*ji*?'"

"No."

"Gurudas, do you know this?"

"Yes," I said. "It is like you end a word with 'ji' to indicate respect for a person. 'Govinda-ji' is a term of respect and affection for the Deity."

"Yes." He continued looking at me. "I want you to invite my godbrothers to our program. Go find Yuk. . . ." I never heard that name before.

Prabhupada's words sounded like "Yuk Chuk Maharaja." Though I had never heard the name I didn't want to appear stupid, especially after he had just corrected Shyamasundar. I would rely on faith, as usual, and go out and look for "Yuk Chuk Maharaja." As an afterthought, or because he was reading my mind, Prabhupada said, "He is near Banki Bihariji Temple."

"Yes, Srila Prabhupada," I said. I went in front of Banki Bihari Temple and asked a passerby, "Do you know where Yuk Chuk Maharaja is?" The second person knew and took me to the alleyway next to the temple. After I knocked, the door was opened and I walked into a cool dark foyer. I saw pictures of Bhaktisiddhanta Saraswati, Prabhupada's Guru Maharaja, and even one photo of Srila Prabhupada when he was secretary of Gaudiya Math and still called Abhay Charan De. I knew then that I was in the right place.

Building the Krishna Balarama Temple

So by Krishna's grace, a nice parcel of land was donated to ISKCON as a site for temple construction. The land was situated in Raman Reti (Enjoyable Sands), outside of Vrindavan's market area. Here, Krishna and his older brother Balarama played as children. Prabhupada put me in charge of the building project.

The Raman Reti land was longer than it was wide. We planned a temple, a guesthouse, a school, and a cow protection area. With renewed excitement I put all my consciousness, sweat, some blood, and many tears into the construction of the Krishna Balarama Mandir.

To start, because of my loyalty to Srila Prabhupada, I was forced to become an enemy to my friend since London, Shyama devi. Shyama devi was a well-known guru of sorts with a large following both in India and the U.K. She too wanted the Raman Reti land, which was one street away from her main Vrindaban temple.

Mr. Saraf, the owner and donor of the land, knew and respected both Prabhupada and Shyama devi, hence he was put into a great conflict and was not sure what to do. So, just as other people do when they become confused in Vrindaban, he decided to put the matter into the hands of Srimati Radharani. Mr. Saraf made up two slips of paper, one with a mark indicating the land and one slip of paper with nothing on it. Sitting at Radharani's lotus feet, he thought of Shyama devi and picked up one slip of paper: blank! He thought of Prabhupada, selected a chit: the land! Thus he chose for our side by the grace of Ksirodakasayi Vishnu, sitting in his heart. Shyama devi was disappointed and angry with this decision. Later she tried to sabotage our project by leaving inauspicious things such as dead animals at the construction site.

Meanwhile, Surabha das and I went around contacting architects, requesting them to design the temple plan. A Mr. Johari, an architect in Delhi, agreed to draw a plan. Time passed, but there was no plan. We weren't paying these architects, so they put our project on the back burner. More time elapsed. Finally, the architect submitted an uninspired square box of a temple, with no arches, windows, or courtyards. We would have to come up with our own temple plan! Prabhupada wrote that we should base our plans on a temple in Vrindaban named Radha Gopala.

I walked over to the Radha Gopala Temple, a beautiful structure. Its openness, height, and sense of space overcame me when I stood in the courtyard, which was bordered on three sides with steps that led to a sitting porch. On the fourth side more steps led to a large Darshan Mandap (platform before the main altar), crowned by the Deities of Radha Gopala. I wondered to myself, "Here I am building a temple; what do I know about building? I had an Erector Set as a kid, I built a small, flower-pot wheelbarrow in wood shop, but this temple is a gigantic project!" I reflected that Krishna and Prabhupada would give me the strength to accomplish this daunting task. Prabhupada would direct me by post and chaitya guru would guide me from within. Nor was I alone, for there were others working with me: Yamuna, Murtidas, Gunarnava from England, and Surabha das.

Surabha was from Holland, and he was an accomplished furniture designer and had an architectural background. Together we viewed the Radha Gopala Temple, the wind racing around us. The breeze was refreshing in the airy courtyard. We would build a temple like this one, and Surabh would draw up our blueprints!

At first he deviated slightly from the plan, but then Prabhupada corrected the drawings so that they were more like his original idea. I was relieved because I argued often with Surabh about keeping to Prabhupada's original plan. The finalized plans were made into blueprints in New Delhi, and I then had to go to Mathura to get the zoning permissions. Conscious of the snail's pace of the bureaucracy in India, I was used to letting the system just drag along, especially concerning my visa renewals. Prabhupada, however, wanted this temple to be built quickly, so this called for special attentiveness and haste on my part. This temple was in Vrindaban; it had to be a jewel, or as Prabhupada said, "the center of our Movement."

I had to deal with permits for building, getting cement, and other construction-related matters, so I rode the tonga to Mathura many, many times. Each time was different; each step provoked some unforeseen and novel delay. I had to ease my way through the approval of our building permit. First, I had to submit our plans, then our intentions. Then they lost our files; then they found them again; then the man who could approve our blueprints was out of station. There were strikes, holidays, and work stoppages. Then all the civil courts took a recess. Totally exasperating!

Then one day I went to the civil offices in Mathura. In a long yard outside the courtrooms were rows of desks: I had reached the final stage of the journey after so many small steps. Nesting there were the lawyers in their usual black coats, worn at the elbows. Young paralegals sat at small tables lined up next to each other. In front of the tables, signs indicated their names and services. On each desk were legal papers and perhaps a small reference book or a briefcase. Rickety, old typewriters churned out submissions for permits, depositions, drafts, and legal documents of every description. These papers were all typed for a fee outdoors in the wind, in the dust, under the bird droppings. Small stones were the paperweights which held down life-and-death situations and decisions for many cases.

Now, after the many trips to Mathura, I waited outside with the solicitors. (I would much rather have been by the banks of the Yamuna River chanting!) Finally, once they saw that no bribes were being offered, and after the plans were again temporarily lost, the proper authorities passed our submitted plans and gave us permission to build our temple.

Prabhupada sent me a bank draft for 300,000 rupees on the Punjab National Bank, our basic funds to continue the temple building project. He asked us to spend the funds wisely and carefully, which I did to the best of my ability. I compared prices and services and got receipts for everything.

At that time India was heavily socialized, so I had to travel to New Delhi again and again to get permits for cement, which was distributed by sanction of the government. A movie-theater complex in Delhi had just been given approval for the last bags of cement in the government quota. Even though our friend, Mr. Dalmia, was going to donate the first ton of cement to us, we needed a permit. I had to go see the Minister of Interior for India to get this simple permit. Try that in the United States! I appealed to the Minister's spiritual side. "We want to build a temple glorifying your culture and tradition, and you want to give the cement for a cinema. A cinema will import Western culture, and not always the highest examples of Western culture." I received the necessary permits.

We had Surabha's plans, and we had all the permissions. Next we had to find a good structural engineer, one who could read the blueprints and who knew about proper building materials. We interviewed four different engineers. Two came from Mathura, and they just seemed too lethargic, too dull. One Mr. Dubai from Vrindaban was a self-effacing man, who hung his head in humility. He was so self-effacing that he effaced himself out of a job. He later became our friend and an assistant engineer for a while. After a day of deliberations we picked a Mr. Sarkar, who thought he was Leonardo Da Vinci or maybe the famous magician, P. C. Sarkar.

(Pardon my digression but this reminds me of a story Srila Prabhupada told me once. The original P. C. Sarkar was one of the most famous magicians in the world. He was very clever and entertaining. He was also an escape artist, and performed prestidigitation tricks that no one else could do.

Once P. C. Sarkar was asked to perform for the Viceroy of India, representing the King and Queen of England, at 8:00 P.M. The guests arrived at the Viceroy's mansion, but there was no P. C. Sarkar. After about ten minutes, people started looking at their watches. Someone asked what time it was. Each person called out a slightly different time, according to their individual watch. Then, about twenty minutes after eight o' clock, P. C. Sarkar walked on stage. The Viceroy arose and shouted out, "What is the meaning of this—to keep us all waiting? You were supposed to begin at eight o'clock!"

P. C. Sarkar stated calmly, "But, my dear sirs, it is eight o'clock."

Everyone looked at their timepieces, and they all showed exactly eight o'clock. But I diverge. . . .)

Mr. Sarkar, our new engineer, looked over the structural drawings. The grounds were measured, and the temple building and the guesthouse behind were marked off. The temple was divided into three sections: an entrance area, a courtyard with raised sides all around, and a darshan mandap leading to a raised altar with three segments. One segment was for Radha Krishna and two Gopis, Lalita and Visaka, one for Lord Chaitanya and the Pancha Tattwa, and the center section was for Krishna and Balarama. Yamuna and I planned the storage space and kitchens behind the altar. We made sure the entrance doors were large enough, and in the walls we placed lots of rings and hooks for hanging Deity clothes, etc. We planned built-in compartments for paraphernalia and storage. Two kitchens were designed, one for the Deities and one for the general population of devotees and guests. The guesthouse had a plan of eighty rooms, a kitchen, a restaurant, a lobby, and reception area. Each room had a balcony and an indoor bathroom. The construction and daily devotional activities were going on nicely.

Suddenly, however, I was called away.

Calcutta Pandal

A telegram arrived in Vrindavan from Tamal Krishna. It was handwritten, as is done in Vrindavan, and read, "Dear Gurudas. Come immediately. Need you to oversee Calcutta Pandal. Tamal ODs."

I recalled from my past that OD meant "overdosed." I thought, "You can't OD on the Holy Name; it must mean 'Tamal OKs.'" (As telegrams in Vrindaban were handwritten, one could not always understand what they said. One time a man came running up to me in the street waving a telegram in my face. He asked frantically, "What does this say?" I looked at the telegram, but I couldn't make out the first word. It said ". . . left." The man then said, "If it's my sister, it means she is on her way to visit, but if it is my mother, it means she has died. What to do?" I told him to go to the telegraph office, next to the phone company and the police station, and to find the man that wrote the telegram and ask him. The man hurried off in the direction of the telegraph office.)

So now I was being summoned to Calcutta!

I took the train, and I arrived there the day before the pandal program. This was the first Calcutta pandal program, and it was to be held at Chowrangi, in the middle of Calcutta. I went to see Prabhupada, but Tamal Krishna intercepted me before I could reach Prabhupada's room.

Tamal said frantically, "The program starts tomorrow! Nothing is done. There is no one overseeing the building of the pandal. The laborers are there. Can you oversee the building of the tent and stage? You're the only one who can do it!"

"Sure," I answered, "I'll go there, but first I want to pay my obeisances to Prabhupada."

Tamal said, "There's no time!"

"There's always time to see Prabhupada," I answered. "I will go to the site immediately after darshan."

He acquiesced, knowing I would go anyway. Prabhupada's door was open, and I bowed down. He was sitting on the floor. He looked up and greeted me.

"You are here from Vrindavan?"

"Yes, Srila Prabhupada—Tamal Krishna has requested me to help with the pandal program." I didn't tell him of the urgency, as I didn't want to tax him in any way.

"What is the report from Vrindavan?" he inquired.

"The building is going on; the foundation is laid, and the pillars are going up."

"Very good," he said, "Is there enough cement?"

"Yes, we have 200 bags in our go-down [storage]."

"Have you eaten prasadam?" he asked.

"Not yet, I just arrived," I said.

"Go and take prasadam," he said kindly.

"Yes, Srila Prabhupada." It felt so good seeing Prabhupada again that my travel fatigue vanished. I felt inspired and energized just being in his presence. My Krishna consciousness was to do whatever pleased him, whether it be overseeing the pandal or obtaining visas. At Prabhupada's order I ate prasadam, and then I took a ricksha to Chowrangi Field, near the Victoria Monument.

As I entered the large field there was no tent, no work going on, no movement except for the occasional body-twitch from one of the workers asleep on the ground. A few of the tent poles were up, and that was it.

I approached the workers and greeted them swiftly and confidently. The foreman, a guy named Nirmal, came up to me and started telling me all the problems they were having.

"How large do you want the tent?" he asked.

"We must have room for at least six hundred people to sit here." I paced off a general area. "Spaces for special seats here, about one hundred people. And the stage can be roughly here."

I took my directions from a rough-drawn plan Tamal had given me, based on the Bombay and Delhi pandal programs. All the problems were soon sorted out, except that the building materials needed to complete the job had not yet arrived. "Can we telephone the supplier?" I asked. Nirmal told me that he had word that the materials were on the way. I looked to the skies and chanted Hare Krishna Hare Krishna.

"In the meantime," I said, "let us work with the materials we have, so when the other supplies arrive something will be done." Nirmal agreed to this plan.

"We will build the pandal first, and then the stage." Nirmal picked up on my enthusiasm and started yelling orders to the workers. Suddenly there was a lot of activity: poles were going up everywhere.

"We must complete this before tomorrow," I told Nirmal.

He said, "Do not worry."

Yeah, right; I had heard this story before here in India. However, time was different here, and maybe something would get done at an appointed time; and then again, maybe not. Just then, trucks rolled onto the field with the rest of the wood, rope, bamboo, tables, chairs, etc.

I walked around the site again, imagining where the stage, kitchen, and prasadam areas were to be set up. I also had to think of chairs for life members, book tables, sound system, porta-potties. I worked with everyone for an hour or so, unloading materials, dragging some *dhurrie* (carpet-like coverings) around, setting up a table, and generally helping out. I thought that if the workers saw me willing to work, they would work harder. Once everything was underway and running smoothly I sat down, watched, and chanted. We stayed up working through the night, and the next morning when I went to the temple the work was still going on.

I washed, had breakfast prasadam, and talked with Tamal and Jaya Pataka Prabhus about the state of the pandal. I suggested that as many devotees as possible come down to the site to help set up. They answered, "We are all going down there now."

So we returned in force. The stage was finished, carpets were laid out on the ground. The kitchen was built, and devotees like Kausaliya started to arrange the pots, fire area, grills for chapatis, and so on. People had already been gathering and watching and wandering around since noon.

By that evening, when the program was to begin, many people were arriving while the last bits of the pandal tent were still being erected. Nobody complained, for this was India. As it turned out, it was Krishna's grace that the tent was not finished yet, because at least eight hundred people showed up, and we had to enlarge the tent by extending it at the back.

I washed and changed into clean dhoti and chaddar and went up on the stage, where the rest of the devotees were already sitting. I bowed down to the Deities. I next checked the sound system and the sturdiness of Prabhupada's vyasasana chair. I sat behind some of the other devotees and chanted japa before my mind could be flooded with some other small detail still undone.

Prabhupada entered with a few others, came up to the stage, sat down, and looked around, surveying the whole scene. Then I heard a loud and disturbing noise to the right of the front entrance where the VIP seats were located. A sign there declared: "Special Guest Seats—One Rupee."

Some Communists were complaining that these seats were selling for one rupee and thus separating rich from poor. Colonel Dutta, an ex-military man who once commanded Fort William Henry in Calcutta, approached the protestors wearing jungle fatigues and hat. This temporarily stopped anyone from rushing into the seats. But they were getting louder. One devotee came up to me. "Prabhupada wants to see you," he said. I went up to the stage, bowed down, and waited.

"What is that disturbance?" Prabhupada asked.

"There are some Communists complaining about the one-rupee seats—they say it is separating the rich from the poor."

Prabhupada thought about this and replied, "The idea of the seats was to allow the elderly Life Members and special guests some facility to sit comfortably. Anyone who might not want to sit on the ground could sit on seats."

I asked Prabhupada what to do about the rowdy Communists. My ear was near him to hear over the commotion, and he said, "Let them sit in the seats."

I went off the stage and invited the discontents to sit in the seats, and they did, as eight hundred others sat contentedly on the carpets covering the ground.

We were finally ready to begin. Prabhupada calmed the objecting Communists further by singing the Brahma-samhita prayers. Peace soon prevailed, and I went back up on the stage to sit to the left of Prabhupada.

Pishima

At the Calcutta pandal program, Prabhupada's wonderful younger sister, Pishima, sat with the devotees up on the stage. Pishima was a very compassionate soul, and her face looked a lot like Prabhupada's face, though her girth was about double. She became my friend and was extremely sincere, kind, soft, and often smiling. She was sitting at the left front of the stage. She also had a personal following of her own, as well as many friends. Oblivious to the fact that Prabhupada was about to begin the program, ignoring the hundreds of other people present, her followers were touching Pishima's feet and making sounds of excitement. Prabhupada called me over and asked, "What is that sound?"

"It is your sister, Pishima—people are showing her respect."

"Ask them to stop; we are ready to begin the program."

Tactfully but firmly I requested that they take their seats. With Pishima's assistance the clamor subsided. I went over to Prabhupada and said, "The noise has stopped; we can begin."

Prabhupada motioned for me to come closer. He whispered mischievously, "I used to quiet her, and I still shall." Then he laughed and began the festivities with kirtan.

Another time Prabhupada told me how he and his sister would fly kites as children. Prabhupada laughed as he remembered that Pishima could get her kite to fly higher by yelling, "Govinda! Govinda!"

Tarun Kanti Ghosh

The Calcutta program was well received, and many praised our singing, dancing, lectures, prasadam, and books. As in Delhi, chief guests came, including Tarun Kanti Ghosh, the minister of tourism for West Bengal. He came from the family that publishes the famous Calcutta newspaper *Ananda Bazaar Patrika*. He always carried a small *Gita* with him and was very influential in India.

Tarun Kanti had a great sense of humor and liked to tease me sometimes. Sometimes, however, he could be a bit superficial. One time he told me he wanted to build a "Disneyland" in India. I scolded him, "There is so much tradition in India—why not make a theme park with Lord Krishna, Laxmi Narayan, and Lord Chaitanya? Instead of fictional, mythical characters you could build dioramas, with the traditional scriptural stories of India, and small parks with virtuous philosophical themes."

Tarun Kanti started crying. He said, "I am rejecting my tradition, and you are accepting it."

The opening ceremonies at Mayapur were soon going to take place, and I wanted Tarun Kanti to be a chief guest at our program. The date was two and a half months away. Certainly my early invitation would give him enough time to put our pandal date into his busy schedule.

"We would like you to attend our function in Mayapur, as you did at our program in Calcutta."

"When is it?" he asked.

When I told him the date, he reacted strangely. "I cannot attend." He closed his hands into fists and punched them together. I was puzzled, and asked why. Again, he punched his fists together and said, "WAR." Sure enough, two-and-a-half months later war broke out with Pakistan.

The Indian government claimed that Pakistan started the war.

> *"A clenched fist cannot shake hands."*
> —Indira Gandhi

Dethroned

Entering his room in the Calcutta temple, which was next to a lake, I found Prabhupada sitting on the floor. "They have dethroned me," he laughed.

"Who, Srila Prabhupada?" I asked.

"The mosquitoes. But I am fooling them. I am sitting on the ground, because they rise to the ceiling." He etched a spiral into the air with his golden fingers fluttering upwards.

After a pause, I asked, "Are there mosquitoes in Krishnaloka?"

He paused ever so briefly and replied, "Even if there are mosquitoes there, they don't bite; they sing."

BACK TO BRAJA

The Calcutta pandal program was a great success, but it was time to return to my beloved Vrindaban to continue helping to build our Krishna Balarama Mandir.

There was a mother owl with five baby owls living in a tree on the Krishna Balarama site. We humans had to build our own houses. Four adobe huts with straw roofs were built: one for Ananda, the cook, one for myself, and another for Yamuna. A fourth hut was for Surabha, the architect, and Murtidas. Gunarnarva and several other brahmacharis also squeezed into the fourth hut. Together we all oversaw the building of the temple.

Large mounds of dirt unearthed for the foundation and used in the cement mixtures dotted the land. A makeshift kitchen and dining area was built in another hut at the south end of the property in front of the guesthouse foundation. We were very fortunate to be in association with a great devotee like Ananda. He was always energetic and jolly. Prabhupada, in a letter regarding Ananda, wrote, "I am very glad to know that Ananda Prabhu is staying with you. Please offer my dandabats. He is my old godbrother and sincere Vaishnava. Please treat him like your father. Do remain in full cooperation. ACBS"

Ananda Prabhu made wonderful prasadam from practically nothing. He picked olive-like fruits from trees and found many vegetables in the wild grasses growing nearby. In many ways, he was like another father to our project. Even though he did not speak English, he was always in an uplifting mood and was a steadying influence on me. The Gaudiya Math came to me often to see if I would give permission for Ananda Prabhu to cook for one of their feast days. When this did not conflict with our plans, I granted the request out of respect and friendship.

A bedraggled dog came coughing up to me one day. He was very skinny and couldn't walk straight. He expelled asthmatic sounds with each step. I felt sorry for him and fed him prasadam. At first Ananda didn't want him around, but he kept coming. Soon Ananda and the others adopted him too. I named him "Dogwood," and he became part of our dining group, which included from three to ten human devotees, "Dogwood," and numerous chipmunks, squirrels, sparrows, and starlings.

One fine Vrindaban morning I decided to feed a peacock that seemed curious about our presence in Raman Reti. I sat cross-legged with some grains. I threw some seeds and grains in front of me, and the peacock came closer. I threw more grains nearer to me, and the peacock followed the trail. Then I held my hands out with grains in them. Very shyly, the peacock came closer and, finally after about a half hour of my patience, he came up to my outstretched hands and pecked out the grains, backed away, saw that it was safe, then came back and ate again. We repeated this ritual daily. As the days floated by the peacock became less afraid and came over whenever he saw me.

Gypsy women, clothed in bright, red-and-yellow, flowing dresses and loose, blue, silk blouses, carried the bricks for our temple on their heads for six rupees a day. They traveled with the construction crews and lived and slept on the site. They wore many silver and ivory bangles all the way up their arms: this was their wealth—and bank. They wouldn't trust their money to a banking institution. To wear your wealth was the old, traditional way of the simple village castes. Prabhupada told me that before banks were established people converted their wealth to bangles. (I once met a couple who had liquidated their factories in India when the Government was nationalizing factories; they converted their assets into gold and bejeweled bangles and went to Iran, sold the bangles, and opened up factories in Tehran.)

Thus the daily life slowly revolved around this Krishna Balarama construction site, which was like a village within a village. We were a group of various personalities, all with different aims and goals, serving together for whatever reasons to build a glorious, wonderful temple, like none other in Vrindaban.

Following are a series of instructions from Prabhupada to me regarding the Vrindaban construction. The letters speak for themselves and show Prabhupada's acute attention to detail and organization.

BOMBAY

19 December, 1972
Vrindavan

My dear Gurudas and Yamuna,

Please accept my blessings. I am in due receipt of your several letters dated November 30 and December 12, 1972, and I have noted the contents with care. I am most pleased to learn from you that the work in Vrindavan is going on very nicely, and that you are both happy in Krishna consciousness. That is the main thing. Of course, I know that you are not trained up for being construction managers, neither that job must be very much tasteful to you, but because you are sincere devotees of Krishna, He is giving you all strength and intelligence how to do it. That is wanted, that is advancement in Krishna consciousness. Not that I must have a very nice place, I must serve like this or like that, otherwise I shall go away. No, Vaishnava devotee means give me simply a place to lay down, little prasadam, whatever little service you have got please give me, that's all. Thank you very much for taking up this difficult work to help me in this way.

Now you are requesting money for supplies, that's all right, but I have not seen the accounts for the money you have spent to date. That you should also supply. But I think Mr. Sarkar is inspired to cooperate with us, and he is very expert, so I do not worry on that account. But record of expenditures must be there, that is standard procedure. I was informed that the party of Yasodanandana and Mahamsa will forward all collections to Vrindavan, but I do not know if they have done it. Mahamsa is coming to Bombay in a few days time and I shall request him to do immediately. We have completed our pandal program of Hare Krishna Festival in Ahmedabad and it was very, very successful. On the last night the huge pandal was filled completely, at least 10,000 or 15,000 attendance. So far Yasodanandana's party, I have just got one letter from them and they shall remain at the following address for one month more: (Secretary's addenda).

In Mayapur they are also requiring about Rs. 50,000 monthly for the work, and for that they are managing with traveling party and temple collection of Calcutta. So you collect from Delhi and spend, and for the rest these other parties will send. I have got report that Yasodanandana has collected more than Rs. 20,000 for Vrindavan, so you have not to worry about anything. But you must keep accurate accounts how it is spent and send me. So far Surabh is concerned, I have left him at Hyderabad to design our temple there on the land donated for that purpose in the busiest marketplace of central Hyderabad city. But if you invite him to come there from time to time, I have no objection.

If you can finish the work by Janmastami next, that will be a very great credit for you, and I shall come there from any part of the world just to install the Deity. But now you must work very, very hard to make good your promise to me, otherwise I shall be very disappointed and become very, very angry upon you. You may purchase Deity from Mayapur-Vrindavan Trust Fund, about that I shall inform you later. One thing is, I have received report that Tejiyas is having difficulty in

Delhi because no men are there to assist him. Delhi is the cultural capital of India, but we have not yet done very much to develop in Delhi. Tejiyas is very sincere and hardworking boy, so we must encourage him. So I have asked Tamala Krishna and Shyamasundar to find some men to go there, and they will do the needful. There are so many intelligent boys and girls in Delhi, that I have marked, and I think there is more potential there than other places in India, so if you and Yamuna go to Delhi from time to time to help Tejiyas with the preaching work, especially preaching to the student class of young persons, that will be nice. If there is shortage of men, we must recruit some men, first-class men, to help us do the work. If that is attempted sincerely, this preaching work, Krishna will provide men to help us. Krishna does not like to see His men suffer or become frustrated and depressed on His behalf, no. If we remain always faithful to Him, working very hard despite all difficulties, very quickly you will meet Krishna face to face, you may know it for certain.

Another thing is, I have heard there is no more CCP for getting our books. But now we are holding a huge pandal festival in the Cross Maidan at Bombay, from January 12th to 21st, so we shall need to take our BTG shipment from the Bombay docks, but they will not allow without CCP. So I hope by now you have got it, and if not, try for it immediately, treat it as urgent matter. And if Yamuna wants to come for that festival here, she may come here for a few days to lead kirtan before my lectures, then return. But I think that Gurudas may have to stay for the work, or if there is opportunity, he may also come, but the work must not be jeopardized. Hoping this meets you both in good health.

Your ever well-wisher,
A. C. Bhaktivedanta Swami

Bombay Pandal

The work was going on at Krishna Balarama Mandir, and competent men were overseeing the construction, so at Madhudvisa's request I traveled to Bombay to help out with the Cross Maidan pandal program.

Prabhupada was keen on pandal programs to help raise funds and educate the public. We had had some success in Calcutta, and from that event I had especially learned from Prabhupada how to invite chief guests and how to set up a kitchen on site in order to provide free prasadam for thousands of people every day.

When I arrived in Bombay we still had to build a kitchen and stage, build booths, set up bathrooms, and install a sound system. To help in the advertising I made a poster in the form of an Indian telegram, with the message of the program, dates, where, and what posted on the telegram. The poster attracted attention because everyone in the world pays attention to messages on telegrams. At first I thought of using a rupee format but decided that that was inappropriate, a little too gross.

When the pandal program started I was busy every moment, but still I always greeted guests. One musician from the Lower East Side of New York, Burton Green, who knew Prabhupada from the Bowery days and who had once given a jazz concert that Prabhupada attended, participated for a few days.

A particularly unkempt person showed up, looking like one of the many sadhu-hippies then traveling in India. I took him by the hand and fed him prasadam. Later on, the young mendicant told me he hadn't eaten for three days. A few days into the program I saw my searching hippie friend waiting in the line for lunch prasadam. As he was looking alone and thoughtful, I sat down next to him and asked him what was wrong. He told me that he had decided to stay since the devotees were so kind to him, and that he was sleeping under the stage. "I was waiting in line for almost two hours. When I got to the serving table, someone called me away to help them. Then they didn't need my help, and the prasadam was gone." I took him to the kitchen and arranged some prasadam for him. Later on I met him again at a reunion party in 1994 at Amekhala and Smarahari's house in London, and he retold the story—as Radhanath Goswami.

Delay

When I returned to Vrindavan I encountered many challenges. It was discovered that Mr. Sarkar was taking kickback money from the cement dealers. Not only did he make a profit by charging us more than the rate, but he added salt to the wound by ordering more cement for the foundation than we needed. I had to fire Mr. Sarkar, and it wasn't easy for me. He was a rogue, a charming one, but he had to go. Prabhupada supported me in a letter: "So far as Mr. Sarkar, our engineer, is concerned, if he becomes too much of a disturbance then you may dismiss him." When I let him go we were temporarily left without an engineer, but we soon found another structural engineer in Mathura who turned out to be all right.

The work continued and, gradually, *tor* (reinforced) steel strengthened the symmetrical pillars that arose out of the foundation. Brick walls filled in the gaps. Limestone plaster and white marble slabs covered the bricks.

Soon the courtyard also took shape. The classic black-and-white tile designs were placed in the floor. Stairs flowed up from the yard to the sitting areas on the sides and to the altar area in front. Marble was laid in the entry hall (*pravash mandap*). A grand, high, wooden door was fitted. The work was progressing nicely as brick cutters, laborers, marble workers, and masons worked sometimes late into the night.

Then, suddenly, the work stopped again. It was harvest time in the workers' villages. Without notice, all the workers left the construction site to pick the harvest in their parents' villages. Was this an act of God? When I questioned the foreman, he was simply reticent. The foreman told me, "They'll be back." But when? He did not know. Two weeks later the workers trickled back.

To complicate matters, there was another cement shortage. The work was held up again. I went to Delhi, and through our friend, Mr. Dalmia, I was able to arrange for more cement to be sent directly to Vrindaban. I had to send six brahmacharis to accompany the trucks. I remember that when the three trucks rolled into our site in the middle of the night, we all cheered and came running.

All of us, myself included, were working day and night to rush the temple completion.

Meanwhile Prabhupada continued to instruct me by letters.

Bombay
31 December, 1972

My dear Gurudas and Yamuna,

Please accept my blessings. Your letters of December 23, 1972, are in hand, along with the very nice photos of the Vrindavan work, as well as the balance sheet and account of materials and supplies. I am very, very pleased to see the photos how the construction is progressing very rapidly under your expert supervision. It appears that at last something is being done solid work. Now you have promised me that it will be completed by Janmastami next, therefore I am completely relying upon you to fulfill your promise to me. Of course, you will have to go quickly before the monsoon by June, but I think by that time there will be sufficient roof to keep everything dry from the rains. If you can construct nice temple in Vrindaban for me in this way, I shall be eternally grateful. Because we are a worldwide movement of Krishna, and if we do not have any nice place at Vrindaban, then what will be the use? Vrindaban is Krishna's land, and in future so many of our disciples will go there just to see, along with many tourists and other friends, so therefore we must have sufficient place for them. That will be our great contribution.

Now, some of our men have met with the Maharaja of Bharatapur here in Bombay, he sent his men to fetch us, and in a bitter mood he requested us immediately to return his idols of silver Radha and Krishna. So let us return them to him, we do not want any ill feeling to be against us. So you may return those Deities to him at earliest opportunity, either at Delhi or at Govardhan. He also has requested his book. I do not know which book that is, but he said that Acyutananda has it and he wants it back without delay, so return him.

Regarding the Deity at Vrindavan, Malati has just now returned from Jaipur, and she has found out one very nice murti of Radha and Krishna more than five feet tall. I want these Deities shall be installed in Vrindaban, so Yamuna may make arrangement to go there and see if they are available, what is the cost, and make all program how they shall be transported to Vrindaban, like that. I think these will be just suitable for our Vrindaban temple, and they will save us time also. You may order the Balarama Deity to be made also by this Murtiwalla. I think Malati has written you one letter in this connection. And if she gets time, then Yamuna may come also for few days to Bombay pandal, being on this side.

I have inspected the trial balance carefully. Of course I do not know what are the prices and so many other things, but I find one discrepancy which you may please make clear to me. The opening bank balance on December 2 is Rs. 7870.50 and for the month of December I find you have deposited twice, on twelfth instant, one sum of Rs. 2630.00 and Rs. 111.00. So the total come to Rs. 10611.50. So far expenditures are there, there is one check drawn on the 5th instant for Rs. 600, one check drawn on the 12th instant for electrical supplies for Rs. 45, one check drawn on the 14th instant for supplies of Rs. 4665.51, and on the 15th instant one check has been drawn for Rs. 3571.26. Subtracting the expenditures of Rs. 8881.77 from the total bank balance including deposits, or Rs. 10611.50, it comes to Rs. 1727.73 as final balance in bank. But you have declared that your figure for final balance in bank is Rs. 1643.79. That means, according to the figures you have given me, there is discrepancy of about Rs. 85.94. Of course, there may be some bank charges, like that, I do not know, or you may have omitted some mention of any other check, but you may inform me why our figures have come out differently.

Hoping this meets you in good health.

Your ever well-wisher,
A. C. Bhaktivedanta Swami

Sydney 18 February, 1973

My dear Gurudas,

    Please accept my blessings. I am in due receipt of your letter dated February 6th, and have noted the contents carefully. My heart has become very joyful upon seeing the progress in Vrindaban construction. When this Vrindaban Temple is completed, it will be a great boon to our Krishna consciousness Movement and devotees from all over the world will come to see Krishna and Balarama. I am very pleased also to see that you are keeping such an orderly account, and as far as further financing is concerned I have arranged with Karandhara das, and he is sending 5,000 copies of *Bhagavad-gita As It Is* to India, and Kartikeya Mahadevia in Bombay, one of our life members, has agreed to distribute 3,000 of these *Gita* at no less than 50 rupees apiece. So that is one and a half lakhs, and I am sending one letter to Kartikeya, informing him that all money collected for these *Gita* should be sent on to you in Vrindaban, and it is up to you along with the other GBC men in India to arrange the sale of the balance of these 2,000 *Bhagavad-gita*s and I think this will provide the necessary finances. I will be traveling here in Australia for a few weeks then I will be returning to Calcutta by March 2nd. So when I return to India we may discuss this matter in more detail. But in the meantime you should work with the senior men there in India to get some concrete plan to finance this program. I have sent you the books and it is up to you to devise a program for distribution.

    You may also discuss together the question of whether a pandal program in Delhi will detract from our collection of funds for the Vrindaban program. I do not think this will be the case, but it seems the collection field will increase with the pandal program. But you please discuss it with the senior men there in India, and then you may send me your joint decision for approval. I hope this meets you in good health.

                      Your ever well-wisher,
                        A. C. Bhaktivedanta Swami

    Prabhupada was pressuring me to have the entire Krishna Balarama Temple completed by Janmastami, 1973. A lot of work was left undone. Money was trickling in, but cement rations stop when a river dries up; construction grinds to a halt when it's harvest time in the nearby villages and the workers just walk off. There were many preparations to be made for the upcoming inauguration of the Krishna Balarama Temple. I went ahead with the plans, even though the temple was still in the construction phase. There were invitations to send, brahmanas to invite, godbrothers and godsisters to feed, elephants to rent, Deity paraphernalia to purchase—and Prabhupada's house to finish.

The deadline came—and went. We simply could not finish everything in time....

Paramahamsa on Lufthansa

Prabhupada was coming to Vrindaban to help us!

When Prabhupada arrived we were all gathered in the front area, dancing happily as he got out of the car and looked around at the incomplete site. The half-completed building and construction site was dotted by large mounds of earth. Prabhupada's quarters had been painted only the day before. His desk table was built especially to his liking, low, and wide enough for water, papers, pens, his dictaphone, and a dish and water for his tilak. We had stained it just one hour before and were fanning it dry with cardboard manila files! The last wet drop of varnish dried literally fifteen seconds before Prabhupada entered the room. We bowed down, and he sat on the cushion behind the desk. We all watched and hoped that his kurta didn't stick to the desk.

"So, Gurudas, what is the news?"

"We are all working hard to complete the temple Srila Prabhupada, but right now there is a shortage of cement, and the workers have gone to their villages for harvest. The Deities are finished, and I have made out the guest list, which I would like you to look over and add anybody—"

"Do you think the temple can be completed nicely very soon?" Srila Prabhupada interrupted.

After a slight hesitation, Yamuna, Surabha, and then I, the eternal optimist, said, "No."

Prabhupada was silent in thought. "We do not want to have a second-class opening; no, it must be *pukka* [first class]. We may open on a later date? What do you think?"

We all agreed that would be better. I was relieved, yet I felt some people were blaming me for the delays, even though I knew there were many ingredients to mold together and I was doing the best I could, working eighteen hours a day. Prabhupada, in consultation with us, decided that the planned date was too soon, and he postponed the opening for another six months.

Prabhupada said, "Do things collectively. We will discuss more tomorrow; now you can take rest." That was his kind way of letting it go for the time being. We bowed down, and as we left Prabhupada's rooms, we were silent with mutual bewilderment, relief, and guilt.

*"Anything you want Krishna will give,
but not perhaps the way we want."*
—A. C. Bhaktivedanta Swami

I Could Set My Watch

Even though I was busy, Prabhupada's example inspired my Krishna consciousness. In the midst of the construction chaos he remained calm and always kept to his schedule. He was always able to chant his rounds and stay regulated wherever he was.

The Krishna Balarama Temple was almost complete. The House of the Lord was adorned with rich colors, scrolled marble shapes, and *jali* windows. Going on the morning walks continued to be a joy and a special time for me, a time when Prabhupada was relaxed and inclined towards intimate talks.

Wherever he happened to be in the world, Prabhupada took his walk at the same time every morning. I remember in Vrindavan we would walk out from the Krishna Balarama Temple construction site, turn right, and head toward the parikrama path. Every morning at 6:03, when we reached a crossroad, a sadhu crossed our path. I looked at my watch when we crossed paths, and if it didn't say 6:03 A.M. I would reset my watch. Eventually, Prabhupada and the sadhu greeted each other every morning.

"Regulation is the preventative of disease"
—A. C. Bhaktivedanta Swami

Shoot Over Their Heads

The purnima, or full moon, effulgence filtered into my hut, and I could not sleep. I got up and checked around the building site. The *chowkidhar* (gate guard) was fast asleep at the gate. I woke him up, as recently some thieves had come in and stolen some tools. The man was useless as a chowkidhar, but I had great respect for him as a former cook for the Radha-Shyamasundar Temple. I woke him up and asked, "Where is your danda [stick]?"

He answered, "Maharaja, I have hidden my stick because the thieves may come and beat me with it." I asked him if he would please return to his duties in the kitchen.

Someone wondered if we should buy a gun to protect the site from thieves. We put it before Prabhupada. He thought briefly and answered, "Yes, you can get a gun, but don't hit anyone. Just shoot over their heads; that will scare them." He illustrated the concept with a story.

Narada Muni had a disciple who was a snake. The snake had been so impressed with Narada Muni and the sound of his *veena* (musical instrument) that he had asked to be made a Vaishnava. One time some neighborhood children were getting revenge for the snake having frightened them in the past. They were cruel. They threw rocks at him and called him names. The snake was sad and consulted his guru, Narada Muni. "What should I do?" he asked. "The children are throwing rocks at me and calling me unkind things."

Narada answered, "It is due to some of your past karma. Now you are a Vaishnava, but you are also a snake—so raise your hoods, but don't bite."

Prabhupada imitated the snake, cupping his hands like a cobra's hood. He made a fierce face: "So," he said, "shoot over their heads!"

> *"We are not against bad men;*
> *we want to change them into good men."*
> —A. C. Bhaktivedanta Swami

Damn Cheap Babu

During the building of the Krishna Balarama Temple, we were engaged in a lot of purchasing, hiring, and accounting. I learned how to bargain, to partially hold back some salaries, and, of course, to account for everything. Still, when some of the devotees had assembled, Prabhupada observed how we Westerners were always being cheated in India. Inventing a fictitious vendor named "Damn Cheap Babu," Prabhupada imitated us, saying, "That's damn cheap, babu, damn cheap."

Prabhupada's Dolls

Winter 1974, and another pilgrimage time arrived in Vrindavan. I was always happy to welcome old and new devotee friends coming to the holy dhama to bask in the mercy of Radharani. This was the third season of pilgrimages to Vrindaban, and Yamuna and I and the others were always trying to improve these pilgrimages for the many prabhus coming from all over the world.

We planned the prasadam menus and hired cooks. I planned workshops that would enable devotees with similar services to have meetings. For example, the treasurers could meet treasurers, medina players could share rhythms and beats with other medina players, and cooks could meet cooks. These workshops were to be interspersed with parikramas (circumambulating) and darshans (receiving blessings) at the many holy spots, tirthas, forests, and temples in Braja Bhumi, ending with a bath in a sacred ghat (pool) every day.

The difference this year was that Srila Prabhupada was in Vrindavan too, the star attraction! I put the workshop idea before him. His countenance brightened, and he said, "This is a very good idea. Do you have a list of the workshops?" I handed him the list I had made and, as Prabhupada looked it over, he remarked, "But there are no doll-making workshops."

As always, I thought, Prabhupada can find the missing link and add one more thing that I missed! His concentration is so sharp. I have seen His Divine Grace look through documents, rooms—and hearts and souls—and always find the missing ingredient, then quietly and matter-of-factly suggest the perfect addition or resolution.

That year we also had to arrange extra sleeping quarters in Fogel Ashram, a few hundred yards down Bhaktivedanta Marg from our Raman Reti Temple construction site, as more than three hundred godbrothers and godsisters were expected! Many of these devotees were staying for a few days and then going on to Mayapur for the Governing Body Commission (GBC) meetings. Having attended quite a few of these meetings myself, and noting their combative nature, I thought of the meetings in Mayapur as "the maya wars." So I stayed in Vrindavan where I thought my service would be more useful.

Soon devotees arrived from all over the world. After settling in and spending a few days visiting the main temples, the workshop idea was implemented, and devotees began to share their experience and wisdom. The workshops were well attended. Prabhupada agreed, "The workshops are a good idea; otherwise they will come here and eat and sleep and gossip."

Here are some of Srila Prabhupada's written comments regarding my suggestions.

... Your suggestion that the devotees visiting Vrindavan engage in preaching and chanting and not in gossiping is very good. I have instructed that this be taken to the GBC and implemented. We have sacrificed our life for Krishna's service, where is there scope for sleeping and gossiping? You can see in my example, not a single moment is wasted. This idleness is the business of the karmis. They can be seen sitting in the park gossiping, "my son-in-law said this," "this man has cheated me." But it has no place in devotional service, so your suggestion is well made.

Your suggestion for groups teaching practical subjects, like book distribution and Deity worship, is also good. These things are wanted.

The installing of telex communications for our main temples is not required. Then they will gossip more through the telex.

So if you apply yourself in helping to prepare and implement

these suggestions for the Vrindavan portion of our festival, that will be very good. Hoping this meets you in good health.
Your ever well-wisher,
A. C. Bhaktivedanta Swami

"Enthusiasm is the backbone of Krishna consciousness."
—A. C. Bhaktivedanta Swami

Krishna Balarama Mandir Inauguration

Once the completion deadline for Janmastami 1973 had been lifted by Srila Prabhupada, we were no longer in such a rush, and we had time to plan and complete the construction properly. Pillars surrounded by scaffolding began to give the temple shape, combining beauty with strength. When the marble arrived from Makrana, the marble cutters showed up. They shaped and carved patterns into the sandstone, jali windows. The wall coverings were carved by hand, an art practiced by only a few artisans in the whole world today. The craftsmen also rounded off and cut shapes in the bricks to form the ornate front entrance. The darshan mandap was covered in special marble from Makrana. Steps rose, the courtyard was roped off and paved, and the bricks began to show the temple structure. The Krishna Balarama Temple was rising quickly and beautifully. Prabhupada oversaw everything, both in person and by letters. Now, two years later, Janmastami 1975, we were finally ready to send out invitations for our grand inaugural festivities.

We invited the obligatory pandit and our Goswami friends from Vrindavan. The best rasa-lila (dramatic dance) company was included in the opening program, and many devotees were invited to attend from all over the globe.

Finally the day of the inauguration arrived. As always there were last-minute arrangements, reversing of problems, and repairs to be attended to. I tried to be everywhere all at once. I helped raise a shelf in the Deity room; I checked the kitchen and helped carry in some fruit. The cooks were preparing a feast for two-hundred-and-fifty guests. Other devotees were mopping and sweeping, and I encouraged and praised them. The pujaris, under Yamuna's direction, were dressing the eight different Deities. I sent someone to check on the rasa dance performers: They were on the way. A book table was placed in the front entrance, manned by Vishal Prabhu. I rounded up any spare devotees with a bullhorn. "Dogwood" came running, as he thought it was time for lunch.

Devotional bhajan singers sat on one side and played harmonium, tamboura, kartalas, and medina drums. The obligatory Vrindavan Brahmins ar-

"Art means full belly."

rived for the opening prayers. Prabhupada and I discussed whether or not the traditional opening ceremonies should be consecrated by local Brahmins. We didn't think we needed them and could do the prayers ourselves, but we acquiesced to the Brahmins so as not to ruffle any local feathers. Vrindavan was, after all, a small village. I sat the Brahmins and pandits in an area for special guests. Some government officials arrived from Vrindavan, Mathura, Lucknow and New Delhi. I greeted them and escorted them to their special, roped-off seats.

The inauguration ceremony began. I was organizing things but had a camera around my neck too. The Brahmins sang the prayers of blessing. Prabhupada led the opening kirtan and spoke some introductory words of welcome. I briefly welcomed everyone. The chief guests spoke.

The rasa dancers performed beautiful pastimes of Radha and Krishna. One of the young rasa players stared right at me. The young boy who played Krishna was looking for me and noticed me standing in the courtyard. I hid behind the Tamal tree, and then I reappeared. There, "Krishna" saw me again. Then I hid behind a pillar, and then I became visible again. This game we were playing was like the hide-and-seek games the cowherd boys played with Lord Krishna. An indescribable phenomenon is present in these rasa-lila plays in Vrindavan. It is said that as the actor dresses in costume, the actor becomes Lord Krishna during the performances.

People swoon and throw money at "Krishna" and treat the actor as a Deity. Was I playing hide-and-seek with Krishna?

The ISKCON gurukula school kids also put on a play. Then the feast was served. Everyone was in a good mood. After the opening, our Krishna Balarama Temple became one of the most visited temples by pilgrims in Vrindavan.

Art Means Full Belly

The place Nandagaon, where Krishna's father lived, is a few kilometers from Vrindavan. One day Prabhupada and I were walking around Nandagaon, looking at some beautiful Krishna-lila paintings on the walls of the main temple there.

Prabhupada said, "Art means full belly." He continued, "People must be well-fed before they can appreciate [the luxury of] art. Similarly, we must feed them before they can appreciate the value of Krishna consciousness."

Baby Kishori

Holding court on his cushions, Prabhupada lay back relaxed as he talked to us. Suddenly, a baby named Kishori rushed at Prabhupada and smacked into the cushion right next to him. He patted her lightly with his hand and she rolled over and giggled. Prabhupada's eyes lit up, and he continued to pat her. Baby Kishori got up, ran back five steps, and rushed the cushions again, and Prabhupada patted her again. They played this game repeatedly, much to my delight.

Twenty minutes of this game passed, and I started to wonder when the game would end. Kishori was like a golden retriever with a ball. After many minutes elapsed, baby Kishori sat down contentedly by Prabhupada's side, laughing lightly to herself.

A baby named Kishori rushed at Prabhupada and smacked into the cushion right next to him.

"Children don't feel austerities, they can manufacture anything into a game."
—A. C. Bhaktivedanta Swami

GEORGE AND RAVI IN VRINDABAN

After the opening of The Krishna Balarama Temple, Prabhupada was preaching and enjoying his new, spacious quarters. A rumor came to the Raman Reti land that Ravi Shankar and George Harrison were in the holy dhama. We sent the word around that Prabhupada would like to see them. They sent word back that they would visit the next morning.

The air was fresh, and a Braja breeze flew into the windows. Four or five devotees were invited into Prabhupada's airy rooms. We could see the front of the property where our guests would arrive. Then we heard the car drive up and stop, and some animated voices. I wanted to run out and see George. I asked Prabhupada if I could be excused to greet George and Ravi, and he agreed.

I ran out, and George and Ravi were coming around the side road. George and I ran towards each other and embraced warmly for about thirty seconds.

We looked into each other's eyes, and he said, "Vrindavan is blissful!" He turned and introduced me to someone I already knew well: "Srivatsa Goswami is showing us around." Then Ravi stepped up and took both of my hands in his and smiled. "We meet again," he said. (We had previously met in San Francisco and London.)

I asked George what he had seen so far in Vrindavan and suggested a few more good spots to see. Srivatsa confirmed that they were already planning to go to those places.

Then I ushered them all into Prabhupada's rooms.

Prabhupada sat erect looking resplendent as they entered the rooms. George and Prabhupada caught up on the news. Prabhupada asked about George's music. "'My Sweet Lord' has the Maha Mantra on it," he told Prabhupada.

"I have heard it," Prabhupada replied. "It is so nice!" Then Prabhupada told George about the successes of the Krishna Book distribution and about how many visitors were coming to Bhaktivedanta Manor (both were funded by George).

As he looked around, Ravi Shankar said, "This new Krishna Balarama Temple is very, very beautiful—the best in Vrindaban!"

Prabhupada looked at me and said, "Our Gurudasji was the in-charge."

They all smiled on me. I blushed at all the benign attention. I said it was simply Krishna's mercy and Prabhupada's direction that had built this temple.

"Is your music getting acceptance?" Prabhupada asked Ravi.

"Yes, Indian music is being heard and appreciated all over the world."

"That is nice, just like our Krishna consciousness Movement is now all over the world."

Prasadam and water were brought in, and we all ate and drank in merriment and felt joyful in the holy dhama with all these great personages.

Money Makes Money

After the Krishna Balarama Temple opened, Prabhupada asked me to arrange for a bank and a post office branch on the land. The manager of the Punjab Bank came out to the property with the necessary papers. During the inauguration of the bank branch, Prabhupada had a handful of money for the first deposit. Before handing the money to the manager, Prabhupada joked, "You should give us some money. I have some money, and money makes money."

The manager replied in fun, "As a representative of the bank, I have more money, so you should give me some money."

Prabhupada retorted, "I represent Krishna; He has the most money, so you should give me money." And everyone laughed.

Vrindavan Darshan

One afternoon Prabhupada said to me, "Gurudasji, you are our panda [temple guide]. Can we go to some temples? Can you arrange? We will go and take some darshan." Later he told me, "Darshan does not mean for you to see the Deity, but rather for the Deity to see you."

I arranged a car. Somehow the news leaked out, and from all sides I was petitioned, lobbied, cajoled, begged, or ordered to take everyone along. Prabhupada arrived and got into the front seat with Aksayananda, who was driving. Prabhupada motioned to Shyamasundar to join him in the front seat. Three of us got into the back seat. Prabhupada then said, "There is more room, come on." Leaders, big guns, GBC, and sannyasis vied for space. Five of us squeezed into the back seat by sitting on each other's laps. Gargamuni showed up, and Prabhupada said, "Come on," and he squashed in too. We were trying to get adjusted to the compacted back seat just as Pancha Dravida Maharaja came ambling along with his staff, eager to join us. We groaned but couldn't refuse him, so he lay across all of us with his hands and legs and danda sticking out the window.

Prabhupada asked me, "Where to first?" From under the pile of Vaishnavas I replied, "Radha Govinda!" When we reached Govindaji Temple, Prabhupada walked out majestically, and we piled out like clowns from a circus car. This scene was repeated as we followed the staggered arati around to all seven main Gaudiya Vaishnava temples, plus some other of Prabhupada's favorite places.

From the Heart

The early, bright stars and the moon were out, and the pastel colors of the Vrindavan dusk sheltered the evening. The night air was refreshing and balmy. Srila Prabhupada was sitting under the black tamal tree in the courtyard of the Krishna Balarama Temple.

I recalled how, during the first days of the temple construction, the plans called for the tamal tree to be cut down. But I thought that temples were more beautiful when there were trees in the courtyards. In many temples benches were built around trees to shade the pilgrims. I petitioned to save the tree, but no one seemed to pay attention. Then Krishna dasa Babaji visited Srila Prabhupada and pointed out that the tree was a tamal tree. Krishna dasa Babaji said that there were only a few tamal trees left in Vrindavan. Prabhupada then took an interest in the tamal tree, and it was spared. The architect's plans were altered so that the courtyard was moved elsewhere. This restructuring enabled Prabhupada to sit under the tamal tree that night and talk and hear about Krishna.

Prabhupada had asked a few devotees to speak that evening, including me, informing us that he would attend. I was anxious because I had overheard some of the speakers practicing Sanskrit verses from *Bhagavad-gita*. I knew some verses also, but my pronunciation was not very good. Many leaders of ISKCON were there for the inauguration, and, sure enough, their lectures were laced with Sanskrit verses. I spoke about how we are not this body and about the value of chanting, serving Radha and Krishna with love, and how to please Prabhupada, who was sitting right there. After I spoke, I went to Srila Prabhupada and sat at his feet. He looked on me and said, "You have spoken so nicely, now I can retire."

Later on that evening, Prabhupada, his sister Pishima, and I were sitting in his rooms alone. Again Prabhupada said, "Now I can retire; you speak as I speak. My sister thought you spoke well, too."

I was surprised again and stammered out, "But Pishima does not speak very much English!"

Prabhupada said very quietly, "She understood your talk, and she told me that you speak from your heart. Now I can retire," he said again.

Teeth

In Vrindavan, Prabhupada and his old godbrother Dr. O.B.L. Kapoor were together again after not having seen each other for many years. They had been friends for more than thirty years and were both disciples of Bhaktisiddhanta Sarasvati. They enjoyed their renewed philosophical discussions and quick-witted, humorous exchanges. Dr. Kapoor, a great scholar and devotee, lived in Vrindavan, and he spent many hours with Prabhupada and his disciples. I was present during one of their meetings.

Sitting together, Prabhupada asked Dr. Kapoor, "Do you have all your teeth?"

Dr. Kapoor answered, "You could say I have all my teeth, if you consider that I keep them in a glass of water at night." We all laughed uproariously. He popped out his false teeth and showed Prabhupada.

Prabhupada puffed out his chest, opened his mouth widely and said, "See—I have all my teeth!"

Parampara

Some people consider all of Vrindavan village a temple and don't wear shoes anywhere in the town. I asked Prabhupada about this.

My question to Prabhupada was, "Should I wear shoes in the holy dhama of Vrindavan?"

"Just follow in the footsteps of your spiritual master," replied Prabhupada. I was walking gingerly, shoeless, on the hot sands of Raman Reti, while Prabhupada was wearing shoes.

More Mercy

My foot was bleeding from a cut, and Prabhupada saw it. He immediately came over with some clean cloth and very carefully, very expertly, bandaged the foot. His touch and humility sped the healing.

Delhi

My duties in Vrindaban also sent me running back and forth to Delhi almost constantly. New Delhi and Vrindaban are but eighty miles apart, so quite often when he came to Vrindaban, Prabhupada would also spend some time in New Delhi. Prabhupada had lived in New Delhi himself, and because it is the capital city of India, he always considered it to be a vital center for the spreading of Krishna consciousness.

"I Will See the Bomb As Krishna"

Another war between India and Pakistan was in progress. Srila Prabhupada and his entourage of foreign disciples were in Delhi when the war broke out. We were staying in a dharmasala in Old Delhi. At night there was a curfew, with a call for windows to be covered and lights to be extinguished during air raids. Prabhupada didn't really do anything differently. We went on our morning walks as usual, and at night we held the usual kirtan programs.

One night at the dharmasala there were about thirty guests and devotees. The sirens began to wail. Some devotees looked to Prabhupada as to whether we should interrupt the program to cover the windows or not. Prabhupada continued chanting and didn't seem to pay any attention to the sirens. As his talk was about to begin, some were still awaiting an instruction. Meanwhile some dharmasala caretakers came in and quietly put blankets over the windows.

No bombs hit Delhi; in fact, the planes didn't make it past the border before returning with engine trouble. I figured something like that would happen, for we were with Srila Prabhupada. Later, as the war progressed, some Pakistani planes actually did make it into India. Indian citizens were frightened.

Reading an article about the India-Pakistan war.

The next day two men were visiting Prabhupada and they asked, "Why didn't you cover the windows? Weren't you afraid of being bombed?"

Prabhupada said, "It is not under our control. If Krishna wants to kill, who can save, and if Krishna wants to save, who can kill?"

The men didn't understand. "But what if the bomb would—"

"You cannot even control your stomachache, your toothache," Prabhupada interrupted: "If I should see the bomb coming overhead"—Prabhupada looked, wide-eyed and trusting toward the sky—"then I will see the bomb as Krishna." He continued to look up, his arms spread wide open, "I will see the bomb as Krishna."

"If a devotee is slapped by Govinda,
he doesn't take it as an insult, but takes it as Krishna's mercy."
—A. C. Bhaktivedanta Swami

Beware of the Dog

On a morning walk in Delhi Prabhupada explained that signs saying BEWARE OF DOG were a symptom of so-called modern civilization. One may walk down the street peacefully, and from behind a large, closed gate a dog will bark at you, "Don't come here!" Each gate separates one man's so-called property from the other man's property. No one shares, and there is no spiritual center.

> "A sweetball manufacturer has no appetite for sweets."
> —A. C. Bhaktivedanta Swami

KING DOG

A rich but miserly man was bragging to me about how he served half-cooked chapatis and a very hot chili-potato dish. Then he brought the guests lots of water, and in this way the water and the half-cooked chapatis bloated everyone's stomachs. When everyone was full, the host brought expensive savories for guests who, by that time, were so full they had to refuse them. The man pretended to be a good host by serving everyone else first, when in fact he wanted to serve himself instead. I told Prabhupada about what the clever man had told me.

Prabhupada replied with a Bengali proverb: "If you make a dog a king, and he is sitting on a throne, if you throw him a shoe, he will run off the throne and bite the shoe." In other words, no matter what position or pretense a person has, eventually his essential nature will emerge.

> "In Kali-yuga it is impossible to control ourselves.
> Lord Shiva could not do it, what to speak of ourselves.
> Chanting will help. That is not artificial."
> —A. C. Bhaktivedanta Swami

DELHI PANDAL

At Prabhupada's suggestion, Tamal Krishna, Tejiyas, and I arranged a grand, week-long Pandal program to take place in Connaught Circus, in the heart of New Delhi. The entire flow of the capital city's traffic—busses, taxis, cars—revolves around this spot.

As in Bombay, I made a poster for the event that looked like a telegram, to catch people's attention. I also invited a Chief Guest for each night to talk about their profession in relation to spiritual life. A famous scientist, Dr. Atma Ram, spoke about the correlation between scientific thought and spirituality. Mr. James George, the Ambassador from Canada, attended, as did movie star Dev Anand, the Poet Laureate for India, and Dr. Lokesh Chandra, president of the Academy of Indian Culture. I asked Prabhupada's old friend, Sri Hans Raj Gupta, the Mayor of Delhi, to preside on opening night.

Swamiji Loves You

Well into the program Prabhupada paused, called me over, and whispered, "Is there a WC [bathroom]?"

"Yes," I said. We had built an outhouse behind the stage area, just in case Prabhupada had to use it during the program.

"Show me where is the WC," he said and gave me his hand as he got off the enormous Vyasasana. I led His Divine Grace off the stage to the left. Some people from the audience came running towards us.

"Swamiji, what did we do wrong?" they cried. "Why are you leaving?" they wailed.

Then about three hundred others took up the call and started following us down the bamboo-covered alleyway to the WC. Prabhupada looked back at the commotion. I continued leading him to the outhouse and then quickly turned to head off the mob at the pass.

I blocked the way and told the three hundred, "Swamiji is coming back. You didn't do anything wrong. Swamiji loves you. He is going to the water closet."

I simultaneously walked and talked, and slowly pushed the crowd back into the seating area. Then I went up to the stage to announce the temporary pause. We sang a short kirtan until Prabhupada returned to the podium.

Hans Raj Gupta

Sri Hans Raj Gupta, the Mayor of Delhi, was a confident, smiling gentleman with an easy sense of humor. He and Srila Prabhupada spent much of their time together laughing. The Mayor had striking, neatly cut, white hair and eyebrows. He was very distinguished looking and, like Srila Prabhupada, had hair growing out of his ears. Crow's feet expanded from his eyes from smiling so much. He usually wore a black Nehru suit and black, khadi-cloth hat, while others wore the conforming white, khadi-cloth suit. The two men had known each other since 1944 when Prabhupada lived in Delhi and founded *Back to Godhead* magazine. Hans Raj told me he remembered how Prabhupada walked all over Old and New Delhi encouraging people to subscribe to *Back to Godhead*, or if he found a qualified devotee, urging them to join the League of Devotees.

The ceiling fan in Prabhupada's Radha Damodara rooms was a gift from Hans Raj Gupta. He became a Life Member immediately, and his name on our list of members influenced others to join. While he was honored for his own deeds, he called Prabhupada a saint. He told me: "There are not many holy men as great as your Guruji." Hans Raj Gupta assisted our work in Delhi, granting any permits we needed for our pandal programs, and he also spoke wonderfully as the Chief Guest one night at our program in Connaught Circus. He served as an advisor and confidant to me when we were starting our Delhi branch of ISKCON. Throughout my five years in India, Sri Gupta had always been supportive and helpful. He visited our Vrindavan temple many times and met with Srila Prabhupada whenever Prabhupada was in New Delhi.

Once Prabhupada and I were invited to Hans Raj Gupta's house in New Delhi. The grounds were well kept, and the large, ranch-style house was open and airy. He welcomed us personally and called for his wife, who remembered Prabhupada. Prabhupada also remembered her. She brought us three cold sorbet drinks.

Prabhupada and Mr. Gupta spoke in Hindi for awhile, and then Prabhupada switched to English. "I want you to help me get some land to build a pukka center here in Delhi. Gurudas and I saw some sites near the Yamuna River. Are they available?"

Sri Gupta was genuinely interested in Prabhupada's proposal, but I could sense that he was restricted in some way. He said, "I know the sites you are referring to, but they are slated for educational use."

Prabhupada replied immediately, "We are educational."

Hans Raj laughed but was a little uncomfortable. He continued, "Those sites are zoned for recreation and education."

Prabhupada said, "We are recreation."

Mr. Gupta laughed again. "There are some religious sites further outside. Are you interested in one of those places?"

"Yes, we are interested, but we don't have to come only under the category of religion; we are education, recreation."

Mr. Gupta said, "I understand, but the government is not so open-minded."

Prabhupada continued, "We are more than a religion; we are following sanatan-dharma. That is why we want a center here to bring the eternal way of life to the people in Delhi."

Mr. Striped Suit

Since childhood I'd heard the name of Kenneth Keating, the senator from my home state of New York. He was now the American ambassador to India, stationed in Delhi, and I thought it would be nice to meet him and to offer my help in some way. As was customary in India, Yamuna and I presented our visiting card at the large gate of the modern American Embassy, a huge compound surrounding buildings, fountains, and pools. To our surprise a meeting was arranged without difficulty.

At the prearranged meeting time I took along with me a few American devotees who had interesting backgrounds. One had been a Peace Corps volunteer, another an architect, another a former Navy cadet.

We were shown into a large, airy room, with tasteful, early-American wallpaper. Everything inside the embassy was American, from the doorknobs to the light fixtures, even to the paper-towel dispensers with the same coarse, tan towels they used in my grade school. No inferior products for the Americans stationed here! They even showed American movies in the private theater twice weekly.

Kenneth Keating, a short, well-groomed, white-haired, kind-faced man, was very cordial at the meeting, and he seemed genuinely interested in our life and work. I began by telling him that "in this life" I was born in New York and had followed his career from childhood. He smiled at that and treated me like a long-lost friend, a fellow American in the Orient. I introduced all my devotee friends, telling a little about each one. (I omitted the fact that the Navy and the devotee had had a premature parting of the ways!) Ambassador Keating then asked each and every one where they were born and why they had become devotees.

He was wearing a gray-and-white, pin-striped suit, and when he sat down he was careful to not muss his pants. We felt at ease, as if a village elder was giving us special time. After the meeting had gone on for awhile, I asked if the United States Food for Peace aid program would donate some food for our prasadam distribution. He picked up the phone and put me in touch with a Mr. Shaunessy, who authorized many tons of W. S. B. ("Wheat Soy Blend") for us. (Unfortunately W. S. B. contained sugar as well, and most Indians found it unappetizing and unpalatable. When we tried to feed it to cows and bulls, even they wouldn't accept it! We created a carob sweet with the stuff, and some people ate it. At any rate, this gesture from the United States Government was nice, and now a connection was in place.)

One day, Srila Prabhupada was staying in Delhi. He called me in and asked, "You are a friend of the American ambassador?" It was more of a statement than a question. "I would like to meet him—can you arrange it?"

I bowed at his feet and said, "I'll try to coordinate it." This meeting had to be arranged rapidly, as Prabhupada was leaving Delhi for Bombay in two days. I had to set up the meeting for the next day.

I rode to the elegant embassy building and found myself at the guard's gate again; the Marine eyed me, but my message was sent in. The Ambassador's secretary sent for me, and I told him of Prabhupada's request. Apparently, Ambassador Keating had given me the green light for anything, and the meeting was arranged for eleven o'clock the next morning.

We arrived with a small entourage and were escorted into a large office and asked to wait. Within a minute, Mr. Keating came in, went straight over to Prabhupada, and shook his hand. The eager Ambassador was wearing the same gray-and-white, pin-striped suit that he wore at our first meeting. Ambassador Keating and Srila Prabhupada sat opposite one another, and the ambassador was genuinely respectful towards Prabhupada.

We took seats around them, forming a small circle. Mr. Keating asked if we wanted tea, and Prabhupada said, "We don't drink tea." So hot milk was agreed upon, and it soon came in cups and saucers with gold rims and the U.S. Eagle insignia on the bottom.

Mr. Keating began by saying how he had met some of Prabhupada's students, gesturing towards me. He said that he was very impressed with us and with our work. Prabhupada glanced at me and smiled briefly. Then Prabhupada said, "I hope that you feel welcome in India. Even though you were born in a different place, we are not so different. We are both giving our ideas to many people."

While Mr. Keating pondered these words, Prabhupada continued, "Our first teaching is that we are not this body, we are spirit soul. We can change our name, our country, our passport, but we are always still the same. The body is temporary and the soul is eternal." Mr. Keating pulled his chair closer to Prabhupada's and gave him his undivided attention.

Prabhupada continued, "Just as you are wearing a striped suit, but you are not the suit. You can change your suit. You are still the same inside the suit. I do not call you Mr. Striped Suit, and you do not call me Mr. Orange Cloth. No, I call you Mr. Keating."

Ambassador Keating appeared like a child, listening in rapt attention to the explanation. He seemed to understand. "If we know this principle," Prabhupada said, "that we are not this body, our life will be successful. Similarly, if we think we are American or Indian, black or white, rich or poor, that this is my real identity, then we are in illusion. Just as we do not drink like this"—Prabhupada pantomimed trying to drink his milk with his elbow and laughed, and then we all laughed uproariously, particularly the ambassador.

The secretary came in, saw the friendliness, and smiled. He said, "Sweden and the other ambassadors are assembled on the front steps of the embassy for a group photograph, and they are waiting for you, Mr. Ambassador." Mr. Keating nodded yes, but he clearly wanted to hear more from Prabhupada.

"When we free ourselves of these temporary bodily designations," Prabhupada added, "then we truly know who we are and why we are here.

Then we can overcome the endless entanglement, the duality of pain and pleasure, always happy-unhappy."

Mr. Keating sat transfixed and completely forgot about the other ambassadors and high commissioners waiting for him on the steps. The secretary came in to again remind him: "The Russian and other heads of state are waiting, Mr. Ambassador."

Disappointed, Mr. Keating said, "I must bring this meeting from the sublime to the mundane and leave you."

Prabhupada answered immediately, "I too must bring this meeting from the sublime to the mundane." He was in a business mood. "I want to meet your president, Mr. Nixon." Mr. Keating said he would try, but he also added that many people had requested to meet President Nixon and that the president didn't seem to be interested in meeting people from India. He reiterated, though, that he would try. The meeting ended in friendship and cheerfulness, and they parted good friends.

On the way back to the temple Srila Prabhupada said to me, "You were able to arrange a meeting with the American ambassador in half a day. You are our Hare Krishna Ambassador."

Kenneth Keating kept in touch with me by telephone and letters and asked about Prabhupada often.

Embassy of the United States of America
New Delhi
April 4, 1972

Dear Gurudas:
Many thanks for your letter of March 30. I am pleased that your discussion with Mr. Shaughnessy was productive. You and your colleagues have my admiration and blessings for your selfless work.
Warm regards.

Very sincerely yours,
Kenneth B. Keating

Department of State
Washington, D.C.
January 31, 1975

Dear Guru das:
Thank you for your letter of January 2 and for your continued prayers for me and my work. As you perhaps do not know, I am now

Ambassador to Israel. I have been in the United States for a couple of weeks but have not been able to arrange for any free time in which I could meet with you and have not been on the West Coast or at any point except Washington and New York. I hope it may be possible at some future time for us to get togeth-er since as you know, I have great respect for you and your associates who serve the Lord according to your faith and perform many good deeds in these hectic days.

Sincerely,
Kenneth B. Keating

The Singing King, Dr. Karan Singh

Once while we were in New Delhi, Prabhupada asked me to arrange a meeting between himself and Dr. Karan Singh. Dr. Singh, whom I had met twice before, was the former Maharaja of what became Kashmir State and was now the Minister of Health and Tourism for India, stationed in Delhi, although he still maintained palaces in Kashmir and other places. (I was once Karan Singh's guest in Kashmir, and I slept in the family museum in one of his palaces.)

Dr. Karan Singh had a palatial home on Malcha Marg in New Delhi. Srila Prabhupada, Giriraj, Shyamasundar, and I arrived at the king's residence early one evening.

We were greeted at the door by a smartly clad servant. The rani (queen), a beautiful woman, arrived from another part of the house, greeted us, and ushered us inside. The rani was dressed immaculately in a colored, silk sari suit; she was decorated with many jewels and perfumed with moog-flower scent. Dr. Karan Singh was dressed in a brown, silk, tailored Nehru coat and matching cap. He was extremely respectful and attentive to Prabhupada and his devotees.

After we had sat there and chatted for awhile, Prabhupada commented on how nicely the rani was dressed, "like a queen." Prabhupada then spoke at length about the meaning of the *Gita*. "Offer everything to Krishna," he said, "and all else will follow." He emphasized that leading men should take up the science of *Bhagavad-gita*, as where the leaders go, all others will follow.

When Prabhupada was finished, I told him how nicely Dr. Karan Singh sang the prayers to the ten avatars (the Dasa-avatara prayers). (The cordial monarch had sung these prayers to Yamuna and me at a previous meeting, and we had responded by singing the verse devoted to Lord Nrsimadeva for Dr. Karan Singh.)

The king gathered himself to sing, sitting in a classic royal pose with one knee on the ground and the other leg bent, back straight, and head erect. He played a large resounding tamboura and sang robustly and sweetly.

Prabhupada listened along and was visibly pleased. Every time I met Dr. Karan Singh after that, he always inquired about Prabhupada.

How White of You

I had an appointment to visit the vice president of India at his home, to invite him to our Delhi pandal program. I arrived at his one-story, white house and was welcomed there by a maid dressed in a crisp, white uniform. The vice president himself was waiting inside, sitting on a white couch. He was wearing a white, khadi (hand-spun cloth) outfit with white, khadi cap, and the walls were covered in white wallpaper. Even the tables and chairs were white. Everything was scrubbed immaculately. The little poodle that wandered into the room was also white. The conversation was like white bread (politically correct). I felt as if we were in a Fellini film. The only thing that was not white was the vice president's skin color.

President

A disciple gushed, "Oh Prabhupada, you should be president."

Prabhupada matter-of-factly replied, "No, you should be president. I will advise."

Meeting Indira Gandhi

Srila Prabhupada first suggested that I meet Indira Gandhi, the Prime Minister of India, in a letter to me dated 7 November, 1970.

Eventually Krishna put me in touch with just the right person to arrange such a meeting. Dr. Lokesh Chandra, M.P. (Member of Parliament), was present in Mr. Dalmia's office in Delhi when Giriraj and I approached Mr. Dalmia to become an ISKCON Life Member. On the spot, Dr. Chandra also became a member. At the time, Lokesh Chandra ran the Academy of Indian and Asian Culture at Hauz Khus Enclave, a posh suburb in south Delhi. From that point on we became good friends, and Yamuna and I would often dine at his house.

The Academy was a large complex on the main road going to the Qutab Minar, that inexplicable column of unknown age and material. A high, plain, brick wall enclosed the Academy grounds, and inside there was a magical, eclectic world. Seven, one-room, guest bungalows were arranged along the back wall. Dr. Chandra and his family lived in a modest five-room house, but Javanese stick puppets, Tibetan mandalas, and Indian stone murtis graced his domain. Dr. Lokesh's father had helped the Dalai Lama escape from Tibet, and subsequently he helped transport monks, sutras, tomes, drawings, rubbings, and other artifacts from Tibet. At one end of a well-lit, large, and long room sat six Tibetan monks working silently, translating writings and transferring stone rubbings. The cranking sounds of a printing press emanated from another part of the building. Shelves and shelves of storage boxes took up half of the house.

On the wall of the living room was a Tibetan mask with red and bulging eyes, its open mouth holding a nest of real baby sparrows. In most countries of the world, like the United States, one would call the exterminator to get rid of the sparrows nesting in a mask in the living room. In India, for sparrows to fly in the house and rest on the ceiling fan is accepted as a commonplace, everyday occurrence. Indian people respect all forms of life, and, for them, function supersedes fashion.

I knew that Dr. Lokesh Chandra had helped Indira win the election and that he was still close to her, so one day I visited Dr. Lokesh and asked him to introduce us to Indira Gandhi. He was able to fix an appointment for us to meet Mrs. Gandhi at a general group audience on the lawn at her residence on Janpath. Dr. Lokesh went with us—Bhanu, Gopal, Yamuna, Giriraj, and me—and introduced us to the prime minister. At that time, as he knew her so well, Lokesh Chandra was able to set up a private meeting with Mrs. Gandhi for a later date.

At the second meeting, we went through the many rooms of her house until we came into a tasteful, large living room overlooking the expansive gardens. We were asked to wait, and very soon after we sat down Indira Gandhi came in. She was a dynamic presence, and she wore a sparkling, beautiful silk sari that was immaculate and neatly pressed. She was very gracious to us as we sat and talked about how people all over the world appreciated East Indian philosophy, spiritual traditions, and culture. She listened politely to what we had to say and didn't say much. We gave her a garland, a set of Prabhupada's *Srimad-Bhagavatams*, and some *Back to Godhead* magazines. She seemed to be enjoying herself in our presence as she formally welcomed us to mother India. Before leaving we posed for a photo together.

Years later, in Mayapur, Prabhupada requested me to go and meet Indira Gandhi again, saying that if she came to our Mayapur temple opening, then Bhaktivinode Thakur himself would personally come and take me back to Godhead!

So I went to Delhi with Tamal Krishna to meet her again. Meanwhile, since I had seen her last, Mrs. Gandhi had seen to it that Yamuna and I were granted long-term visas (unheard of in those times)!

Tamal and I arrived at Janpath and were taken to her immediately. Indira came in, again immaculately dressed and coifed. She asked, "How is your good wife?"

"She is fine, thank you," I answered. This time we brought Prabhupada's *Bhagavad-gita*, a garland, and a jar of pure, yellow ghee from our ISKCON farm in Holland. (In India the ghee often looks more white than yellow.)

As we presented her with the ghee, one drop of ghee from the cap of the bottle got on her fingers. She gave the ghee to an attendant, who probably had to test it before she had any. Then she took out a small, lace handkerchief and wiped her fingers before she would touch the *Bhagavad-gita*. She had that much respect for the holy book of India. She received the sacred words of Lord Krishna to Arjuna and gave the volume to her assistant.

I turned the conversation to her attending our Mayapur opening celebration. She politely declined, saying that India has a secular policy towards spiritual groups and she must not pick one over another.

She said, "If I go to your function, then everyone will want me to go to theirs, and I will not be able to get any work done."

I pressed on: "We are not a religion—we represent a way of life, the best of what India has exported. Many chief guests, from all professions, have already agreed to come."

She politely declined.

I was waiting for Tamal Krishna to press our case, for he could usually argue the skin off a snake and get anyone to change their minds by sheer perseverance. Tamal said nothing. "A fine time for him to be reticent," I thought to myself.

"She seemed to be enjoying herself in our presence as she formally welcomed us to mother India." Left to right: *Gopal, Gurudas, Yamuna, Indira Gandhi, Giriraj, and Bhanu.*

After this, the atmosphere became slightly tense. Oh well, Bhaktivinode won't drag me back to Godhead this time. I changed the subject. A photo of our Ratha Yatra festival in London happened to be on the front page of the *Hindustan Times* newspaper that day. I turned to her and brightly said, "Did you see the picture of our London Ratha Yatra festival in the *Hindustan Times* this morning?" She laughed like a little girl, both surprised and delighted, as the newspaper was sitting right in front of us on the table!

We parted as friends, and from Dr. Chandra I heard that from time to time Indira Gandhi helped us secretly behind the scenes, informing others to let us carry on our devotional work in India unmolested.

Visas Forever

As I was based in Vrindavan, just eighty miles from New Delhi, one of my services was to take care of visa problems for foreign devotees in India. For most visa extensions I found a system that worked, especially in the provinces outside the larger cities of Calcutta, New Delhi, and Bombay. The best way to get the visa handled was to apply for an extension right before the expiration date. The pending decision then dragged on through office after office, in triplicate, and by the time they granted the extension, it was time to reapply. The delays allowed me and many others to stay in India for years! My visa status was perpetually in limbo. I did not bother to push it through any faster than the nature of that beast.

Good Old Days

Everyone was excited: Prabhupada was about to arrive in Delhi. Many devotees awaited his arrival, including many ISKCON leaders, so rather than bicker over what aspect of the arrival I would perform, I let the others bargain. "I want to give a garland," said one person. "You get his luggage," said another. "I want to wash his feet," someone else informed us. All the devotional duties were assigned, and I was left. No one had volunteered to lead kirtan, I thought to myself.

Prabhupada's arrival was very formal on this occasion, and he hardly looked at anyone as he walked into the airport waiting lounge. He offered pranams, but kept a stern look. While he passed through the devotees, I began to bellow out the Hare Krishna mantra to the old, traditional tune we used to sing in New York and San Francisco. Prabhupada, still aloof, heard the chanting and saw me with the kartalas, then his reticence became a bright, wide-open smile. He gave me a big wave. As he got into the car, he invited me in. "I like that tune very much," he said, smiling contentedly.

I answered, "Like we sang in San Francisco."

We rode together for awhile and were quiet. I asked Prabhupada, "Do you think the first days together in San Francisco were special?"

"Oh yes," Prabhupada answered emphatically.

SANNYASA

*"Sannyasa means becomig a world preacher,
thus making the whole world your family."*
—A. C. Bhaktivedanta Swami

Always Moving

ONE DEVOTEE WAS SITTING COMFORTABLY at Prabhupada's lotus feet. He gushed, "Oh, Prabhupada, I want to sit at your lotus feet forever." Prabhupada smiled down mercifully and said, "But my lotus feet are always moving, so you cannot sit down!" Later he explained, "The business of a sannyasi is to always be moving. Rupa Goswami never stayed in a place or under a tree for more than three days so he wouldn't become attached to any one place." Regarding Rupa Goswami, Prabhupada also said, "Rupa Goswami taught that you should not follow rules and regulations if you have not realized the meaning first." Prabhupada then added, "Adwaita Acharya would not read a verse in the *Srimad-Bhagavatam* or *Bhagavad-gita* if he didn't understand the meaning of the verse he was reading."

Moving On

The Krishna Balarama Temple was built and was being maintained nicely. There was no need for me to be there anymore. I passed the presidential baton to Akshayananda Maharaja, who had been helping me. He spoke Hindi and was very serious about his devotional service.

It was late 1975, and Yamuna and I were exhausted, overworked, and stressed. I had just overcome typhoid fever after fighting it for twenty-seven days. I had almost died. Yamuna and my godbrothers Yasodananda and Rishi Kumar had nursed me back to health and perhaps saved my life. Yamuna moved into the hospital room that also housed a big dog, and she cooked for me when I was able to eat. When Prabhupada heard of my illness he was very concerned. When I was released from the hospital, Prabhupada invited me to Hyderabad and fed me personally with his golden, lotus hands. His Divine Grace praised me and made sure I was on the road to recovery.

Yamuna and I returned to Vrindavan. We had decided, after five years in India, to leave and go back to the United States.

We asked Srila Prabhupada if that was all right, and he acquiesced.

I had not seen my family, and especially my kindly father, for many years. My father was the successful manager of an insurance office who would rather have been a writer or a scholar. He went back to school in his sixties.

He always encouraged my Krishna-consciousness path, which to him was better than the beatings I suffered in the South during the civil rights movement.

My father was the first man to hire an African-American for Metro Life Insurance. He sponsored immigrant couples from Eastern Europe and found them jobs. He was open-minded and wise. One time he came to my defense in New York's Central Park when I was being harassed for chanting Hare Krishna. People had been mocking us and laughing and shouting over our chanting. My father stood in front of the crowd and asked them to quiet down. When they did, he pointed to me proudly and said, "That's my son."

My father was also the person the company sent to fix any problem in branch offices. He was able to go anywhere as a troubleshooter. I tried to emulate him. He was also very tolerant. A fastidious dresser, one time when he went to the New York temple in a pair of new shoes, he could not find his shoes afterward, so he borrowed a pair of old sneakers and went off to his office in his nice suit and sneakers!

Yamuna and I felt out of place in my father's retirement village in central Florida. When I saw my father again, he looked old and tired. He welcomed me as usual. He arranged for me to talk to a gathering of forty people in his house. They asked thoughtful questions, but they wanted to know why my father's son would join a cult.

I addressed the assembly: "Try to understand that we are not so different from anybody else. Many of you are Jews and Christians and were previously persecuted for following your beliefs. We too are only following our hearts, seeking love of God. Yet we are laughed at, spit upon, and harassed, in the same way believers in the past were misunderstood. Now the descendants of those who were once persecuted are now in power and are being narrow-minded and laughing at new "cults." We are not a cult. The majority of people in India read the *Bhagavad-gita* and worship as I do. My guru is the best example of God Consciousness I have met. He has achieved spiritual self-realization, yet he has tremendous managerial skills, he travels all over the world, he has meetings with fascinating people like the Beatles and Indira Gandhi—and he has nurtured my love for God."

The guests gradually became more accepting, showing by nods and smiles that they understood. So I continued: "We need not be ashamed for our beliefs. Nobody who follows their dreams and intuitions should be blamed, even if they make a mistake. That's how we learn. All of us, at one time or another, did something that was looked upon with cynicism or suspicion. Unless we are shallow conformists, we won't deviate for our principles. I followed my heart to my teacher. Following beliefs is the way the great inventions and humanitarian reforms came about. I urge you all to hear your heart calling. Cultivate your love of God. Even though others may not understand, stay the course. Criticisms and myopic thinking are only obstacles in our path, and they should be tossed away. My Guru Maharaja has said, 'When the elephant caravan passes, the dogs will bark.' Now is the time for you all in your later years to rekindle your God Consciousness. Say the holy names that you believe in.

"This path we are all searching for can be found by anyone at any moment. We all have this questioning aspect in us, and although outward spiritual formats may appear different, essentially the paths are similar, leading us to love for God.

"I found my Guru, and I am fortunate. He has given me so much. I stand on the shoulders of my preceptors, ancestors, mentors, and saints. They guide me and are part of my inspiration.

"Please don't be ashamed, any fellow seekers, for following your hearts and trying something different and challenging. Follow your true heart; don't cheat, because the only one fooled in the long run is ourselves. There is no bluffing in bhakti-yoga, true spiritual life, the yoga of devotion to God. Our whole life is dedicated to serving God and humanity, and this has taken me around the world in the process. I owe so much to my father here and to my spiritual father. I love you both."

A few days after visiting my father, Yamuna decided to leave and move to a farm in Oregon. I was very confused. It was a very painful time for me and bad timing all around. I went to join my friend, Abhirama, in the Coconut Grove temple, and then I moved on to the Atlanta temple. My father died a few days later. Abhirama accompanied me to the funeral of my father. I was devastated. I needed to be with Prabhupada.

Prabhupada was in Philadelphia; when I inquired, he called me there to be with him. As always, Prabhupada was my kind father too. His divine mercy comforted and consoled me in the loss of my earthly father and the separation from Yamuna. He encouraged me to give up householder life and become a sannyasi, a renunciate. Previously, in his letters, Prabhupada had brought up the subject of sannyasa to me. Although many others coveted becoming a sannyasi, up till now I did not seem to have this inclination. There were about fifteen ISKCON devotees who had already taken sannyasa initiation by that time. I was now being asked by my Guru Maharaja to embrace the renounced order of life. Now, because Prabhupada was personally asking me to take sannyasa, I agreed. I felt as if I'd been thrown out of the nest, still grieving and confused. Now I was to embark on a new phase of Krishna consciousness. I think Prabhupada sensed my restlessness as he encouraged me by saying, "You are a great preacher." He then informed me that he would perform my sannyasa initiation in Berkeley, California, in two weeks time.

SANNYASA

On the appointed day, many old friends and other people showed up for the ceremony. Prabhupada spoke frankly; he said that Yamuna and I were great devotees, that he was pleased with me, and now that Yamuna was gone I could go on myself as a preacher, a sannyasi, and in this way continue to serve Lord Krishna. After the initiation I asked him if there was any particular service he had in mind for me. Prabhupada requested that I join Vishnujana and Tamal Krishna as a preacher with the Radha-Damodar traveling bus party.

I began managing a bus party that went around to universities in the Pacific Northwest of the United States. My Radha Damodara bus party included Jayananda Thakur and Paribrajakacarya Swami.

"*I managed a bus party that went around to universities in the Pacific Northwest of the United States.*"

Later, I managed traveling bus parties in Europe, Northern Ireland, and Lebanon. Prabhupada also requested me to go to the Communist countries, and he guided me as I traveled into Poland, Romania, Yugoslavia, Czechoslovakia, Bulgaria, and East Germany. These forays into Eastern Europe were extremely slow and clandestine, and in the beginning success was measured in small doses. Many devotees were persecuted at that time in places where now there are thriving ISKCON temples. Although I did not often have Prabhupada's personal darshan when I was preaching throughout the world, he often seemed to be guiding me from within and from without.

Swami Bhaktivedanta put his toe into the waters of material nature, and slowly small ripples of purification changed the polluted mire into pure, fresh, liquid devotion. His divine presence agitated the waters of nescience, and these waves of purity have agitated the whole ocean. Each drop of purity that his followers add to this world, each sincere recitation of the holy names that we pass on, bears fruit to the prophesy that Hare Krishna will be heard in every town and village on the planet.

With this humble offering, I pray that I have transmitted to you all a glimpse into the greatness, compassion, and saintliness of His Divine Grace, through my memories of his pastimes.

Not a day goes by without his guidance.

The Guru lives through his teachings. I carry on by Prabhupada's instructions, words, his caresses, and by his example.

DROPS OF NECTAR ALONG THE PATH

*"Krishna consciousness is simply wonderful.
It is sweet no matter where you taste it."*
—A. C. Bhaktivedanta Swami

HOMESICK FOR VRINDABAN

His first year in New York was sometimes hard for Swamiji. He told me that when he was feeling homesick for Vrindavan he would visit the customs office where all the ship schedules were kept. Once, a customs officer who got to know Prabhupada asked him, "Swami, you have been coming here and inquiring about ship times to India, but when are you going back to India?" The Swami knew that simply by going to the customs office he could allay his homesickness and satisfy his desire to return home.

PURIFICATION OF A THIEF

This reminded him of the story about a thief who became a Vaishnava. The reformed thief realized that he got as much enjoyment from watching peoples' reactions to the theft as he did from the wealth he had stolen. He missed these reactions so much that he was tempted to become a thief again. He consulted his guru, who told him just to move his fellow devotees' belongings to other rooms when they slept. He did this, and when the devotees awakened they began looking for their missing things. It was quite a mix-up—and thus the thief was satisfied. He told the devotees, "My dear brothers and sisters, I was previously a thief, and now I have become a Vaishnava; therefore, I cannot steal someone else's belongings. However, I missed the reactions of my former victims, so Guruji told me to hide your things and to observe your reactions. Now I don't have to steal anymore. Thank you very much."

AMERICA SINGING

Swamiji told the story of a priest sermonizing to some coal miners. Doing both voices, he said, "If you don't worship God, you will go to hell."
The miners asked, "What is hell like?"
"Oh! Hell is dark and hot, and deep underground."

The miners said, "This hell sounds like where we work every day—it's not so bad."

The priest thought a moment and said, "There are no newspapers in hell."

"Oh," said the miners, "then we don't want to go to hell!"

Telling this story Swamiji would laugh softly and say, "We must find what attracts people and show them how Krishna is the all-attractive."

Snow

Swamiji told me that when he first saw snow falling from his window in New York, he thought that it was lime, and he wondered why people were throwing lime down from the roof.

Spread the Krishna Arts to Every Town and Village

One time in Los Angeles we were preparing for the arrival of Srila Prabhupada. My job was to arrange tours of the temple facilities for influential people. Our office answering machine message announced: "This is the office of Gurudas, Purudas, Dharma [Dharmadyaksa] and Sidd [Siddhesvar dasa]." The many attractions of the tour included artists painting in the studio, the ancient Bengali art of straw-doll-making for dioramas, the temple room itself, and the dance and theater troupes. I saw Satarupa and Prajapati, of the dance troupe, and they looked despondent even though Srila Prabhupada was coming. When I inquired, they told me that they were not being appreciated here, and that they wanted to go to India to study dance and perform. I thought about this dilemma and came up with an idea. I suggested that when Srila Prabhupada came they could do a miniperformance in the courtyard on the front lawn.

The ensemble of seven prepared, and soon Prabhupada's car pulled up. He was surrounded by admiring devotees, many of whom were seeing him in person for the first time. Prabhupada smiled profusely as the wave of devotees bowed down before him. The dancer/thespians then appeared out of the sea of white and orange dhotis and multicolored saris. Balarama was on the back of the Pralambha demon, and they towered above the crowd. Prabhupada, still sitting in the car, looked up and smiled. The other dancers circled, displaying mudras of Krishna playing His flute and fluttering their hands in depiction of His sweet words. I took what I thought was a timely opportunity to approach the car window. As we looked into each other's eyes, Srila Prabhupada smiled his abundant blessings upon me. I said, "Srila Prabhupada, how are you feeling?" He shook his head from side to side, the Indian way of saying so-so or okay. I continued, "The dancers want to perform for you—is that convenient?"

"Yes," he answered.

"When?" I asked.

"Tomorrow, in the temple."

Another tomorrow, I thought.

The next day the temple room was full to capacity with expectant devotees as Prabhupada presided over the whole scene from his high Vyasasana. Then the play began. In the Krishna books, Pralambha is larger than Balarama. However, in this production Prajapati, the actor playing Balarama, was larger than the actor playing Pralambha. Pralambha started to fall with the excessive weight on his shoulders, and he had to hold on to some curtains and then to the wall. I looked over to see Prabhupada's reaction. He was laughing kindly. The rest of the play went on smoothly. A brief Bharat Natyam dance performance followed, which Prabhupada seemed to enjoy thoroughly.

The next day Prabhupada and about six others, including myself, were walking through the big, hangarlike warehouse that housed Bhaktivedanta Books. Prabhupada was listening to Ramesvara talk about the book distribution. Ramesvara painted a very bright picture of his operation. We came upon Srutashrava driving a forklift. Ramesvara said, "This is a forklift." When he saw Prabhupada, Sruta bowed down right on the floor of the forklift. His head was on the pedal that made the forklift rise. The prongs continued rising unchecked until they crushed some neon lights hanging from the high ceiling.

Fortunately, by Krishna's grace, we were out of harm's way as falling glass hit the ground. Prabhupada then asked Ramesvara, "Are there many accidents?"

Ramesvara protested loudly that they had a one-hundred-percent safety record. His New York accent was grating. I said, "Except for today." Everyone laughed. We walked around the debris.

Prabhupada then said, "Where is Prajapati?" Someone ran to get him. Soon Prajapati came in, partly walking, partly bowing, partly fawning, awaiting Prabhupada's instruction. "That was a very nice performance last night. You also do dance?" Prabhupada asked.

"Yes, Srila Prabhupada," Prajapati answered.

Prabhupada turned to everyone and, focusing especially on Ramesvara, said, "Then let us spread the Krishna conscious arts to every town and village, just like we do with our books."

Prajapati couldn't help but say, "Jaya!" I was pleased too.

As we continued our tour, we rounded a corner and came upon a small, darkened room. It was empty. We started to pass it, but Prabhupada paused and went inside. We tried to crowd in behind him. I peered around the corner, as there was not enough room for all of us, but I wanted to see what was going on. I pushed my head inside the space. Prabhupada took his cane and pointed to a small box under a table next to the wall: "What is that?"

Ramesvara was deeply embarrassed and confessed, "Those are the records of book returns." They had been hidden, and, as usual, nothing could be hidden from Prabhupada!

We went through a hallway and came out into a corridor where a new bhakta was sleeping in a chair. He woke up to find all of us, including Prabhupada, looking at him. Surprised, he changed colors and wasn't sure what to do. Prabhupada saw his discomfort, then noticed some Q-Tips nearby. He said to the youngster, "I need some of those—how do you say them?"

The boy answered proudly, "Q-Tips."

He had the presence of mind to give the box of Q-tips to Prabhupada, who said, "Thank you. This is Vaishnava prasadam."

The youth was blessed. We all walked on.

You Are Not This Body

One of the most important, simple and yet misunderstood elements of our philosophy is "You are not this body." Srila Prabhupada introduced this idea to us when the Movement was young, before there were many books available, when we knew very few prayers, and before we were able to grasp the complexities of Vedic, devotional science. Still, even after eleven years Prabhupada reiterated and reiterated the same idea, "You are not this body."

"We must give up these bodily designations."

"You can change your country but you cannot change your eternal identity."

"You are not this body; you are spirit soul."

We must constantly be reminded about the bedrock principle of Vedic philosophy: "We are not this body."

Proud Disciple

My Guru's Spiritual Master was Bhaktisiddhanta Saraswati. He was a great scholar and staunch devotee. Bhaktisiddhanta Saraswati was called the "living encyclopedia" because he remembered everything he ever read.

The relationship between the spiritual master and the disciple is special. The disciple must choose his guru carefully and then follow his instructions and example. Some disciples consider the guru a possession, and this phenomenon was quite popular in the Sixties. Many people were following the various teachers who came to the West. Some followed a guru only briefly, according to how it suited them, and they considered the guru as just another possession. At parties they would conveniently quote, "My guru says this or that." The guru is not a pet or a fad or a vicarious extension of the disciple. Bhaktisiddhanta Saraswati taught that the guru is a representative of Lord Krishna and not to be taken lightly.

The genuine guru blesses all his students equally, yet sometimes a disciple may feel specially favored and proud of his relationship with his guru. Bhaktisiddhanta Saraswati had this to say regarding a disciple feeling puffed-up and favored by the guru:

> *"If a student feels favored, he is like a mosquito perched on the lap of a king, thinking, 'All these people are my subjects,' but all he can really do is bite the king."*
> —Bhaktisiddhanta Saraswati Maharaja

> *"Try your best, and even if you don't succeed there is no loss."*
> —A.C. Bhaktivedanta Swami

The Richest Man in India

The Birlas are one of the richest families in India. On a morning walk in the Hanging Gardens, Bombay, a devotee was saying, as some gentleman was passing, "That's B. R. Birla!" Another devotee said, "No, that's R. K. Birla!" Prabhupada joked, "Any Birla will do."

Equality Once More

Regarding rich and poor, Prabhupada once remarked, "Water tastes the same in an iron pot or a gold pot."

Elders

The eldest member of the Birla clan visited Prabhupada. Regardless of their different positions in society, Prabhupada treated Mr. Birla as his elder, with special respect. On other occasions I always saw Prabhupada treat his elders, whether they be rich or poor, with the same respect.

Faulty Logic

There was a doctor who could cure pneumonia but not colds. Prabhupada told the story that this doctor instructed his patients who had colds to soak themselves in cold water, so that when they contracted pneumonia the doctor could then cure them.

WHAT IS IMPORTANT

"Why are you photographing me?" Prabhupada asked. "You should be photographing something important, like people chanting Hare Krishna in the streets. Preaching is more important."

The disciples of Srila Prabhupada are known as the Hare Krishnas. We are not known as the Prabhupadas or the Bhaktivedantas—unlike many other groups that are named after the guru, like the Guru Maharajis or the Rajneeshis or the Sai Babas or the Maharishis.

Sometimes Prabhupada was so humble that he would stand in a long line with everyone else at an outdoor event. He would always accept whatever Krishna gave him, from his simple rooms in Vrindavan to a palatial mansion in England or Detroit.

KRISHNA IS EVERYWHERE

When questioned if he could see Krishna, Prabhupada answered, "Yes. But if you do not see, that does not mean that I do not see. If I see my lover, does that mean you can also see my lover? If I see my wife, you cannot say that I cannot see her. If I say I can see Krishna, you cannot say I cannot see Krishna. You ask me to show you God. The *Bhagavad-gita* says, 'I am the taste of water.' I am showing you Krishna, but you don't accept. If you do not know, how do you know I have not seen him?"

PRABHUPADA DEFEATS MAYA

I first met Mr. Nair in his office in Bombay (now Mumbai). He had a reputation for being rude to devotees, so sometimes just for the challenge devotees went to his office to try to convince him to become a Life Member. This was considered good training. One time Giriraj and I went to Mr. Nair's office. When we arrived, instead of offering us a cold drink or some form of the usual hospitality, he offered us some cold words: "Why should I become a life member, when I am Krishna! I don't need your books to read about Krishna; I am Krishna! Ha ha!" He ranted on like this for several minutes.

When he had finally ceased his braying, I said, "Krishna created the oceans and skies—did you do that? And Krishna spoke the *Bhagavad-gita*, was that you speaking? Krishna—"

Mr. Nair interrupted. "Yes, I am Krishna," he bleated. There was no reasoning with him. He was standing now, red-faced and flailing his arms. I picked up his glass paperweight and dropped it on his desk. It made a large, sharp, thudding sound. He stopped his histrionics. Giriraj and I looked at each other and decided that the best thing to do was to leave.

Later on I came in contact with Mr. Nair again, as Prabhupada had been trying to negotiate with him for a piece of property he owned in the Juhu section of suburban Bombay. The property was suitable for our plans for a temple, library, and hotel. At first Mr. Nair offered the land, and then suddenly he retracted his offer. He seemed to take delight in disrespecting and aggravating Srila Prabhupada and the devotees.

One day Prabhupada called me into his rooms and said, "You should try to convince Mr. Nair to sell us the land. You get along with everyone." Then Prabhupada pondered a moment and said, "But you have no business sense." He paused again and then said, "*Hmmmm*, Tamal Krishna, you should try to get Mr. Nair to sell us the land. You have good business sense—but you don't get along with anyone...." Then, almost as if he were a child having a realization, he said, "The only one who can do this is me. I must deal with Mr. Nair." So this realization instantly became the plan.

Eventually the land negotiations came to a showdown between Prabhupada and Mr. Nair, who brought along a strong yogi with him. It was said that this yogi had many mystic powers. Tamal Krishna and Shyamasundar were also sitting in the room with Prabhupada. Prabhupada fed lunch to Mr. Nair and the yogi and then invited them to rest after the meal in another room. They both fell asleep. Prabhupada then requested Tamal to awaken Mr. Nair but to leave the yogi sleeping. In this way, although Mr. Nair was still somewhat uncooperative, Prabhupada was able to wrangle some concessions from him.

However, despite Prabhupada's long patience and tolerance, Mr. Nair's intransigence caused him to sabotage the negotiations time after time, and ultimately the papers never got signed. Nair even sent police and gundas (hired thugs) to harass the devotees.

Soon after, Mr. Nair died.

Later, I happened to be in Bombay for a meeting between Mr. Nair's widow, her attorney, and Srila Prabhupada regarding the Juhu land. Several of us had been invited by Prabhupada to sit with him in the room. When I entered the room, everything felt old-fashioned—as if we were in a past century. The atmosphere was genteel and peaceful, like the calm after the storm. The decorations on the walls were older; the furnishings were antiques. The pens could have been feather quills. Mrs. Nair's sari looked like a gown from an earlier age, and Prabhupada was in his saffron dhoti and chaddar.

Now the terms of the agreement flowed blessedly into place, and the documents for the Juhu land were signed that day. After the signing, Prabhupada called Mrs. Nair his "daughter," and she broke down in tears. She cried for a while. She said to Prabhupada with great emotion, "It was my husband that did not want to sell you this land for your temple, not me." She cried again, and Prabhupada comforted her and softly patted her head a few times.

I watched the construction begin soon after, growing into the grand temple, library, and residences that can be visited at Hare Krishna Land, Juhu Beach, Mumbai.

Be Bold

"If you are going to rob, rob the government reserve, and if you are going to hunt, hunt the rhinoceros, because if you fail, everyone will say, 'Oh, that was impossible anyway,' and if you succeed, they will say, 'That was a glorious feat!'"

What Great Men Do

"Whatever action is performed by great men, common men follow in his footsteps, and whatever standards he sets by exemplary acts, all the world pursues." (*Bhagavad-gita* 3:21)

One morning we were riding in a car with Srila Prabhupada on our way to visit the ancient temple of Thakur Haridas. Even though Shyamasundar, the driver, had to honk the car horn constantly on the crowded road, the atmosphere of the Bengali countryside was restful, and we were intrigued and interested by the many surrounding scenes: cows and dogs wandering about, women drying and sifting dahl, rickshas going here and there, and pedestrians quickly scurrying to the side of the road when they heard the horn. Probably because it was used so much, the horn broke and became silent. Consequently, we came close to hitting some people beside the road. Someone started shouting "Hare Krishna" loudly out the window at anything that moved. This only seemed to scare people instead of warning them, but it would have been all right had they suffered cardiac arrest because the holy name was being yelled into their ears!

Suddenly Prabhupada turned in his seat and said, "Give me my plate." He took his cane and banged on his metal plate out the window whenever we neared a bicycle or some pedestrians. Sure enough, they would veer automatically to the side of the road. Prabhupada repeated the banging a few more times and then handed the plate and spoon to Aksayananda Prabhu. "Now you do it." Akshayananda banged the plate successfully.

Prabhupada laughed and said, "They will think it is a new American invention and want to imitate it!"

Child's View of a Great Man

"He's not so great; he's just my father."

Great Renunciate

A man who had known Prabhupada many years ago during his business days in Allahabad wondered, "Will Swamiji remember me?" Prabhupada not only remembered the man but also his family and history as well. I saw this phenomenon repeated several times. Once I met a Sikh man from Allahabad on a train, and, after talking to the gentleman for some time, I told him about my spiritual master, A.C. Bhaktivedanta Swami Prabhupada. The gentleman said, "I knew your guru. I used to go to his pharmacy, De's Pharmacy." The Sikh continued, "He was a very learned and kind man. Then one day we saw him just walking out of town, away from everything, just walking away, and he disappeared."

My Questions Answered

From a letter:

"Your first question about the jiva's form with particular reference to *Bhagavad-gita* (8.18). You quote from the purport, "During the nighttime they have no form." This means that there is no material form. The simple understanding is as we are transmigrating from one material form to another, so actually in this material world we have no fixed form. Similarly, when we are spiritually perfect we develop the spiritual form to live eternally in the spiritual world. In the spiritual world there are exactly the same things as we see here, namely the land, water, trees, birds, beasts, human beings, etc., and all of them are spiritual as all the varieties here are material.

"So these things can be understood when one is advanced in self-realization. The real form of the living entity is eternal servant of Krishna. Now, this spiritual form is developed when he enters into the spiritual world.

"Regarding your second question, "Where in our scriptures is there mention of Lord Jesus Christ as recognized and what is the purport?" We do not find in the scriptures Lord Jesus Christ's name. There is mention of Lord Buddha's name, which is described in our Srimad Bhagavatam. So far we are concerned, we have all our obeisances for Lord Jesus Christ because His whole life was devoted to the service of the Lord.

Lalit Prasad Thakur

Our car was driving deeper and deeper into the jungles of West Bengal. Prabhupada was on his way to meet with Lalit Prasad Thakur, Bhaktivinode Thakur's son and younger brother of Bhaktisiddhanta Saraswati.

We arrived and parked the car under some thick palm fronds. The lush jungle was shading the whole compound around an ancient temple where Lalit Prasad lived. A brahmachari taking care of the ninety-six-year-old devotee welcomed us and took us to two rooms. He showed us where to wash and rest after our long journey. Soon three people were bringing prasadam, good Bengali style, stuffed portals, and other preparations like bitter melon that Prabhupada loved.

After respecting the delicious yet simple meal, we rested for a short time. The room was alternately in light and shade as a breeze stirred the surrounding overgrown jungle. The murmuring jungle sounds enhanced my peaceful rest. I soon awoke and was astounded to see Prabhupada rise suddenly from a sleep state refreshed and ready to go in an instant. We were led to Lalita Prasad's simple house, and when he saw Prabhupada, Lalit Prasad brightened. Lalit, young in demeanor, didn't stand up but bounced up and down on his cot like a happy puppy. Although ninety-six years in age, his eyes and manner were much more youthful. The soul-force surged through him and reached out as a benediction to us all. Prabhupada treated him as an elder and bowed, but Lalit Prasad bowed right back so fast it was difficult to distinguish who was bowing to whom.

Lalita Prasad and Prabhupada were speaking in Bengali, but I could tell how very fond Lalita Prasad was of Srila Prabhupada. I could tell he was praising Prabhupada's preaching mission and results. I could understand some of the words and concepts. They spoke about the possibility of some of Prabhupada's ISKCON disciples maintaining two nearby temples. Lalit described how Gaudiya Math stole his father's books and writings. He also described the philosophical difference between himself and his brother Bhaktisiddhanta Saraswati regarding the Babaji worshiping mood and the strong type of preaching methods Bhaktisiddhanta employed.

The two elder Vaishnavas talked and laughed. Whenever Lalit got excited—and this seemed to be all the time—he spit all over the place: on me, on Prabhupada, on himself, into Gokula Vrindavan, everywhere. Prabhupada didn't seem to mind the saliva, nor did I, because we felt transcendentally blessed by this great devotee. Then Prabhupada motioned to me and Shyamasundar that it was time to leave. Lalit Prasad hugged us all as we left. Dousing me again with transcendental water from his lotus mouth, Lalit Prasad called me a "stout-hearted bhakta." I felt elated. I was invited to return any time, and I did return several times to receive his darshan, the blessing of Bhaktivinode's living son.

CONCENTRATION

Prabhupada told a true story that illustrates how we can become so focused that we do not notice the things in front of us. An author in Calcutta was so absorbed in his reading that he was unaware of his surroundings. One day a huge traffic accident happened right outside his window. Yet when the author was questioned as a witness, he was unable to describe anything, because he had been concentrating so much on his work he didn't even see or hear the accident! Concentration on sense gratification, which is the deluding power of Maya, will distract us so much we can't see Krishna, even though He is everywhere around us.

MOTHER THERESA

I had heard of this kind, saintly woman who housed and healed otherwise-abandoned souls in India. She would pick up and nurse sick and forgotten people from the railway platforms and streets of Calcutta, including lepers, outcastes and untouchables. This was certainly in the spirit of Lord Chaitanya, who also welcomed all souls regardless of status, race, or religion. Mother Theresa, like Lord Chaitanya, had the ability to see into souls and to heal the sick. I knew that though most of the people she rescued were Bengali, thus Hindu, she herself was a devout Christian. I thought that since she may not have known any Bengali bhajans (spiritual songs), I would go to her and offer to sing bhajans to members of her suffering flock at the time of their passing.

The hand-pulled ricksha wove its way through the exotic, aromatic, crowded streets of Calcutta. We passed men struggling to pull long carts heaped with wrapped goods; others carried huge bundles on their heads, skinny legs protruding under heavy loads. (The ricksha-wallah with his small, dull cowbell/horn was carrying his load too: me!) We passed the Chinese stores, went down the street where musical instruments were sold, and crossed over small bridges spanning dried-up streams. Occasionally the narrow alleyways widened into tree-lined streets, loud with car horns and choking in exhaust fumes. I chanted on my beads. At last we wheeled down a small lane, past a hidden palace, and I found myself across from a ramshackle school at the front of Mother Theresa's small hospice.

The doorbell was on a rope. I pulled on the rope, and a clean-faced smiling sister appeared at the door. "I'm looking for Mother Theresa," I smiled.

"Please come with me." The nun, in a white sari with blue border that signified her order, took me into a simple, cool front room. There was a small desk and chair and nothing else except a picture of Lord Jesus Christ and one of Mother Theresa herself. A few minutes later the sister came back and asked me to follow her. We passed through several hospital wards and through a final door. Standing before me was Mother Theresa, cradling a baby in her arms. She was quite small, yet powerful, like Srila Prabhupada. She comforted the child and patted another emaciated boy. She smiled openly and warmly on me. She recognized me as another servant of God and welcomed me.

As we walked through the hospital rooms, she reached out to touch sad faces and yearning hands and bodies. Through an interpreter I told her about our temple in Calcutta. I offered to sing Bengali bhajans to the sick and dying, so that they had the option of thinking about God at the time of death. She immediately agreed, but later on her other staff rejected the idea for sectarian reasons.

Still, I felt privileged to be in her glow. I had the intuitive feeling that she was a selfless, compassionate person. Mother Theresa had the softest hands, which she held out to me when we parted. I marveled that I could hold these same hands that had comforted and blessed countless souls.

Memories of Mother

Prabhupada told me how much his mother loved him and even admitted that she spoiled him as a child. Once, after little Abhay insisted, she had given him two toy guns, one for each hand. Another time he was sent to his room without dinner for being naughty. His mother was so caring, however, that she couldn't bear to think of her darling child being hungry, so she relented and brought plates of prasadam to him to eat while he was confined to his room.

> *"Take hot jalebis for a cold."*
> —A. C. Bhaktivedanta Swami

Blind Following

Prabhupada once told a story to illustrate the folly of following someone blindly: At a famous bathing ghat, people used to bring a brass cup shaped like a leaf to dip holy water from the Yamuna River and pour it into another identical cup to make oblations while reciting prayers. During the Gayatri mantra, when devotees say prayers on their brahmana threads, everyone's cups were on the bank of the river. After prayers, people had to look for their two cups that looked like everyone else's cups. One day, a man had the bright idea to put a small clay ball from the riverbank in each of his cups to distinguish them from the others, so he wouldn't have to search or argue. After putting the clay balls in his cups, he said Gayatri with his eyes closed. When he went to retrieve his cups, the man found that all the other cups on the bank had clay balls in them too! Everyone thought that his way was the proper ritual, so they copied him.

> "Philosophy without practice is speculation;
> practice without philosophy is fanaticism."
> —A. C. Bhaktivedanta Swami

Gopal Bon

Prabhupada was very adept at telling jokes, and some of his favorite jokes were about Gopal Bon, a fictional Bengali character who time and again demonstrated his absurdity while thinking he was very clever. For example, one day Gopal Bon was walking with a basket of grain on his head. A wind came along and blew the grains onto the ground all around him. Gopal Bon then said, "Well, I was going to distribute the grains anyway."

Full Circle

One day many people were standing in a long line to give Srila Prabhupada gifts and receive his blessings. He turned to me and said, "Just see how they are treating saintly people."

Many people were touching Prabhupada's feet. He said to me, "When someone touches your feet, you may have to take on their karma. Gurus who are strong in spiritual potency can absorb other people's karma." Then he joked, "That is why a guru pats someone on the head, to give the karma back." We laughed together, as His Divine Grace mock-demonstrated his technique on an imaginary supplicant.

Clear Mind

To demonstrate the unadulterated nature of the mind during past ages, or yugas, Prabhupada told this story.

While he was meditating one day, a yogi happened to witness an argument between two adversaries. The case was brought to court, and the yogi was called as a witness. He went up before the court and recounted the argument verbatim. To the surprise of the court officials, when the yogi was questioned further they discovered that he could not speak the language spoken by the two litigants, but his memory was so clear that he was able to repeat the discussion exactly as he heard it.

> "Essential truth, spoken concisely, is true eloquence."
> —Chanakya Pandit

Nature

Prabhupada often told this story.

One time a scorpion wanted to cross the river. He came upon a camel who was about to cross the deep river. The scorpion said to the camel, "Please, Mr. Camel, take me across the river."

The camel replied, "Oh, no: your reputation proceeds you, and I am afraid you will sting me."

The scorpion said, "Why should I do that? For if I did sting you, both of us would drown!"

That made sense to the camel, who thus invited the scorpion onto his back. In the middle of the river the scorpion stung the camel on his hump. Prabhupada demonstrated this by imitating a scorpion's tail with a fast, downward thrust of his arm. Then Prabhupada imitated the camel, who looked up questioningly at the scorpion. "Why did you do that? Now we shall both drown," the camel asked, his voice quivering.

"It's my nature," the scorpion replied.

Taming the Demon

One time a snarling dog charged at Srila Prabhupada. It looked like the Salva or Kesi demon charging Lord Krishna. Prabhupada raised his stick and said, "Come on!" The dog stopped short. Prabhupada gestured ever so slightly with his cane, and the dog sat down, still growling softly. Then Prabhupada threatened again, and the dog lay down and whimpered.

When we rounded the block for the second time, the whole performance was repeated; but by the third time we rounded the block, the dog had changed into Prabhupada's friend. The dog then tagged along with our group for awhile—the canine had now become a tamed servant. I thought of the dog as one of my godbrothers, taking training from Srila Prabhupada just as I did.

> "A devotee doesn't praise or reject a dog or a pandit.
> All are in diseased condition; all are part and parcel of Krishna.
> We must engage them in the service of the Lord."
> —A. C. Bhaktivedanta Swami

Sports

Walking across a soccer field in Gorakpur, India, I asked Srila Prabhupada, "Did you ever play sports in school?"

"Yes," he replied, "I was captain of the debating team."

FIRST YOU MUST KNOW THE *GITA*

At a *Bhagavad-gita* conference in Gorakpur, sponsored by Hanuman Prasad Poddar of the Gita Press, Prabhupada was asked to preside and speak on one of the appointed lecture days. Prabhupada had been looking at some of the *Gita* translations being displayed at the conference. He spoke on how the discussions at the gathering overlooked Krishna as the speaker of the *Gita*. He pointed out that they were arguing about what the *Gita* said, but they did not understand who spoke the words of the *Gita*. There was a big push to distribute the *Gita* all over the world, he said, but, "First you must know the *Gita* before you can distribute it. Krishna says, 'I am God,' and they are saying it is not Krishna talking. First, you must know that Krishna is God, then you can distribute *Gita*."

PREACHING IS MORE IMPORTANT

If Prabhupada's regular assistant were away, whoever was available among the devotees would sometimes have the opportunity to give Prabhupada his daily massage. Getting the chance to massage Srila Prabhupada was considered by all devotees to be a very special mercy. I have heard many stories throughout the years of how massaging Prabhupada was the high point in someone's devotional career.

One day Nara Narayan prabhu was asked by Prabhupada to try massaging him. Nara Narayan was a passionate, burly carpenter and sculptor. As he took his shower to be clean for the massage, his mind was in great conflict. "My hands are too coarse to touch the soft skin of His Divine Grace. These rough appendages are not worthy even to be near the holy self of Prabhupada! What should I do?" ran his tormented mind.

Meanwhile Prabhupada was waiting and waiting. Finally he asked someone else to try. As the devotee was about to start, Nara Narayan burst into the room and shouted, "I am ready, Srila Prabhupada!"

On another occasion, someone new was massaging Srila Prabhupada. While he sat there being massaged, Prabhupada was telling me about the history of the Home Bill Act during the British period in India. Prabhupada quietly said to the person massaging him, "Move the oil bottle, otherwise it will tip over." The devotee didn't follow Prabhupada's instruction, and, sure enough, he soon tipped the bottle over with his foot.

One day my turn came to massage Prabhupada. I relished the experience, having massaged His Divine Grace twice before. When I entered the room, Prabhupada looked at me and said, "Don't you have something more important to do? Anyone can rub oils. You can go out and preach. Not everyone can preach like you. Preaching is more important." He did however relent to my massaging him that day, and he said I did a good job. Touching his golden skin rejuvenated me as well. The sweet scent that emanated from Prabhupada was a reward in itself. His frame was strong and lithe. I derived great pleasure whenever he nodded off to sleep during the massage, a sure sign of effectiveness, according to Srutakirti, who was his regular assistant. By massaging His Divine Grace, I also felt I was able to preach more effectively.

WITH YOGI BHAJAN

I happened to be present when Srila Prabhupada met the famous Sikh guru Yogi Bhajan in Berkeley, California. Prabhupada was friendly, and Yogi Bhajan returned the kindness. Prabhupada seemed like an older brother to Yogi Bhajan. Yogi Bhajan talked about how he had obtained his immigration status and how his teachings were catching on in the Western world. Prabhupada listened and reminded Yogi Bhajan again of the importance of teaching the messages of *Bhagavad-gita* purely, acknowledging Krishna as God.

"Someone said that Guru Nanak has accepted Krishna as the Supreme Father. Is it a fact?"

Yogi Bhajan replied, "In the *Guru Grantha*, Krishna is accepted as incarnation of God."

Srila Prabhupada replied, "Incarnation and God, there is no difference."

Yogi Bhajan said, "Guru Govind Singh says Krishna is an avatar."

Then Srila Prabhupada quoted Lord Krishna speaking in the *Bhagavad-gita*: "All created beings have their source in these two natures. Of all that is material and all that is spiritual in this world, know for certain that I am both the origin and the dissolution." Prabhupada continued, "There is one God, one supreme Lord. If Guru Nanak accepts Krishna as God, as we do, why not put this God as one God? Why not present this God all over the world: '*Yad yad acharrati shresh taha.*' If you carry this message—it is not my message—it is the message of Krishna. I have not manufactured this message. I am imperfect, but I am presenting the perfect message; that is my business. I don't say I am perfect, I am simply carrier. When a peon delivers a money order for one thousand dollars, it is not his money. He simply carries. So my business is to carry Krishna's message, that's all. Whatever I am saying, I am quoting from *Bhagavad-gita*. You have seen it. I never say 'It is my opinion,' or 'I think'; I never say like that. If we want to do something substantial, we must come together on a common platform. That common platform is already there in every line of *Bhagavad-gita*. It is so nice."

Yogi Bhajan could only agree and shake his head in accord.

> *"Krishna consciousness means to be
> obligated to Krishna, to be a little grateful."*
> —A. C. Bhaktivedanta Swami

S. S. Radhakrishnan

One time we rode by train with Prabhupada to Madras, South India, for a spiritual conference and radio show. A meeting had been arranged in Madras between his Divine Grace and S. S. Radhakrishnan, the former vice president of India. S. S. Radhakrishnan had translated a widely read version of the *Bhagavad-gita*, but one that had left out the importance of Krishna as the speaker and instead glorified the song. S. S. Radhakrishnan's *Gita* was another impersonal interpretation. We all knew this.

After some cordial greetings, the former vice president asked Prabhupada how many temples existed in the West. Prabhupada quickly changed the subject and asked why and how Dr. Radhakrishnan did not recognize Krishna as God. Prabhupada continued, "Krishna says in *Bhagavad-gita*, 'Offer a leaf to Me.'" (9:12).

Dr. Radhakrishnan could not answer Prabhupada. He tried to change the subject and soon became flustered. This formerly powerful man just silently sat there, trembling. We left soon after this, and I could feel Prabhupada's displeasure. Srila Prabhupada said, "Just see, the great vice president of India does not know the meaning of *Bhagavad-gita*!"

Unlimited

Walking by the ocean in Madras one day, Prabhupada said, "There are more demigods than waves in the sea." On another occasion, while walking on the same path, he said, "The waves look beautiful from the shore, but when you are in them it is very difficult." He explained that the ocean waves are like the captivating effect of Maya: "She appears attractive, but is entangling."

Krishna's Mercy

Late at night, when everyone else was asleep, was a nice time to be with Prabhupada. He was usually in a very mellow mood, so if I wanted to have his precious darshan I would sometimes stand outside his door and make slight noises so he would come out to see what the noise was and invite me in. We were staying in the new quarters at Mayapur, in the first of the four, large residence buildings. The sky was overcast. I was yearning for Prabhupada's association, so I went near his rooms and made walking and chanting sounds. No servants were around, so Prabhupada came out himself saying, "Who is that?" He saw me chanting, smiled, and came all the way out of his quarters.

Srila Prabhupada walked up and down on the balcony with me, then turned towards the fields and walked to the balcony railing. He looked out and said, "The farmers beg Krishna for rainwater." He paused briefly. "All right, take it!" As Prabhupada swept his hand down as if dispensing rain, a lightening bolt crashed; suddenly the sky opened and rain came down furiously.

"Take it," he said quietly, and walked into his rooms.

*"The nightingale desists to sing
until it has something pleasing to say."*
—Chanakya Pandit

APPENDIX

Vyasa Puja Offerings

IN 1969, SHORTLY AFTER WE had moved into the Bury Place temple in London, which was only two blocks from the British Museum, I began to search through the archives of the India Office library and the British Museum library for the writings of Bhaktivinode Thakur, Rupa Goswami, Krishna das Kaviraj, or any other authors in our Gaudiya Vaishnava tradition. I found many treasures, including the *Poriad* by Bhaktivinode Thakur, a Bengali *Rasa Mitra Sindhu*, some original paintings of the Jagannatha festival in Puri, India, and photographs of past spiritual masters in our tradition!

The British Museum library is one of the largest in the world, and it houses books from around the world. Since the British Empire once included India, many old books from India found their way to Great Russel Street. Each culture influenced the other immensely.

The most exciting treasure I found was a 1936 issue of the *Harmonist*, the magazine founded by Bhaktisiddhanta Saraswati, my grandfather guru. I held this booklet in my hands, thinking that perhaps it had been touched by those same saintly hands! Inside was even more of a gift, for the magazine contained a poem by my Guru Maharaja, A. C. Bhaktivedanta Swami. For the birthday anniversary celebrations of His Divine Grace Srila Bhaktisiddhanta Saraswati Prabhupada, at the Bombay Gaudiya Math in February, 1936, my guru composed and read his poem.

1.
Adore adore ye all
the happy day
blessed than heaven
sweeter than May
When he appeared in Puri
the holy place
My Lord and Master
His Divine Grace.

2.
Oh! my master
the evangelic angel.
Give us thy light,
Light up thy candle
Struggle for existence
a human race
the only hope
His Divine Grace.

3.
Misled we are
all going astray
Save us Lord
Our fervent prayer
Wonder thy ways
to turn our face
Adore thy feet
Your Divine Grace.

4.
Forgotten Krishna
We fallen souls
Paying most heavy
The illusion's tolls
Darkness around
A human race
the only hope
His Divine Grace.

5.
Message of service
Thou hast brought
A healthful life
As Chaitanya wrought.
Unknown to all
it's full of brace.
That's your gift
Your Divine Grace.

6.
Absolute is sentient
Thou hast proved,
Impersonal calamity
Thou hast moved
This gives us a life
Anew and fresh
Worship thy feet
Your Divine Grace

7.
Had you not come
Who had told
The message of Krishna
Forceful and bold.
That's your right
you have the mace.
Save me a fallen
Your Divine Grace.

8.
The line of service
As drawn by you,
Is pleasing and healthy
Like morning dew.
The oldest of all
But in new dress
Miracle done
Your Divine Grace

—*Abhay Charan dasa*

I sent a photocopy of Srila Prabhupada's poem to him. He was so very thankful, and it was relayed to me by others how much he appreciated my finding it. Later, he commented, "I thought I had lost it [the poem]."

The following are my own meager Vyasa Puja Prayers, written over the years, that I have humbly offered at the lotus feet of my spiritual master, His Divine Grace A. C. Bhaktivedanta Swami Prabhupada.

Vrindavan, August 1972

Dear Srila Prabhupada,

I am sitting in the very rooms you resided in and started our movement in, hearing the same bells you heard, writing this in the same spot in which you wrote and translated the immortal *Srimad-Bhagavatam* (bringing the higher world of Krishna to the lower world of matter), and seeing the formidable jewel-like form of Rupa Goswami's samadhi, steady and encouraging. Your old stove stands in the corner, and I can again taste the prasad you cooked for us back in 1965. What a trick! Who would have thought that you could bring order and responsibility to those Kali-yugites, dedicated to chaos and irresponsibility. I sit and stare, and the blank page stares back at me. It is again the time to write a Vyasa-puja homage, though it should be done at every moment. How do I glorify you, who are so unlimitedly glorious? It is hardly expressed in a few thousand words, and I cannot aptly put my overwhelming feelings for you down on paper (just as I must desist from adding a humble, self-effacing statement to all others herein, since I cannot begin to deface what is already so low). It is you who give us the taste for the spiritual. I am not so serious, but love for you keeps me plodding along, and I pray that all of us may continue to back you with fuller convictions, as you still show us the way back home.

In these rooms, I see advertisements for your first three volumes of *Srimad-Bhagavatam*; I see "League of Devotees" pamphlets; I see "De's Pain Liniment." I see old membership books, chemistry beakers, bookstore distribution lists, etc. I see all the services we are presently engaged in, and you have already done them. I think I should just recount some of the examples of your preaching in Vrindavan, since this is being written on behalf of the Vrindavan devotees. This will be my glorification to your limitless, wonderful qualities.

Once, I awaited your arrival at New Delhi Airport. You requested me to arrange a car to go to Vrindavan. "Vrindavan doesn't mean buying a ticket. It is an attitude, a way of accepting the special mercy of the dhama." You were not only arranging the ticket, but escorting me through the gate yourself. I thought that if I could choose the highest pleasure—spiritual or mundane—of all the unending pleasures available, that pleasure would be to be with you in Vrindavan. The purest devotee and the purest place combined. Now the desire is being fulfilled.

Vestiges of sentiment and romanticism still needing to be dispelled from our brains, and cut by your sword of correctness lay waiting to be smote down like untrained soldiers.

Before having come into your direct contact, we read books of so-called spirituality, ideas with no applicable basis. The books spoke of a neophyte disciple waiting before the door of his guru with quiet determination, while excessive heat and cold attacked the beatific devotee. After three days of patient austerity, the gate opens, the guru stands there, and the neophyte becomes a disciple. But you saw that we cannot even stand in one place for five minutes. So you engaged us in Krishna's service. Another of these books told of a disciple's not eating for many days. But you saw how we grow restless if we don't eat, so you fed us Krishna-prasad. You, in fact, teach us the perfect balance of sanctity and activity, of work and play, of bhajan and preaching, of action and inaction, of devotion and preaching, of pancharatrika and bhagavad-viddhi. And so with the idea of the highest pleasure of you and Vrindavan together, I anticipate your arrival in Delhi's Palam Airport. There are only two of us to greet you, but you accept our garlands and sandalwood and rosewater with a grace that makes us bashful, as if the whole world were there greeting you. The car pulls up, and we await some words. You hand me your (at the time) small white satchel, which you carry our movement around in; but still you say nothing. You glide into the front seat, and we get into the back with your traveling secretary. Exchanging whispered news of devotees and activities around the world, we talk in low, subdued voices, so as not to disturb you. Minutes pass like hours as we await your transcendental words, some instruction, some acknowledgment. But transcendental as you are, you remain silent. I have another realization: there is no need for you to acknowledge or appease us. By now our Society has begun to establish itself as it should be—catering to your mood, not ours. If you want to be silent, that is correct, and we should not expect or push anything else. And so from that time on, whenever meeting with you I let you establish the mood, not me. If you want to joke, I joke; if you want to chastise, I bow my head remorsefully; if you want to talk business, I talk business; if you want to talk philosophy, I talk philosophy. I remember in Calcutta once when being sent on a special mission I came in and stated with importance, wanting glorification, "I am going now," and you simply turned and walked into the bathroom.

Yet, in the car, we still anticipate some divine instruction, some words of Wisdom—anything—as you, in all your natural beauty, sit relaxed in the front seat. At a red stoplight, the Indian version of the Hell's Angels roll up next to your open window. You turn your head slightly and say "Hare Krishna," and the young grease-ball says "Hare Krishna" back. He jabbers to his friends, and they jabber back, and they turn into Gandharvas and young innocents by your grace. We still await, murmuring the maha-mantra silently. We glide to the outskirts of New Delhi on the way to Vrindavan. Your voice of authority and patience finally breaks the vacuous silence. You say, "Cement." Another realization—here again all those romantic books about perfumed saints and do-nothing sadhus vanish like bubbles popping in the air. The practical application of devotion instead.

You point to a large water tower and say, "We should build one like that in Vrindavan." We are on the way to finalize all the arrangements of a piece of land given to us by the grace of Srimati Radharani, after the promises of court jesters, kings, mice and men all failed. You had sent me to Vrindavan to scout land and/or already-built temples. We narrowed down our choice to this piece of land in holy Raman Reti ("enjoyable sands"). When we arrived in holy Vrindavan, your ever-bright eyes became even brighter. We are staying at Saraf Bhavan, and you set up camp on the top floor, like a field general. The floor consists of six small side rooms around a long hall, and we are preparing for the next few days of amazing events. Somehow or other, without any advertising or announcements, your old friends, godbrothers, officials, etc., start showing up. Summoned by some silent incomprehensible means, they begin to appear—like silent natures out of jungle thickets, an enigma to the common covered man. We first arrange for a ground-breaking ceremony with the ex-owner of the land in Raman Reti, the present site of our Krishna-Balarama Mandir, while in the next room another dissatisfied person, who wanted the same piece of property, waits. Police and retired members of parliament appear, and you talk to them, and they convince the agitator that any thoughts of getting the piece of land are in vain. One Goswami, hardly able to see, led by his son, comes from Radha-Damodara, while his archrivals—two other Goswamis—arrive simultaneously. You spring up from your seat faster than a speeding bullet and put the enemies in different rooms to avoid their fighting (although they live in the same temple compound, they haven't spoken to one another for years). You satisfy each one of them separately; they each take you as an ally, and you discuss and draw up papers which arrange our stay at some rooms at the top of Radha-Damodara Temple. Your secretary is simultaneously drawing up the contract for accepting the Raman Reti property and the contract for the rooms at Damodara. Some babajis (in their off-white cloth) and your slightly bearded godbrothers arrive, and you at once host them and then feed them amidst all the other agreements and arrangements. You are like the great ringmaster we used to see as children, running the whole show, the central attraction, training all—a dancing bear in one ring, a tightrope walker in another ring, and the lions in another ring—you continue to control from your seat this great transcendental circus in this most transcendental arena, Vrindavan.

I remember one time a dog charged at you, snarling, looking like Salva or the Kesi demon charging Lord Krishna. You raised your stick and said, "Come on." The dog stopped short, you gestured slightly with your stick, and the dog sat down, still growling. Then you threatened again, and he lay down and whimpered. When we rounded the block for the second time, the whole performance was repeated, but the third time we saw that the dog was your servant and friend; he was tamed. I thought of him as my companion or godbrother, remembering how you similarly trained us all.

You then explained how "Beware of the dog" was a symptom of modern false civilization, where one may walk down the street peacefully and from behind a large closed gate the dog barks at you, "Don't come here"—each gate separating one man's property from the other man's property, no one sharing, no spiritual center.

I was beginning to learn by your example the balance between practical hard work for Krishna and temple devotions which sanctify that hard work. In Krishna consciousness there is no room for dry rituals. "Necessity is the mother of invention," you told, and I could see that "devotee" means whatever Krishna wants, that's all. We are His toys. The sincerity of the offering is the essence, not the wealth. "Anyone in any part of the world may offer a fruit, a flower, some water, to Lord Krishna, and He will accept," you taught. And so you engage us to work hard, day and night, for Lord Krishna. "We should not waste a moment," you recently wrote me in a letter. "Take my example, not a moment is wasted. The karmis sit in the park and say, 'My son-in-law said this, etc.'" The next day I came to see you, and some more transcendental instructions were being given by you to Subala dasa:

Srila Prabhupada: You do not like to live with the devotees?
Subala: No.
Srila Prabhupada: Why is that?
Subala: They gossip and talk nonsense.
Srila Prabhupada: Then you must change the gossip into transcendental talks. So many people come to me with nonsensical talks, and I transform them into transcendental talks.
Subala: We are always fighting.
Srila Prabhupada: You must consider it to be your fault. If each person thinks in that way, there cannot be fighting. If someone calls me "prabhu," and I think I am their master, that is wrong.
Subala: I just want to stay in Vrindavan.
Srila Prabhupada: It is better that you give Vrindavan to others. If I did not leave Vrindavan, you would not know Vrindavan. Rather, you should go out, preach, and then come back and build a skyscraper (pronounced "scrapper").

The next day on the morning walk, we saw many devotees, sadhus, etc., as regular asarati, who came to you to pay respects (they are so regular you can set your watch by them). We started to walk towards Raman Reti. You tell how the neem tree is medicinal. We see women picking up cow dung, and you say, "Everything is used in India. That is proper." I say, "Cow dung is purer than other dungs; it does not attract as many flies."

You smile mischievously and say, "Oh, you have done research?" Then you say, "Therefore this is proof that cow dung is antiseptic."

I say, "Yes," and you order me to study nature, for that will reveal many truths of the *Bhagavatam*. This is especially true in Vrindavan.

"Living in Vrindavan is like lying on the lap of Krishna," you say, but later you qualify that, "Krishna is not loitering in Loi Bazaar." And over the years you come and go, you come to speed up the construction of the temple, you taste the water, you stand and count the bags of cement used.

You question our actions in much detail. "How much is the price of atta (flour)?" I say Rs. 1.60 a kilo, and you split up all the prices to how much an average devotee can eat. For instance, "A devotee eats one quarter of a kilo of rice. The rice costs Rs. 1.80, so a devotee eats one quarter of that. Therefore, Rs.0.45 is spent per man on rice." And you break up all the items, including spices, wood for cooking, and still you cut down on the amount we are spending to feed the devotees. One of the items, a vegetable, you ask what is the cost per kilo. I say, "60 paisa." You tell the story of "damn cheap babu." The foreign babu comes and gets the local prices and says, "damn cheap, damn cheap" while he is being charged twice the amount as the local residents. "Sixty paisa," you say. "It should cost 30 paisa." I quip that those are the prices in 1953. (I remember seeing your account book in your rooms at Radha-Damodara and how much you would spend, and you would account for everything.) You then say, "Do it that cheaply anyway," and we do it by your empowered potency. You ask not only the price of vegetables, but the cost of cement, steel, as well as the timings of the Frontier Mail, the Toofan Express and the Punjab Mail Trains.

You expect me to know all the local residents, and you introduce me to them, as they come to see you. You initiated me into the vast etiquette and intrigues of Vrindavan society, and sometimes send me on seemingly impossible missions, like the time you sent me to borrow three crores of rupees (Rs. 30,000,000) from the Home Minister of India, to be paid back in foreign exchange, or the time you sent me to ask the American Ambassador to India to allow us to live in one of his houses free, or when a king wanted Rs. 50,000,000 for his palace and you told me to say that since we are brahmanas and you are king, you must give to brahmanas. If we see all these things in the transcendental light, they are not outrageous; rather, it is the mundane darkness that is outrageous.

I remember the time we were walking on the banks of the Yamuna, the full moon still in the morning sky. You point with your cane to the moon and say, "They say the moon is dust. Why are those sands [pointing to the Yamuna] not shining and those sands [pointing to the moon] shining? If it is reflection of the sun as they [the scientists] claim, then the sun is there—why are those [the moon's] sands shining and those [the Yamuna's sands] not?" The moon-talks intrigue us all as we press close to one another to hear you.

Sometimes, we walk through the back alleys of this vast wonderland. Your cane rings on the red stones. You decided to reside one night again in your old rooms, and four of us are fortunate enough to accompany you, sleep in a heap in your kitchen to keep warm, in the post-Karttika night chill.

Slowly, the Krishna-Balarama construction begins, a well is dug, but the water is salty. But then another, producing sweet water blessed by Balarama, awes the neighbors, who all have salt water. The construction rolls on slowly, a string of endless obstacles, no money, no materials. You push us harder; you come there yourself, and you solve everything. You come and live at Sethji's house nearby, a pandal cover is erected to fuel your preaching fire, and you speak how the true bhakta is the only unmotivated yogi, whereas jnanis, yogis and karma-yogis all are tarnished by motivated liberation-wishes. During another mass pilgrimage, the devotees stay at Laksmi Rani Kunj, and you deliver the famous *Nectar of Devotion* series of lectures at Radha-Damodara Temple. After the lectures, devotees and guests all squeeze into your small rooms.

You talk to me many times about vairagya, how we should give up material attachments. You also teach tolerance. I asked you whether it is sometimes very hot or cold in Vrindavan to test how much one loves Krishna by staying here, and you answered, "Yes, sometimes Krishna tests that way." Titiksa must be developed.

Your house is finally being completed. I remember the frantic rush to put everything in order for your first viewing; the floor and your newly varnished desk dried literally thirty seconds before you walked in. Of course, this is not unique, as probably every temple in the movement has experienced this same rush before your arrival and how miraculously everything comes together almost the same instant as you step your lotus feet inside.

Your old godbrothers come, and you host them in your new rooms, along with the late afternoon stream of guests from every part of India. You sit back relaxed and talk to them, enlighten them, until night comes and the bright stars appear in the Vrindavan sky. Again, your magnanimity is all-embracing. I remember one night you say to me, "Let's go to some temples. Can you arrange? What time is their darshan?" Later you tell me, "Darshan does not mean for you to see the Deity, but rather for the Deity to see you." I arrange a car; by that time the news has leaked out, in the unexplainable way of our

Krishna conscious grapevine-communications, more speedy than any modern telecommunications system, and suddenly I am being petitioned, lobbied, cajoled, begged, and ordered that I take everyone along. You get in the front seat along with the driver, and then you motion to one devotee, "Come on," and as the front seat is filled, you say, "There is room in back, come on," and the back seat is filled by the pillars and big guns of our Krishna Consciousness Movement. A stack of GBCs and sannyasis squash in the back seat.

After it is filled, Gargamuni Maharaja shows up, and you say, "Come on, come on," and so he squeezes in the already overburdened and crowded back seat. As the car is ready to limp off, Panca Dravida Maharaja comes ambling along with his danda, eager to join, and we can't refuse him. He lays across all of us, with his hands and legs hanging out the window. You ask, "Where to first? Where to next?" and my muffled reply comes from under the Vaishnava bodies. When we reach Govinda temple, you walk out majestically, and we pile out, like the clowns in a circus, all getting out of the small car. During the morning walks, we sit down by the side of the road, and you teach the whole varna and ashram system.

Your personal friendliness knows no bounds. Like a kind father, you instructed me to invite all the Goswamis and special people of Vrindavan to our first Vyasa-puja ceremony at Krishna-Balarama Mandir. The temple was decorated gloriously, and many special guests came. We had just finished washing your lotus feet. I was drying your lotus toes one by one by one, and you looked at me and asked, "Have you invited such and such?" As I worked very hard to make everything nice for you, I readily said, "Yes, he told me he would be a little late," and you looked pleased. After we bathed and dried your feet, the senior devotees began to offer flowers and offer dandavats (prostrating themselves) three times. As I was offering dandavats for the second time, you called me again. I thought, "Uh oh, who did I forget to invite?" Srila Prabhupada always catches all of our mistakes, and I leaned close to you. Instead of asking anything, you simply took your fingers and so affectionately ruffled my sikha and the top of my head. All the devotees crowding around cried, "*Ahhh!*" in one well-wisher's voice. I felt my years of service again rewarded. You are so Krishna conscious that every time your finger extends, your lips open, your eyes look, or your eyebrows twitch, it is great preaching. I begin to become astounded at how much of your precious time you have given to us.

Recently, when I went to see you in your new rooms in Bombay, I say, "I don't want to take too much of your precious time."

You reply, "No, no, you can come any time, and also bring some honey." You then ask, "How do you like these rooms?"

I say, "They are wonderful because you are in them now, but if you were in another place, they too would be wonderful. Because of Your Divine Grace they are a tirtha."

Tirthi kurvanti tirthani, you corrected my pronunciation and said, "Yes, one who keeps Krishna always, one who remembers Krishna—yoginam api sarvesam mad-gatenantaratmana sraddhavan bhajate yo mam sa me yuktatamo matah—that place becomes Krishna conscious." Then we both at the same time, as if by magic, said: man-mana bhava mad-bhaktah.

Each minute with you is the fulfillment of a dream, a special event, and you have given the treasure-house of many hours. (You have changed our vocabulary, so we talk like you.) We gesture like you and give the same answers to questions as you do, and we try to preach like you. We embrace the parampara not out of duty, but because we are attracted to your way of doing things. Your defense of Krishna is boundless, and we watch in awe at your untiring strength as everyone except simple devotees are exposed to be fools and rascals.

A simple proof of your changing us is that the word 'duty' was unknown and unused in our upbringing. No one taught us a sense of duty, because no one knows what or whom to serve. The whole system of dharma and duty has become a practical engraved truth to many now, as you have brought duty to us, and even though many ideas from the ancient Vedas at first seemed unattractive, they now constitute a way of life for thousands. These truths shown, by your example that have changed so many lives, are wonderfully unique and obviously graced by Lord Krishna. The general society may not understand us, but they have to recognize us. A judge recently stated in court that we are bona fide, which in itself is a great step for what was an unknown teaching just eleven years ago. It took Moses, Muhammad and Jesus Christ much longer to establish their teachings as bona fide in the courts of law. Now, it is our duty to change the scientists, who are the modern smarta-brahmanas and high priests of today. You tell me, "Our movement is sublime, the books are sublime, and Krishna is supplying everything. Now go out in Poland and Russia and arrange for meetings with the scientists."

I say, "Communist scientists?"

You say, "Why not? Two plus two equals four both for the Communists and Capitalists. It is not that because I am Communist, I can say two plus two equals five. You must convince them of this Krishna consciousness. I predict that Russians will become first-class theists."

I said, "Yes, because there are less sense objects to distract them."

"They will view my books carefully. They have respect for Indian culture, and the Sanskrit texts. The Jagais and Madhais will change. Even Valmiki was a dacoit and he changed, so you go and arrange everything."

One of your greatest gifts is your great understanding of every situation in perfect perspective. They (the lawyers in New York) wanted to end the "brainwashing" litigations, but instead you wanted to extend them for fourteen years, using your books as evidence: "Exhibit A—*Bhagavad-gita*." Only you can come up with the most remarkable ideas, using each situation in its best capacity to give Krishna consciousness to everyone. Where we are shortsighted, you see all sides of each situation and apply it. So many times I have watched as we, your disciples, have wanted to condemn, but you see and you can explain properly another, perhaps conflicting, point of view. This fairness, according to time and circumstance, must be learned. You have said about someone we were criticizing, "He is not to be blamed; he was taught what he knows, as you have been taught what you know, so rather than blame him, rectify his teachings."

For example, one day as we were shooing away ducks in our path, we said, "You rascals," but you calmly replied, "As you are thinking they are rascals, they are thinking you are rascals." So you always teach that preaching means seeing from the perspective of Lord Krishna's viewpoint, and attracting others also to Krishna's Vedic version. We owe our gratitude to you only. What I feel when in your association—that strength, that determination, that enthusiasm, that ecstasy—is an unequaled feeling, for only you are the great touchstone of deliverance. I pray that we all can remember these feelings and remain steady in our devotional service.

Vrindavan devotees

August, 1973

Dear Srila Prabhupada,

We offer our heartful obeisances to you, the best spiritual father of the whole cosmic situation. As you beckon us, we follow you with the faltering steps of babies entering the realm of purity. "Don't be afraid, Krishna will protect," you say with your chest expanded like Bhismadeva, to encourage us to become 'Abhay Charan dasa'. How fortunate we are to be called Vaishnavas. By your example everywhere, you represent all the great acharyas for all time and space. You are the acharya with all potency, as grave and exact as His Divine Grace Bhaktisiddhanta Prabhupada, warm, personal, compassionate, a knower-of-all-worlds and encouraging like His Divine Grace Bhaktivinode Thakur. We see you sitting and writing at night as Bhaktivinode did, the sound of the gas motor fan puttering in the background; all of Navadvipa meets your gaze. As renounced as Gaura Kishore dasa Babaji, chanting for the whole world to hear it, you see all souls as devotees just as Sri Jagannatha dasa Babaji saw the tiger. You sing with soft-throated authority just like Sri Narottama dasa Thakur, and you are just like the embodiment of Sri Visvanatha Cakravarti.

You represent Sri Rupa Gosvamipada, the Rasa-tattva. You inspire Sambandha, Abhidheya and Prayojana as Sanatana Gosvami's Siddhanta-tattva. You are the embodiment of Vidhi-tattva as seen in Sri Gopala Bhatta's Hari-bhakti-vilasa. As the servant of Sri Raghunatha Goswami, you are eternally honoring all Vaishnavas, and as Sri Raghunatha Bhatta Goswami reads, so when you read the holy Bhagavatam, your eyes fill with tears. As the great Sri Krishna dasa Kaviraja has envisioned, you are bringing the holy maha-mantra to the lips of middle-aged women polishing their Formica kitchens and to over-stuffed businessmen jostling one another in crowded subways. You teach with such clarity and simplicity for we common men could not hear you any other way, being so dulled by the material modes. Just as Sri Jiva Goswami, you know every aspect of Krishna's Vaishnava philosophy. On morning walks you see in the leaves of trees examples of Govinda-bhasya in the clouds, the Vedanta-sutra in the animals. And then you ask us questions to let us realize what you see, just as the magician pulls rabbits out of top hats, you pull krishna-prema-bhakti out of stone hearts.

You carry on the tradition of Jagat Guru Sri Madhavendra Puri and defeat the impersonalists; in the line of Sri Madhvacarya, you satisfy the hearts of all devotees that surrender to you. How fortunate we are to contact your lotus feet, to know anything about Lord Chaitanya Mahaprabhu, the *Srimad-Bhagavatam*, the Hare Krishna mantra, the *Srimad-Bhagavad-gita*, the arca-vigraha of Their Lordships Radha and Krishna, the endless associates of the Supreme Lord, and now all of the wonderful and glorified Godbrothers that have gathered at your lotus feet. If you had not come to preach all this, we would not have had the opportunity to learn it, and revive others. What have we done, we who are so full of greed, envy, umbrage and lust, to deserve to serve you in Holy Vrindavan Dhama. It is incomprehensible to us how vast your mercy is upon us. For now we are forming a close team, joyously building a wonderful Nanda Maharaja's house just for Krishna and Balarama. We jump and work in the sands of Raman Reti, wash in the water of the embracing Yamuna River, respect the holy prasad prepared by Anand Prabhu, place our heads at the feet of Sri-Sri Radha-Madana-Mohana, Sri Radha-Govinda, Sri Radha-Gopinatha, Sri Radha-Raman, Sri Radha-Gokulananda, Sri Radha-Damodara, Sri Radha-Shyamasundar, and Sri Radha-Giridhari. We are cooled from the scorching heat by the sandal-tulasi tastes of maha-prasad. We are washed by the caranamrta of the Lord, and take the parikrama of Govardhan and Radha-Kunda.

Here all of your examples of the species functioning in the modes of material nature become manifest: pigs eating stool instead of halva, camels eating thorny twigs, elephants rolling in the dust just after the bath, monkey mothers carrying their babies precariously swinging in the treetops, asses working like asses just for a mouth full of grasses and then kicking each other for some sex life, cows grazing peacefully in the forest, and peacocks dancing with feathers unfurled like a whole kirtan party with arms upraised. "Hari Bol!"

Last night a nimba tree fell down in a storm and just missed hitting our house, but, as always, Krishna protects his devotees, and no one was harmed. We expected rather to see Nalakuvera and Manigriva emerge resplendent with helmet and jewels!

Now you have allowed us, these unserious devotees, to serve you in your eternal home town. We beg only to follow in your footsteps by following your instructions and nothing more. Eternally you reside here in Vrindavan with Sri-Sri Radha and Krishna, the cowherd boys, headed by Lord Balarama, the demigods, and the host of pilgrims whose sins have been washed away by the River Yamuna.

You are the center of our life, just as Lord Krishna is the center of life in Vrindavan Dhama. Here the holy name is on every mouth, tilak adorns every beautiful face and bead-bags are the extensions of all the hands. The work is hard, the service is trying, but the rewards are too great. Here everything is done for Your Divine Grace, our dear most spiritual master and father.

> *sri-guru-carana-padma, kevala-bhakati-sadma*
> *bando mui savadhana mate*
> *jahara prasade bhai, e bhava toriya jai*
> *krsna-prapti hoy jaha ha'te*

> *sri-guru karuna-sindhu, adhama janara bandhu,*
> *lokanath lokera jivana*
> *ha ha prabhu koro doya, deho more pada-chaya,*
> *ebe jasa ghusuk tribhuvana*

Our goal is to remember your instructions at every moment. By so doing we may one day become Krishna conscious and then, representing you and your Guru Maharaja, we may obtain the goal of life that we seek. We must always remember that we are representing you and must act as you do with all our heart and soul. We are eternally thanking you again and again for accepting us as your disciples.

Gurudas Adhikari
Yamuna devi dasi
Satyavrata dasa brahmachari

Tatpur dasa brahmachari
Gunarnava dasa brahmachari
Anand Prabhu (Srila Prabhupada's Godbrother)

AUGUST, 1976

Meeting with Our Guru—Krishna-Balaram TSKP

You call, "Where is Gurudas!" I come, expectant, eager to serve, prepared for the unexpected. Nama om visnu-padaya: I offer my obeisances to the lotus feet of you, Srila Prabhupada. Krsna-presthaya bhutale: you are very dear to Lord Krishna. Reverently, I bow down, an air of eternity pervades the room, a seriousness of purpose found nowhere else. Conviction sets the mood and inspires me also, offering some small service, it becomes secondary, to the adventure for our mutual Lord, a small bluish boy. He can do so much. I try to write this, but cannot properly express your greatness, nor my great love for you. Your one knee is up in the air, like a great building of the future, your hand rests on the peak of your knee, your head rests back, relaxed, but you see everything.

When coming to see you, gravity is always there, even in our light joking, which occurs often, interspersed with the business at hand. I watch interview after interview, with others also, sometimes in Hindi or Bengali, although the words are a montage passing by, the words still convey the same dedicated, serious love of Lord Krishna; you are dhira—engaging whomever you meet, changing their thinking, towards a higher philosophical understanding, or to render some service, or if nothing else to accept some prasad. "Give them prasad," you say as people are going. Now, after watching you for so long, I automatically do this, without asking.

People come to you, never taking your darshan lightly. You want to give them the highest goal of life, Krishna consciousness. You want everyone to be happy, sometimes you have to administer the medicine by coaxing the seemingly bitter pill of surrender into them, sometimes cutting out the diseases we still carry, sometimes you engage us, as if we are holding a horse's mouth open and forcing the medicine in. Then with an encouraging word, whoever receives your mercy runs out of your room eager to execute the service you prescribe.

Anything may happen in your presence—you are transcendentally situated. You may question a new idea very carefully—"What makes you think your contribution is different?"—or you may ask, "What is our goal?"

"To love Krishna," we answer.

"Why?" you challenge.

Or you may ask, "How do you know Krishna is God?" You propose the answer and if it is not exact enough—"That is your dogmatism." You want us to be sure of what we are doing; many times you seem to question just to see if we are convinced or determined; if challenged and we remain silent "silence means affirmation," affirmation of whatever the opposing viewpoint is.

Another time you questioned like a tornado, question after question. Each question was harder to answer. The questions took on technical rather than philosophical qualities, no bluffing, no abstractions, Srila Prabhupada's voice thundering like a cyclone and tornado combined. I simply said, "I am a great fool."

You said extremely quiet and soft, "One must remain a fool before his spiritual master. Lord Chaitanya said that." Then the mood became philosophical. By your questioning you train us to be careful, hard as iron, soft as a rose.

Sitting in your new Mercedes 200 SL Lotus Chariot, our elbows sometimes touching, you speak to a life member in the front seat. You are so quiet, contained, sure, peaceful, powerful. All of Lord Krishna comes from you; you are not separate from Lord Krishna. Lord Krishna stays in His abode, yet runs faster than everyone. You also stay, and we cannot keep up with you, and when you travel we cannot keep up with you. You told of a Bengali proverb: an intelligent man can make thirteen rupees by sitting, another less intelligent man gets twelve rupees by traveling. Either way, whether you travel or sit down we cannot keep up with you. Sometimes, you sit so still your automatic watch stops.

Assorted facts of life fill the air; you are a storehouse of transcendental grandfather wisdom:

"Hot jalebis cure colds."

"Some rich men used to bury a live child with their hidden treasure so when the child dies, he would become a ghost and guard the treasure."

"Mustard oil on the body, not in the body."

"Now as we import dry milk from the West when before there was an abundance of cows, now we are importing brahmanas from the West."

"A language does not consist of yes, no, very good."

"Do things cooperatively, for if you fail, no one person is to blame and if there is success, all persons get credit."

"The scientists research useless things. They say the poison is colorless, odorless, and tasteless. How can they test that the poison is tasteless?" (And you imitate a dying scientist whose last words are, "It is tasteless!")

"There were yogis who were able to eat mercury and then make gold from their urine." Then you laugh, "That is how they maintain themselves."

"They say that you don't see Krishna. How they can say you don't see, if they don't see? Just like you may have a lover and when you think of that lover you see him, but the other person doesn't see your lover. They cannot say that you do not see Krishna. A man in Bengal was a writer and there was an accident in front of his window. He did not see because he was absorbed in writing. We are so absorbed in Krishna, we can see Him." Little anecdotes spice your teachings.

As the Bengali countryside passes, I think of the years you have sacrificed for us all, leaving the wonderful shelter of Radha-Damodara to execute your Guru's orders. We too must go where you bid us, do what pleases you the most.

Floating down the roads of Bengal, we ride silently in your new 200 SL Chariot, you view everything with clear blazing vision, curiosity with spiritual perspective combined. I too, like a child, try to view everything that passes by the window, so much going on, so much to see, everything living, everything personal, children, bullock carts, straw huts, bathing ghats, water buffaloes, dogs, bicycles, dahl drying on the road, palm trees.

So much to see, a variety for the senses, yet I am pulled to see you, to disregard all that is going on around, and to gaze on your lotus face as the Bengal scenery floats by, as if the planet's zooming instead of the trees. That is your divine trick, I see you instead of the externals. You sit with your hand in the air, a flower between your long golden fingers, caressed by you, remaining ever fresh, unharmed during the whole journey. Your face concerned for the whole of humanity, your eyes beam compassionately, eyes no one can equal, combined with an unshakable strength, you see everything, your feet planted firmly on the ground, relaxed, sure of Lord Krishna's protection, you inspire the devotees of the world.

I see you instead of the variegatedness; you have attracted me to the divine instead of the mundane; you constantly trick everyone this way, "Think of Lord Krishna, not maya," and because every movement of your eyes is preaching, you constantly engage in Krishna's service anyone who meets you.

You scoff at the material world, the same one that everyone embraces, yet you remain a gentleman in its domain. You tell humorous story upon story to describe the absurdity of fallible soldiers of illusion, and through humor we can laugh at ourselves, at humanity's useless struggle, and then try to embrace a higher taste. You tell that material life means fall down, still the foolish man embraces the temporary pleasures and pains despite his seeing everything decay before him. Despite his brothers being jailed, he steals.

You mock the foolishness. A man is sawing a branch (you demonstrate), sawing himself on the limb, cutting in such a way that he will fall. His friend comes and says, "If you cut that way you will fall down." "Don't tell me how to cut, I know," says the blinded fool, and when he falls on the ground he says to his friend, "Oh, you are a great astrologer, you can see the future."

Another story teaches us to be responsible for our actions. A man is beating someone with a stick, the police constable comes and charges, "You are beating that man." "Oh, no, it is not me beating him, it is the stick." You demonstrate that we must be responsible and not blame others. We blunder with the blunt tool of narrow minds, not seeing that you want us to understand Krishna in a living spontaneous manner. Instead, we try to make His teachings a geometric cement and steel formula. You teach us to be real devotees, not artificial, but joyous and loving, sages who honor time and circumstance, and we still choose to embrace hard and fast rules.

I remember years ago how you told us of the smarta brahmana who had two fish-shaped brass little dishes, kosit and kosu. This brahmana was pouring oblations of Ganges water back into the river. After finishing the oblations he put his two brass fish-shaped cups on the river bank and went to say his Gayatri mantra. After Gayatri, upon returning to the bank to get his cups, he saw cups of the same size and shape. The other brahmanas had left them on the bank. The next day, to avoid the same mix-up, he placed a small clay ball in the cups, before saying his Gayatri. When he went to retrieve his cups he saw all the brahmanas' cups had little clay balls in them, as they thought that the clay ball was an esoteric ritual that they did not know, so being smarta brahmanas they imitated blindly.

How can we count the gifts you give us, you are training us all, lions, tigers, dogs, cats, gangsters and cheats, like a lion tamer in the circus of illusions. Mad men prisoners in the material world, you point out "who is crazy and who is sane." For ten years I meditate on how you try to show us that we are not this body. We still take refuge in this cage of mucus, bile, stool and bone. If we realized this simple fact, there would not be any fighting. Again you illustrate with example and story. "When someone calls you prabhu, you should not think 'Come here and wipe my shoes.'" We are like children beating their father while arguing over which part to massage. The tendency to be envious is recounted by this dialogue: "Did you hear of such and such a high court judge?" "No, it cannot be, he is not qualified to be a high court judge." "No, no it is true, he is a high court judge."

"All right, he may be a high court judge, but he must not be getting any salary!" You warn us not to cheat, and I realize that you know that we are not very advanced. It is not a cheap thing. We vacillate from devotee to cheat a thousand times daily. Again, you have to spoon-feed us with stories, as the *Srimad-Bhagavatam* and *Bhagavad-gita* are not imbibed in our frivolous state. This you illustrate with the story of a motivated devotee, the fictitious man from Bengal, Gopala Bon, who is stringing a garland of bokul flowers. (Bokul is a flower as well as a vegetable when fried and mixed with other vegetables.) His friend asks, "What are you doing?" "Oh, I am making a garland for Lord Krishna," says Gopala. "Do you mean to say that Lord Krishna will come here and take this garland from you?" his friend asked. "That is my plan. If Lord Krishna doesn't come and take this garland personally, then I shall fry it up and eat it." Another time, Gopala Bon is walking down the road with a basket of wheat on his head, and a strong wind comes and scatters the wheat in all ten directions. Then, Gopala folds his hands together, and says "Govinda bhoga."

Riding in the car, back seat, sitting next to you, the "Krishna Meditation" tape penetrating, the joyous sound of your unmatchable harmonium filling our hearts with glee, you turn and say, "Gurudas Prabhu, can you play the harmonium like that?" and I realize that you are the best in everything. So many muscular youths fall behind in your transcendental wake. I feel proud sitting with you in the car, not only because it is a special privilege, but because I am proud of you and proud of being your son and disciple. You outclass us in all respects, as you have the qualities of Krishna. Therefore, you are the guru. You can walk farther than any of us in the mornings, dance nicer, think quicker, quote more slokas, open more temples, preach more miles, write more essays, poems, books and letters, eat less prasad, eat more prasad if the mood strikes, sleep less, read more, think of Krishna more, sing the most beautifully, distribute the most books, attract the most members, make friends with the most devotees, remain transcendentally aloof, the most detached, non dependent, the most dependent on Krishna, a traveling mendicant and simultaneously the most wealthy, able to smile broader than all, and then one second later appear the gravest. Softness caresses the corner of your eyes, fire blazes from the center, intelligence from the middle, you are able to hold a flower longer than all of us without crushing it, you know us all, we do not know you, and you allow familiarity. You become childlike and then suddenly if we misuse this, you cut us down like a banana tree in a whirlwind, you disappear as Lord Krishna did when the gopis became proud. You encourage us again and again, using a story as you coax us to be bold for Krishna. We ask can we put on dramatic plays in the street, you say, "Why not, do it with Nrsimha faces, what you do all will follow. It will become a style."

Then you again tell of a Charles Chaplin film you saw fifty years before. As follows: Charles Chaplin was at the ball dance (fancy dress ball) and when he went to sit some rascal nailed down his tailing coat. When Charles Chaplin got up, his tailing coat tore in the middle, he did not know it, and when he danced everyone was looking at his torn coat. Charles Chaplin went into the private room and saw in the mirrors that his tails were torn up the middle and so he tore the tails all the way up to the neck and he danced harder as they flapped around. All the people saw this and they too went into the private room and tore their tailing coats and danced. It became the style."

Later: "Be bold, if you're going to hunt, try for rhinoceros, and if you're going to thieve, try for the government reserve. If you fail, everyone will say 'it was impossible,' and if you succeed, everyone will say 'How great.'"

You taught us again as we rode to Thakur Bhaktivinode's Dvadasi Mandir in Bir Nagar, West Bengal. The horn of our old green car failed. Bhavananda Swami and myself were yelling Hare Krishna out the window at all the obstacles on the road, so as to try and warn them of the car coming, but they sometimes did not hear. You then said, "Give me my plate," and you then took your cane and banged the plate and said, "This is our horn." It worked. We banged all the way to Bir Nagar and you laughed. "They will think that this is the latest American style horn and will want to imitate," and you laughed again.

In your history of India lessons to me you made the same point, that anything "made in Britain" was considered first-class. You told how the English came to India and instilled the whole population with the idea of buying British cloth, and how the British administrators were paid in gold via "the home bill," thus depleting the gold reserve, making India dependent on England. Because of this dependency India felt sheltered by Britain and so anything "made in England," done in England, was the style. It still exists today, you go on, "The villager asks if I vote for the British, will they care?" All these stories would not be necessary if we were able to hear you correctly.

The shastra simply states the same thing:

> *yad yad acarati sresthas*
> *tat tad evetaro janah*
> *sa yat pramanam kurute*
> *lokas tad anuvartate*
> (Bg. 3.21)

"Whatever action is performed by a great man, common men follow in his footsteps. And whatever standards he sets by exemplary acts, all the world pursues."

But we need spoon-feeding and you take your precious time to do this like a caring mother dropping nectar in our yearning beaks. So we follow in your footsteps and follow your standards and exemplary acts. Now let the whole world pursue.

Your eyes moist, everyone awaiting your next move, you grace us all individually, all different personalities, yet one in your presence. One frivolous becomes serious. The dry become juicy. We must not forget you, we must remain dhira always. We must understand time and circumstances and mostly, Prabhus, we must not fight anymore. We must read your instructions, your books daily and chant in-between. You have given us the mercy. Recently on a walk I asked, "How does krpa-siddhi work?"

You turned on me suddenly and said, "If I give you a hundred thousand rupees and say 'Take it, take it,' that is krpa-siddhi"; and then to emphasize you put your hand in my stomach giving me the imaginary 100,000 rs., saying, "Take it, take it! And when you spend, you realize—krpa-siddhi."

It is you who are giving us Krishna. We must take His lotus feet on our head. This is our goal, nothing else. You and He are not separate, that we must realize. I love you, you make me happy. Guru-krsna-prasade paya bhakti-lata-bija. "Now go on and help me push on this Movement." We leave your chambers, a new determination. Krishna, please engage me in your service.

Hare Krishna.

Your servant,
Gurudas Swami
Krishna-Balarama
Traveling Sankirtan Party

ABOUT THE AUTHOR

GURUDAS FIRST MET His Divine Grace A. C. Bhaktivedanta Swami Prabhupada, on January 17, 1967, at the San Francisco Airport.

He and Yamuna were initiated on April 7, 1967. As an instrument in Lord Krishna's plan, Gurudas helped in the beginning with the San Francisco Sri Sri Radha Krishna and New Jagannath Puri Temple. Three San Francisco devotee couples, including Gurudas and Yamuna, were then sent by Prabhupada to London, where Gurudas became president of the ISKCON temple at 7 Bury Place.

Sriman George Harrison agreed to record some singles and albums of the devotees, and the "Hare Krishna Mantra" single soon became the fastest selling hit for Apple Records, even faster than the Beatles singles. Gurudas helped in obtaining the Bhaktivedanta Manor from George.

Prabhupada then requested that Gurudas lead a party of seventeen devotees into India, where he helped form the Bombay, New Delhi, and Calcutta temples. Prabhupada then asked Gurudas to try to get a Maharaja's palace for the site of the Krishna Balarama Temple in Vrindavan. Instead, a site was found in Raman Reti, and Gurudas was put in charge of the temple building project.

Gurudas met with the United States Ambassador Kenneth Keating and introduced Prabhupada to him. Through this contact, we procured grains for prasadam distribution, from the U.S. Food for Peace program. Gurudas met and dealt with Indian Prime Minister Indira Gandhi, as well as many Indian cabinet ministers and officials.

The Radha Damodar Traveling Sankirtan Party was formed after Gurudas' sannyasa initiation, and he then went on a Pacific Northwest speaking tour. Back in Europe, Gurudas took a bus to civil-war-torn Northern Ireland. In 1975, Prabhupada asked Gurudas to go to the Communist countries. He and Gyanashyam went to Poland, Yugoslavia, Czechoslovakia, Romania, and Bulgaria.

In 1977, Gurudas was requested to go to another warring place, Lebanon, where, by Krishna's grace, Gurudas spearheaded a United Nations ISKCON food distribution program. Since then, Gurudas has written four books and made three films, and he carries on a counseling and healing practice in San Francisco, California.

MAHABHARATA

The Greatest Spiritual Epic of All Time

As the divinely beautiful Draupadi rose from the fire, a voice rang out from the heavens foretelling a terrible destiny: "She will cause the destruction of countless warriors." And so begins one of the most fabulous stories of all time. Mahabharata plunges us into a wondrous and ancient world of romance and adventure. In this exciting new rendition of the renowned classic, Krishna Dharma condenses the epic into a fast-paced novel—a powerful and moving tale recounting the fascinating adventures of the five heroic Pandava brothers and their celestial wife. Culminating in an apocalyptic war, Mahabharata is a masterpiece of suspense, intrigue, and illuminating wisdom.

"A well-wrought saga that will be appreciated by Western readers. Highly recommended."—*The Midwest Book Review*

"...very readable, its tone elevated without being ponderous."—*Library Journal*

"...blockbuster treatment...Moves effortlessly, often as racily as a thriller, without compromising the elevated style and diction."—*India Today*

"Its truths are unassailable, its relevance beyond dispute, and its timelessness absolute."—*Atlantis Rising*

"I could not tear my mind away!"—*Magical Blend*

Condensed Version
$19.95 ♦ ISBN 1-887089-25-X ♦ 6" x 9" ♦ Hardbound ♦ 288 pgs.

Complete Unabridged Version
$39.95 ♦ ISBN 1-887089-17-9 ♦ 6" x 9" ♦ Hardbound ♦ 960 pgs.
♦ 16 color plates ♦ 20 Illustrations

To order call toll-free 1-888-867-2458, or visit www.torchlight.com.

RAMAYANA

By Krishna Dharma

A THRILLING NEW RENDITION OF THE WORLD'S OLDEST EPIC

Ramayana is both a spellbinding adventure and a work of profound philosophy, offering answers to life's deepest questions. It tells of another time, when gods and heroes walked among us, facing supernatural forces of evil and guided by powerful mystics and sages.

Revered throughout the ages for its moral and spiritual wisdom, it is a beautiful and uplifting tale of romance and high adventure, recounting the odyssey of Rama, a great king of Ancient India. Rama, along with his beautiful wife, Sita, and his faithful brother Laksmana, is exiled to the forest for fourteen years. There, Sita is kidnapped by the powerful demon Ravana. Along with Lakshmana and a fantastic army of supernatural creatures, Rama starts on a perilous quest to find his beloved Sita.

"A spellbinding adventure and a work of profound philosophy, offering answers to life's deepest questions... *Ramayana* is a beautiful tale of romance and high adventure...Faithfully preserved and passed on in varied forms for countless generations, the *Ramayana* is recognized by many Western scholars as a literary masterpiece. Now Krishna Dharma has provided the English-speaking reader with a superb opportunity to discover and enjoy this ancient and influential classic."

—The Midwest Book Review

"(*Ramayana*)makes for lively reading as a good adventure and love story as well as a guide to spiritual practice.This version breaks up what was originally seven long chapters into smaller, easier to handle units. Recommended for any library in need of a first copy or a contemporary and highly readable rendering of this ancient Indian classic."

—Library Journal

$27.95 ♦ ISBN 1-887089-22-5 ♦ 6" x 9" ♦ Hardbound ♦ 488 pgs.
8 color plates ♦ 10 B&W Drawings

To order call toll-free 1-888-867-2458, or visit www.torchlight.com.

Diary of a Traveling Preacher

VOLUME 4 (September, 2001–April, 2003)

by Indradyumna Swami

From the snows of Siberia to the deserts of Kazakhstan, from the Polish seaside to the sacred dust of India, accompany Indradyumna Swami as he travels throughout the world to spread the divine name of Kṛṣṇa and the message of Śrī Caitanya Mahāprabhu—often against fierce opposition.

Savor the bliss and challenge of preaching on four continents; introducing people young and old, rich and poor, learned and simple, to Kṛṣṇa consciousness.

Price: $14.95

To order call toll-free 1–888–867–2458,
or visit www.torchlight.com

TORCHLIGHT PUBLISHING
P. O. Box 52, Badger, CA 93603